Teaching and Learning Second Language Listening

"This book is a very well worked out approach to listening from a metacognitive viewpoint. It is firmly based on research and experience and combines both theoretical and practical aspects of listening in a very readable way. It will be of great value to those who have an interest in learner strategy development, learner autonomy, and the metacognitive development of a language skill."

I. S. P. Nation, Victoria University of Wellington, New Zealand

"Vandergrift and Goh, two highly accomplished and skilled thinkers and writers, have produced a volume that will have an important place in the applied linguistics literature for many years to come. The authors have a keen sense of where the field of L2 listening pedagogy is right now and where it needs to go, and the volume most definitely assists us in getting there."

Andrew Cohen, University of Minnesota, USA

This reader-friendly text, firmly grounded in listening theories and supported by recent research findings, offers a comprehensive treatment of concepts and knowledge related to teaching second language (L2) listening, with a particular emphasis on metacognition.

The metacognitive approach, aimed at developing learner listening in a holistic manner, is unique and groundbreaking. The book is focused on the language learner throughout; all theoretical perspectives, research insights, and pedagogical principles in the book are presented and discussed in relation to the learner.

The pedagogical model—a combination of the tried-and-tested sequence of listening lessons and activities that show learners how to activate processes of skilled listeners—provides teachers with a sound framework for students' L2 listening development to take place inside and outside the classroom. The text includes many practical ideas for listening tasks that have been used successfully in various language learning contexts.

Larry Vandergrift is Professor, Official Languages and Bilingualism Institute, Faculty of Arts, University of Ottawa, Canada.

Christine C. M. Goh is Associate Professor, English Language & Literature Department, National Institute of Education, Nanyang Technological University, Singapore.

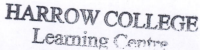

HARROW COLLEGE
Learning Centre

ESL & Applied Linguistics Professional Series
Eli Hinkel, Series Editor

Visit **www.routledge.com/education** for additional information on titles in the ESL & Applied Linguistics Professional Series.

Teaching and Learning Second Language Listening

Metacognition in Action

Larry Vandergrift
Christine C. M. Goh

Routledge
Taylor & Francis Group

NEW YORK AND LONDON

First published 2012
by Routledge
711 Third Avenue, New York, NY 10017

Simultaneously published in the UK
by Routledge
2 Park Square, Milton Park, Abingdon, Oxon OX14 4RN

Routledge is an imprint of the Taylor & Francis Group, an informa business

Library of Congress Cataloging in Publication Data
Vandergrift, Larry.
    Teaching and learning second language listening : metacognition in action /
Larry Vandergrift, Christine C.M. Goh.
    p. cm.—(ESL & applied linguistics professional series)
    Includes bibliographical references and index.
    1. Language and languages—Study and teaching. 2. Listening—Study and teaching.
    3. Second language acquisition—Study and teaching.
    I. Goh, Christine Chuen Meng. II. Title.
    P53.47.V36 2011
    418.0071—dc22   2011012507

ISBN: 978–0–415–88371–9 (hbk)
ISBN: 978–0–415–88372–6 (pbk)
ISBN: 978–0–203–84337–6 (ebk)

Typeset in Sabon & Gillsans
by Swales & Willis Ltd, Exeter, Devon

To our respective spouses Kathy and Paul,
for their love and faithful support;
and to our children,
Michael, Ellen, Andrea, and their families; and Nicole;
for cheering us on.

Permissions

The authors and publishers thank the following for permission to reproduce in whole or in part the following figures and tables:

Taylor and Francis Group, LLC, a division of Informa plc
Figure 2.1, copyright 2011, from *Handbook of Research in Second Language Teaching and Learning, Volume 2* by E. Hinkel (Ed.).

Figure 4.1, copyright 2006, from Development and validation of the Imhof-Janusik listening concepts inventory to measure listening conceptualization differences between cultures. *Journal of International Communication Research, 35*, 79–98 by M. Imhof, & L. Janusik.

Wiley-Blackwell Publishers
Table 2.2, copyright 1997, from The Cinderella of communication strategies: receptive strategies in interactive listening. *Modern Language Journal, 90*, 338–352 by L. Vandergrift.

Figure 5.4, copyright 2006, from The Metacognitive Awareness Listening Questionnaire (MALQ): Development and validation. *Language Learning, 56*, 431–462 by L. Vandergrift, C. Goh, C. Mareschal, & M. H. Tafaghodatari.

Appendix A, copyright 1997, from The strategies of second language (French) listeners: A descriptive study. *Foreign Language Annals, 30*, 387–409 by L. Vandergrift.

Mouton De Gruyter Publishers
Figure 3.1, copyright 1993, from Language use in normal speakers and its disorders by W. J. M Levelt. In G. Blanken, J. Dittmann, H. Grimm, J. C. Marshall, & C.-W. Wallesch (Eds.), *Linguistic disorders and pathologies* (pp. 1–15).

University of Toronto Press
Figure 5.2, copyright 2003, from From prediction through reflection: Guiding students through the process of L2 listening. *The Canadian Modern Language Review, 59*, 425–440 by L. Vandergrift.

Contents

PART III
Listening in Other Contexts

Preface

There have been positive changes in the teaching of second language (L2) listening over the past few decades, but learners still face challenges in the classroom and beyond as they try to improve their ability to listen. This is true in spite of the fact that many learners, particularly at beginning and intermediate levels, want to learn the skill of listening, a skill over which they feel they have the least control. Listening receives limited attention in many classes, often without sustained support to guide learners through the process of learning to become more successful listeners. In addition, the way in which listening activities are planned and taught often creates anxiety in learners, instead of the confidence they need to keep trying. A holistic approach to listening instruction is therefore needed. In this regard, a metacognitive perspective may provide an answer.

Purpose of Book

The purpose of this book is to help teachers understand the process of listening, the role of metacognition in listening development, and how to teach listening more effectively. It explains the process of L2 listening and the factors that affect success to provide readers with a rich theoretical understanding of what L2 listening involves. Based on our research and many years of L2 classroom experience, we identify practical pedagogical principles and discuss how to plan and carry these out in listening activities. The emphasis is on *teaching* listening in order to motivate and assist learners in their efforts to improve listening skills in and out of the classroom.

The role of metacognition in listening development receives detailed attention in the analysis of available research studies on listening and in teaching practice. We present a metacognitive approach that engages learners in listening and thinking about their listening through an active and reiterative process, while they practice listening skills, within an integrated, holistic approach to learning. The aim of this approach is to help language learners become self-regulated listeners who maximize opportunities for listening inside and outside the classroom and develop skills for real-life listening. They are empowered to do this through strategic actions, individual reflection, and collaboration with others.

The activities in the book are designed to improve how listeners process a listening text in the target language and help them use strategies to control these processes more efficiently and effectively. The book also shows how learners can develop phonological awareness of the features of the spoken form of the target language and relevant perception skills that enable listening comprehension to take place. These activities will help to sensitize learners to listening and strengthen the overall process of learning to listen.

The text is designed to be both a textbook and a reference book for professionals in the field of second language acquisition. As a textbook, it serves teacher education courses that deal specifically with L2 teaching worldwide, especially at the level of Diploma and MA/M.Ed courses. Practicing teachers and other professionals will find it useful as a reference tool for developing a deeper understanding of listening skills and how these skills can be developed through focused attention in programs of instruction. The discussions about listening processes and environments for learning to listen will also be of interest to readers keen on keeping abreast of recent research and theoretical perspectives.

The approach in this book focuses on the language learner throughout; all theoretical perspectives, research insights, and pedagogical principles are presented and discussed in relation to the learner. The metacognitive approach we propose provides teachers with a sound and coherent framework for L2 listening development to take place inside and outside the classroom. Using knowledge of how listening processes work, materials are provided to raise learner awareness of the nature and demands of L2 listening. This leads to strategies that can facilitate comprehension in different contexts and methods for teaching them within integrated language courses.

In addition, we present pedagogical models that teachers can easily use or adapt. They are designed to provide a coherent framework for listening development inside and outside the classroom. The first, a metacognitive pedagogical sequence, provides a combination of a tried-and-tested sequence of listening lessons and activities that show learners how to activate processes of skilled listeners. This model is integrated into the discussion of all dimensions of listening, such as perception activities, authentic listening tasks, extensive listening projects, and interactive listening activities. The benefits of this model for teaching listening, grounded in listening theories, is supported by recent research findings. The second model is built on principles of task-based learning, which enable learners to practice listening for communication and meaning and at the same time develop their metacognitive awareness about L2 listening.

Overview of Book

Part I, consisting of four chapters, introduces our pedagogical perspective within a historical context and discusses the foundational aspects of L2 listening comprehension and instruction.

Chapter 1, "Challenges and Opportunities in Listening Instruction," discusses changes in listening instruction over the past 50 years. It argues for a more holistic approach that focuses on the process of learning to listen. The goal is to develop the necessary knowledge and control of internal cognitive and affective processes.

Chapter 2, "Listening Competence," focuses on understanding what listeners do to comprehend speech in both one-way and interactive listening contexts. It discusses cognitive processes, knowledge sources, and the unique features of interactive listening.

Chapter 3, "A Model of Listening Comprehension," describes a theoretical model that encapsulates into one coherent system the cognitive processes and concepts involved in listening. It illustrates how the components in this model might operate during one-way and interactive listening.

Chapter 4, "Factors That Influence Listening Success," examines a range of cognitive and affective factors that influence the quality of processing in listening and can lead to different results for different learners.

Part II, consisting of six chapters, explores in depth the role of metacognition in learning to listen. We discuss what it means to put metacognition into action and illustrate in very practical ways how teachers can do this in the classroom.

Chapter 5, "A Metacognitive Approach to Listening Instruction," explains the theoretical foundation for a metacognitive approach to L2 listening instruction that helps learners engage effectively with spoken input and guides them in their overall listening development in and out of the classroom.

Chapter 6, "A Metacognitive Pedagogical Sequence," shows how the metacognitive processes of planning, monitoring, problem-solving, and evaluation can shape a pedagogical sequence that leads learners to activate the processes in real-life listening. Various listening activities are presented to illustrate how this pedagogical sequence works.

Chapter 7, "Activities for Metacognitive Instruction," presents a number of additional activities to help learners develop metacognitive knowledge about the process of listening and to focus on themselves as L2 listeners in areas such as self-concept, motivation, and anxiety.

Chapter 8, "Developing Perception and Word Segmentation Skills," discusses the bottom-up component of listening comprehension in greater detail. It examines the research literature on how listeners segment speech, and presents classroom-based activities to develop bottom-up skills as part of the learner's metacognitive knowledge about listening.

Chapter 9, "Task-Based Listening Lessons," presents an activity-based, process-oriented approach to L2 listening development. The tasks, which include pre- and post-listening activities and metacognitive activities, are designed to enrich listening practice by moving beyond a narrow focus on comprehension alone.

Chapter 10, "Projects for Extensive Listening," presents planned, process-based projects to extend listening practice beyond the classroom. They are designed to help learners deepen their understanding of listening, use listening and learning strategies, and practice perception and interpretation skills.

Part III, consisting of two chapters, discusses the development of L2 listening in multimedia environments and the assessment of listening competence.

Chapter 11, "Listening in Multimedia Environments," explores the potential of technology for teaching L2 listening. It examines research on the use of technological tools such as video, textual supports, transcripts, and captions to help listeners mediate their comprehension efforts. It considers the implications for learning and teaching, with a special focus on real-life listening skills.

Chapter 12, "Assessing Listening for Learning," discusses L2 listening assessment within the framework of metacognition, particularly the importance of formative assessment for developing self-regulation. We examine the differences between formative and summative assessments and discuss related issues in light of fundamental criteria such as validity, reliability, and authenticity.

All chapters open with a scenario that highlights one or more of the issues in the chapter. Each scenario is followed by a pre-reading reflection on the issues or central theme of the chapter. Each chapter concludes with a set of tasks, discussion questions, and suggestions for further reading on the topic.

Our goal is to open up discussion about listening instruction for learners of any second language. The discussion questions and tasks are designed to help readers from all contexts examine the relevance of the ideas for their own situation. Some of the tasks are designed for use in teacher preparation or professional development courses, where participants have the benefit of working with others to further develop their understanding through discussions and feedback from instructors and peers. While most of the specific examples in the book refer to the teaching of listening in English, the broader relevance is highlighted in analysis, questions, and tasks.

The field of metacognitive listening instruction is evolving. Our goal is to explain and demonstrate how to *teach* listening so that teachers plan lessons that avoid the pitfalls of earlier practices that merely tested what was heard, and instead tap into the processes involved and the potential that learners themselves bring to improve L2 learning. We acknowledge there may be limitations to some of our ideas. All aspects of this approach have not yet been fully researched. However, since a metacognitive approach has rarely been presented with both principles and practical examples, we hope that this book will be helpful to extend existing discussions and lead to more improvements in the future.

Acknowledgments

Many years of classroom teaching led each of us separately to recognize the importance of listening in language learning and to investigate the nature and role of learning strategies in listening comprehension. The results of our doctoral research, one in French second language classrooms in Canada and the other in English second language classrooms in Singapore, led to the same conclusion: learner metacognition plays a crucial role in learning to listen and understand another language. We became aware of each other's work through our respective publications and that led to collaborative efforts, such as development of the Metacognitive Awareness of Listening Questionnaire (MALQ) and, eventually, this book. It is our hope that this book will help teachers around the world better understand the process of listening comprehension and become more effective in their efforts to develop successful language learners.

In writing this book, we have been encouraged and supported by many people. We would like to acknowledge:

- the support and encouragement of our respective families;
- the formative role of colleagues Anna Chamot, Andrew Cohen, David Mendelsohn, Rebecca Oxford, Joan Rubin, and Anita Wenden, and their encouragement of our work;
- the useful feedback from colleagues who have read one or more chapters: Albert Dudley, Patricia Dunkel, Bill Grabe, Volker Hegelheimer, Amelia Hope, Catherine Mareschal, Rebecca Ranjan, Alysse Weinberg;
- the help provided by Josée Légaré in creating, formatting, and revising figures and tables;
- the editorial support by Kathy Vandergrift who helped make our writing clearer;
- the meticulous work by Karim Mekki in preparing the references and verifying all the details for manuscript submission; and,
- the encouragement from Naomi Silverman and Eli Hinkel at Routledge to embark on this book project.

Larry Vandergrift
Christine C. M. Goh

Prologue: Reflection on Issues Related to Teaching and Learning Listening

Before reading this book, we ask you, the reader, to take a moment to reflect on your own experience and approach to teaching second language (L2) listening. The way you were taught to listen in language classes, your encounters with target language speakers, and your teaching experiences have likely influenced your perceptions about how to teach others to listen. It is important to understand your own assumptions and beliefs—why we do what we do in the classroom—and critically examine the impact of our own practices for learners. Only then can we consider other perspectives that lead to new approaches and different outcomes.

The statements on the next page summarize some common perceptions, right or wrong, about learning and teaching L2 listening. Read these statements and take a few moments to reflect on the degree to which you agree or disagree with each one. In order to clarify your assumptions, we encourage you to discuss your responses with a colleague or a classmate.

As you read through the chapters of this book, recall these statements and the questions that surfaced as you considered your own response, or debated the issues with your colleagues or class. We will revisit these statements in the Epilogue, after you have read and critically examined the various dimensions of teaching and learning L2 listening discussed in this book.

Strongly disagree	Disagree	Slightly disagree	Partly agree	Agree	Strongly agree	
1	2	3	4	5	6	

1. Compared with the other language skills, listening is a passive activity.	1	2	3	4	5	6	
2. The most important thing in listening instruction is that students get the right answer.	1	2	3	4	5	6	
3. Learner anxiety is a major obstacle in L2 listening.	1	2	3	4	5	6	
4. Listening means understanding words, so teachers just need to help learners understand all the words in the sound stream.	1	2	3	4	5	6	
5. Teaching listening through video is better than audio alone.	1	2	3	4	5	6	
6. Learners with good listening ability in their first language will also become good L2 listeners.	1	2	3	4	5	6	
7. When teachers provide learners with the context for a listening activity, they give away too much information.	1	2	3	4	5	6	
8. Interactive listening, conversation with another speaker, is more difficult than one-way listening (i.e., radio and television).	1	2	3	4	5	6	
9. Letting students listen on their own, according to their interests, is the best way to develop listening skills.	1	2	3	4	5	6	
10. Captions and subtitles are useful	1	2	3	4	5	6	

Part I

Learning to Listen

Chapter 1

Challenges and Opportunities in Listening Instruction

Scenario

It is time for Class 2B to have their listening lesson. Miss Campbell tells her students to take out their course book and look at the listening exercise on pages 28 and 29. She tells them that they will be listening to a passage about wedding rites of a group of people who live in Asia. Next she tells them to read the questions and the multiple-choice answers for the listening passage very carefully. She explains that this will help them find out what the passage is about as well as what to listen for when the recording is played. When the class is ready, she plays a CD recording of a listening passage.

The students listen attentively and select what they think is the correct answer to each question. When the recording ends, Miss Campbell plays it a second time so that learners can check their answers. After this, she goes over each question and gives them the correct answer. Finally, she checks how individual learners have performed and then goes over some of the difficult questions and explains the correct answers. When this is done, the class moves on to the next part of the lesson, which requires them to write a short composition based on what they have heard from the passage.

Pre-reading Reflection

1. Does this listening lesson resemble any of the listening lessons that you have experienced as a learner or taught to your students? What are the similarities or differences?
2. Do you think it is useful to ask learners to preview the comprehension questions? Why or why not?
3. Some people would say that this lesson tests listening rather than teaches it. What is your response to this statement?

Introduction

Listening is an important skill: it enables language learners to receive and interact with language input and facilitates the emergence of other language skills. Compared with writing and reading, or even speaking, however, the development of listening receives the least systematic attention from teachers and instructional materials. While language learners are often taught how to plan and draft a composition or deliver an oral presentation, learners are seldom taught how to approach listening or how to manage their listening when attending to spoken texts or messages. Although they are exposed to more listening activities in classrooms today, learners are still left to develop their listening abilities on their own with little direct support from the teacher. A possible reason for this is that many teachers are themselves unsure of how to teach listening in a principled manner. We believe that every language teacher needs to have a clear understanding of the processes involved in listening and in particular how strategies can be used to manage comprehension efforts. A teacher also needs to know how to harness the potential for learning inherent in every student, so as to help them achieve success in developing listening and overall language proficiency.

Listening activities in many language classrooms tend to focus on the outcome of listening; listeners are asked to record or repeat the details they have heard, or to explain the meaning of a passage they have heard. In short, many of the listening activities do little more than test how well they can listen. Because learners are often put in situations where they have to show how much they have understood or, more often, reveal what they have not understood, they feel anxious about listening. In addition, when they not only have to understand what the person is saying but must also respond in an appropriate way, learners' stress and anxiety levels increase even further.

In addition to anxiety, learners also face the challenge of not knowing how to listen when they encounter listening input. Although pre-listening activities are a common feature in some classrooms, these activities mainly provide learners with the background knowledge they need to make listening easier. Learners are "primed" to listen to a specific piece of text through a pre-listening activity, but they are seldom taught how to listen once the audio or video begins. For example, many learners need time to get used to the speaker's voice or "tune into" the message. They often miss the first parts of an aural text and they struggle to construct the context and the meaning for the rest of the message (Goh, 2000).

Once learners begin listening, they are often expected to complete the listening task without any help along the way. The nature of spoken text, experienced in real time, does not normally allow the listener to slow it down or break it down into manageable chunks. Many teachers also feel that they should ask learners to listen to the input without any interruption or repetition because this mirrors real-life communication. The downside of this practice is that learners are constantly trying to understand what they hear but never get a chance to step back and learn how to deal with the listening input. Unlike reading, where the teacher can direct learners' attention to specific parts of a reading passage or ask guiding questions to scaffold their thinking and comprehension, listening lessons do not typically offer such opportunities for learning. As a result, learners do not learn about strategies they can use to improve their listening ability, nor do they understand the processes that are involved in learning to listen in a new language.

Another instruction gap is the lack of guidance on how learners can self-direct and evaluate their efforts to improve their listening. Many learners who desire to improve their listening participate earnestly in all class listening activities in the hope that these will help them become more successful listeners over time. They also look to their teachers to show them how they can improve their listening abilities. Usually, the advice is to listen to songs more, watch more movies, listen to the radio or watch the news on TV, and find native speakers as conversation partners. Most of these activities, when planned by the teacher, are accompanied by "homework" that requires learners to demonstrate some outcome of their listening. These outcomes might include writing a summary of a movie or TV news report they have watched or giving a response to something they have heard. Efforts to improve, however, are sometimes not sufficiently monitored or supported. Learners may try their best to engage in listening on their own outside class time, but they may not know how to take advantage of these opportunities to improve their listening proficiency. Second language (L2) learners need to be supported and to understand the listening processes they are using. In short, teachers need a way to engage learners' metacognition in teaching listening.

Metacognition, or the act of thinking about thinking, refers to the ability of learners to control their thoughts and to regulate their own learning. It plays an important role in learning to listen. There is a general consensus among researchers in the fields of comprehension and second language (L2) learning that metacognition enhances thinking and comprehension (Baker, 2002; Wenden, 1998).

Although metacognition is a crucial aspect of learning to listen, it does not have a significant and explicit role in many language classrooms. A survey of the various approaches to listening instruction shows that listening has gained greater prominence in language teaching, but listening lessons have, until recently, been mainly text-oriented and communication-oriented rather than learner-oriented. The focus of much listening instruction has been on getting learners to comprehend, on their own and with little support, the meaning latent in a piece of spoken text. With time the focus has shifted to the comprehension of details and the gist of messages that have a communicative purpose. More recently, we see a greater emphasis on how learners listen; however, even in situations where the learners and their learning have become factors for consideration in the planning and delivery of the lesson, more could be done to engage learners directly in improving their listening comprehension and managing their own learning.

Listening Instruction: An Overview

Although frequently neglected, listening has had a place in the language classroom for about 50 years. Over this time period the way in which listening activities are conducted has changed. Broadly speaking, we have witnessed three types of listening instruction over the years: text-oriented instruction, communication-oriented instruction, and learner-oriented instruction.

Text-Oriented Instruction

Brown (1987) noted that listening instruction was heavily influenced by reading and writing pedagogy in the 1950s and 60s, even though listening activities were carried out for the purpose of comprehension. There was a heavy emphasis on decoding skills, as well as imitation and memorization of sound and grammar patterns. Typically, learners had to discriminate sounds, answer comprehension questions based on a listening passage, or take dictation of written passages. Under such circumstances, learners had to reveal precisely how well they understood what they had heard. Instead of learning how to listen accurately, listening activities tested the accuracy of their comprehension. According to Morley (1999), this type of instruction is sometimes called a "quiz show" format, where learners have to answer different types of questions based on traditional reading comprehension exercises. Instead of writing out their answers, learners were required to respond in the form of short answers or to select answers from options given. When tests and examinations began to make use of multiple-choice questions, these response formats also made their way into many course books and classrooms. This tendency to test rather than teach listening continues in many classrooms to this day. Table 1.1 summarizes the key features of text-oriented listening instruction and outlines some key challenges that learners face in their attempts to develop listening skills under these conditions.

In text-oriented instruction, the emphasis is on recognizing and understanding different components of a listening input. These include individual sounds and phonological features, as well as key words and phrases.

Table 1.1. Features of Text-Oriented Listening Instruction

Learning objectives	• Decode sounds: phonemes, word stress, and sentence-level intonation • Listen to, imitate, and memorize sound and grammar patterns • Identify relevant details from oral input • Demonstrate understanding of the meaning of the passage
Listening input	• Words, phrases, and sentences read aloud • Written passages read aloud
Classroom interaction	• Learner–teacher • Individual listening
Learner response	• Discriminate sounds at word- and sentence-levels • Write dictation of written passages • Answer comprehension questions based on the listening passage • Complete written texts with details from the listening passage
Challenges for learners	• Listening is not taught as a language skill • Learner comprehension is constantly assessed informally • Listening passages are often dense and do not reflect the linguistic features of spoken texts

An explanation for this emphasis is found in the early ideas of cognitive psychology. Meaning was presumed to be built in an incremental manner from individual sounds to words, to strings of words and, eventually, to a complete text. The listener's understanding of the message was presumed to develop with each stage. Learners were also often asked to write down what they heard as a way of reinforcing the input.

Another feature of text-oriented listening pedagogy is the dominance of the written language. Listening texts were traditionally written passages read aloud. These passages were frequently written without due consideration of the difference between written and spoken language. They were often lexically dense and grammatically complex, and they did not reflect the linguistic features of spoken texts. The language produced when we speak is seldom, if ever, identical to the language produced in the written word, even when we are talking about the same thing. Evidence of this difference was convincingly demonstrated by linguists such as Halliday (1985). He showed, for example, that written texts were more tightly "packed" with complex sentences and therefore had a higher "lexical density." More recently, the differences between spoken and written discourse have also been empirically demonstrated through corpus studies of the spoken language such as the CANCODE project (Carter & McCarthy, 1997; McCarthy & Carter, 1995). With these insights, it became clear that many texts chosen for listening practice were totally unsuitable for use in listening classes. More importantly, these same texts often created additional challenges for language learners due to the heavy cognitive demands made on working memory.

Communication-Oriented Instruction

The position of listening as a distinct and important skill in language learning received a much-needed boost when the Council of Europe set out a model of the communicative needs of the archetypal adult foreign language learner in the early 1970s (Howatt, 1984). Proposals by Munby (1978) on communicative syllabus design, based on the original work of the Council of Europe, provided models for each of the four language skills. Listening was presented as a complex set of skills and micro-skills. It was no longer perceived as something that could simply be "picked up" by language learners, but as a complex communicative skill that had to be learned as one would learn other language skills such as reading and writing. Soon other models and taxonomies of listening skills and sub-skills for different types of communicative situations were published and these directly influenced how listening was presented in many course books. Many of these models were influenced by cognitive psychology and emphasized the importance of listening comprehension as active meaning construction. Richards (1983), for example, presented a taxonomy based on listening skills organized within the context of conversational and academic listening. Rixon (1981) proposed a five-stage framework that included: knowing objectives; understanding language (making guesses if language is not understood); filtering for relevance; checking against own knowledge; and applying information.

The success and influence of the communicative language teaching (CLT) methodology that emerged in the 1970s engendered much discussion about innovative methods for teaching, as well as criteria for selecting materials, designing tasks, and developing materials (Johnson & Morrow, 1981). Teachers were encouraged to move away from using long written passages in favor of authentic materials, such as songs, movies, and recorded conversations for listening. With the availability of portable radio cassette recorders and video recorders, this quickly became a reality in many classrooms. Pre-listening activities were also introduced to engage learners in preparatory activities that enabled them to use their background knowledge for the topic during listening (Anderson & Lynch, 1988; Underwood, 1989; Ur, 1984). Table 1.2 summarizes the key features of communication-oriented listening instruction. It shows that, even in lessons with a communicative purpose, learners could still face challenges such as a neglect of listening in favor of speaking or four-skill integrated units and the indirect assessment of comprehension.

Table 1.2. Features of Communication-Oriented Listening Instruction

Learning objectives	• Develop both macro and micro skills for listening • Develop specific enabling skills for listening
Listening input	• Spontaneous learner–learner talk • Scripted or semi-scripted texts with a high degree of authenticity • Authentic listening/oral interaction materials
Classroom interaction	• Learner–learner • Learner–teacher • Individual listening
Learner response	• Respond to spoken texts in socially and contextually appropriate ways (e.g., inferring attitude, taking notes, identifying details) • Complete missing information in texts or discourse • Use information from listening text for other communicative purposes
Challenges for language learners	• Listening often neglected in thematic lessons that integrate the four language skills • Listening neglected in oral communication activities which focus more on speaking • Learners indirectly assessed for comprehension

CLT methodology (including variants such as task-based learning) typically promoted the development of all four language skills. Listening, speaking, reading, and writing were taught in a series of lessons or units so that learners could practice each skill in relation to the theme. In classrooms that adopted an integrated skills approach, listening activities were used mainly to provide background knowledge or important vocabulary for subsequent tasks that typically focused on the two production skills of speaking and writing. Once again, listening was carried out in the language classroom in the service of something other than itself. Unlike the role it played in audio-lingual classrooms, listening in a communicatively-oriented classroom was typically carried out to prepare learners for major writing or speaking outcomes.

In oral communication activities, where both listening and speaking were involved, the emphasis was mostly on the speaking component. For example, in an information gap activity, where learners gave information to their assigned partners, teachers tended to pay more attention to how those pieces of information were communicated orally. Less attention, if any, was given to how learners should listen for and comprehend the information. Thus, even in classrooms where plenty of oral activities took place (as is indeed the case in many CLT classrooms), listening was often the sleeping partner in the business of oral communication. Once again, language learners did not get sufficient support in learning how to process and manage the listening input they received.

Although self-access learning centers were a common feature in many language learning institutions, little attention was given to learner efforts at listening outside the classroom. While these centers provided a rich collection of recorded materials for listening practice, few provided learners with help and instructions on how to self-regulate their learning. Self-regulated learning refers to the ability of learners to proactively control their thoughts, actions, and feelings in order to learn—that is, to master their own learning processes (Zimmerman & Schunk, 2001).

Learner-Oriented Instruction

Several learner-oriented developments in the field of language teaching and learning in the last three decades have had an influence on listening instruction. In late 1970s and 80s, applied linguists began to focus on why some learners were more successful at learning a language than others (O'Malley & Chamot, 1990; Oxford, 1990; Stern, 1983; Wenden & Rubin, 1987). In what has come to be known as good language learner research, examination of learner strategies was broadened subsequently to cover individual language skills, including listening.

New evidence-based approaches to teaching listening have been suggested, particularly in the area of listening strategies (see reviews by Macaro, Graham, & Vanderplank, 2007, and Vandergrift, 2007). Chamot (1995) and Mendelsohn (1994, 1998) have called for a strategy-based approach to listening instruction. O'Malley and Chamot (1990) noted that strategies had cognitive and affective bases. The model they developed to classify learning strategies contains an executive or meta-cognitive function to direct learning, in addition to the operative or cognitive processing function that involves interacting with the material to be learned or applying a specific technique to a learning task. Socio-affective strategies, on the other hand, account for the influence of social and affective processes on learning or the motivational and affective states of the learners. The strategic approach works within a socio-cognitive paradigm to train learners how to apply various strategies in order to handle the demands of listening (Mendelsohn, 1998). Teachers were advised to use techniques such as teacher modeling to show learners some of the mental processes that took place as they constructed their understanding of listening texts. Some examples of how this was done include thinking aloud by the teacher (Chamot, 1995) and demonstrating the use of cognitive strategies for verifying informed guesses (Field, 1998). Teachers were also advised to use pre-communication activities as a way of raising learners' awareness about listening processes (Buck, 1995).

Learner-oriented instruction comes closest to teaching learners how to listen. It was developed as an answer to the problem of "testing camouflages as testing" in listening classes (Mendelsohn, 1994). Teacher modeling and scaffolded listening practice in metacognitive processes were clearly valuable for helping learners *learn* how to listen. The suggested techniques helped in some ways to demystify the sub-skills involved in successful listening by making explicit to novice listeners the implicit processes of skilled listeners. Learners were shown tangible ways of managing their mental processes for listening. The features of learner-oriented listening instruction are summarized in Table 1.3. This approach, which focuses mainly on the use of cognitive strategies, may not go far enough in helping learners develop the metacognitive aspects of learning. These include awareness and the use of a range of strategies, as well as developing habits of mind that improve self-regulated learning, both within and beyond the classroom.

Vandergrift (2004, 2007) and Goh (1997, 2008) take the learner-oriented approach further by proposing a metacognitive approach to teach listening in a holistic manner. This metacognitive approach focuses on what learners can do to help themselves listen better when engaging with aural input. Especially important is the potential of this approach

Table 1.3 Features of Learner-Oriented Listening Instruction

Learning objectives	• Use listening strategies for enhancing comprehension and coping with problems • Develop metacognitive awareness about L2 listening
Listening input	• Spontaneous learner–learner talk • Scripted or semi-scripted texts with a high degree of authenticity • Authentic listening/oral interaction materials
Classroom interaction	• Learner–learner • Learner–teacher • Individual listening (self-directed)
Learner response	• Respond to spoken texts in socially and contextually appropriate ways (e.g., inferring attitude, taking notes, identifying details) • Complete missing information in texts or discourse • Prepare reflections and self-reports on use of strategies
Challenges for learners	• Learners become aware of strategies but the lessons do not always allow them to experience the use of these strategies in more tangible ways • Learning to listen is often an individual affair and listeners do not benefit sufficiently from the knowledge and experiences of others • Learners lack a variety of structural support that could assist them in their overall development of listening abilities

to provide systematic support to learners for overall listening development in varied and creative ways, from the classroom to various domains outside it.

Towards a More Holistic Approach to L2 Listening Instruction

In spite of positive developments in communication-oriented and learner-oriented types of listening instruction, text-orientated activities still persist in many language classrooms. Ideas and practices recommended by researchers and language educators are not always translated or translated successfully into the classroom and everyday activities. One such practice was asking learners to answer comprehension questions based on a listening passage, or the "quiz show" mode mentioned earlier.

If we examine current course textbooks or talk to teachers, we would find that these comprehension-based techniques are still commonplace today. For example, learners are still required to demonstrate their understanding of listening passages or videotexts by choosing the correct answer from a number of options, writing summaries, or selecting words from the computer screen to complete sentences from the listening passage. Communicative language teaching highlights the importance of practicing core listening skills, such as listening for details, listening for gist, predicting, listening selectively, and making inferences. The main goal of these listening lessons, however, is typically the achievement of successful comprehension. With a focus on the product of listening, every activity becomes a test of the learners' listening ability only, rather than a means for understanding the social and cognitive nature of developing and using these listening skills. Although scholars have warned against using listening activities as a disguised form of testing (Sheerin, 1987), this practice is in fact quite commonplace in many language classrooms, even today.

The goal of this book is to show that some of the intrinsic challenges within the three types of listening instruction can be addressed by teaching within a metacognitive framework. Teachers need to enhance the current strategy approach to engage learners in a wider range of metacognitive activities about listening. These metacognitive learning activities should aim to deepen learner understanding of themselves as L2 listeners, raise greater awareness of the demands and processes of L2 listening, and teach learners how to manage their comprehension and learning.

Research in first language (L1) and L2 comprehension shows that learners who successfully use metacognitive knowledge of listening and strategies to improve their comprehension, will also experience increased motivation. Goh (2002a, 2008) focused on a metacognitive approach that helps learners become more self-regulated and self-directed in their efforts to improve their individual listening abilities. In this book, we will show how these ideas can be incorporated effectively into a holistic learning experience for L2 listeners. For example, you will be introduced to a research-based metacognitive pedagogical sequence (Vandergrift, 2004, 2007) designed to help learners integrate the use of multiple strategies while focusing on the process of listening. At specific stages in a lesson sequence, learners are prompted to use strategies to regulate their comprehension and achieve successful comprehension. In addition to pursuing comprehension, the sequence guides learners through important metacognitive processes such as prediction, verification, monitoring, problem-solving, and evaluation—processes used by effective listeners and effective learners. This sequence not only raises learner awareness about the listening process, it also offers much needed scaffolding so that listeners can learn from each other while working with listening texts. We refer to this as metacognitive instruction for L2 listening. It is an approach to listening instruction that explicitly elicits and enhances learner knowledge about learning to listen, as well as teaching effective strategies for managing comprehension and overall listening development.

Summary

Listening, often the weakest skill for many language learners, receives the least structured support in the L2 classroom. Over the last five decades, listening has slowly become more important in the language curriculum, and more time and attention have been allocated to it. While this is a vast improvement from the time when listening was merely exploited to further other pedagogical goals, the time has come for language educators to rethink how they teach listening.

This chapter has outlined why learners need a more comprehensive approach to learning to listen. Developments in teaching methodologies over the last five decades have addressed some earlier weaknesses but there are still some gaps and limitations that need attention. The practice of testing learners for their understanding of listening input, rather than teaching them how to process and manage that input, is still predominant. A new approach for listening instruction is needed to give learners tools for self-regulated learning to develop listening beyond the classroom. This chapter has argued for a more holistic teaching approach that focuses on the process of learning to listen so that L2 listeners can develop the necessary learner knowledge and control of internal cognitive and affective processes, as well as the external social demands that influence comprehension success.

Discussion Questions and Tasks

1. Select a language teaching course book along with all its accompanying resources for listening. Examine the activities and types of

listening input used. Do they have any features of the types of listening instruction described earlier? Comment on the benefits of the types of instruction used in the book and the challenges that learners might face.

2. What is your understanding of a holistic metacognitive approach to teaching listening? How is this different from an activity where learners listen to the input and answer the questions based on it?

3. Think of a group of learners that you know or teach. What are their problems with learning to listen? What kind of support do they get from their teachers to deal with these problems?

4. Interview a few language learners to find out what they typically do in a listening class and how they feel about these activities. Ask them what else they would like their teachers to do to help them improve their listening.

5. Here are some important terms introduced in the chapter. What do they mean to you?

   a. Metacognition.
   b. Self-regulation.
   c. Learner strategy.

Suggestions for Further Reading

Larsen-Freeman, D. (1986). *Techniques and principles in language teaching*. New York: Oxford University Press.

Chapters 2 (Audio-lingual method) and 9 (Communicative method) are particularly interesting for insights into listening instruction as part of these language teaching methods.

Morley, J. (1999). Current perspectives on improving aural comprehension. *ESL Magazine, 2*(1), 16–19.

A readable overview of the evolution in listening instruction up to and including the communicative language teaching era.

White, G. (2006). Teaching listening: Time for a change in methodology. In E. Usó-Juan & A. Martínez-Flor (Eds.), *Current trends in the development and teaching of the four language skills* (pp. 111–135). Berlin: Mouton de Gruyter.

A readable chapter tracing some of the developments in listening instruction over the past 30 years and arguing for a more learner-centered approach to improve the teaching of L2 listening. Examples of activities are presented and discussed.

Chapter 2

Listening Competence

Scenario (excerpts from student listening diaries)

Usually when I listen to the radio or watch TV I can hear clearly most of their words and paragraphs, but I can't connect the words quickly. So sometimes I couldn't catch what they said. On the other hand, when I talk about something to someone, mostly I can understand them. I think it is because that when I talk with somebody I make myself into the language surrounding but when I listen to the radio or watch TV, I don't. (Abdul)

I think it is important to relate the things we heard to the things we experienced. I often find that it will be easier for me to understand the speech in English if I've known something about the topic in Chinese. The second method to grasp the main idea is that I notice the junction of several parts. We often get confused when we don't know the structure of the whole speaking. (Zhifei)

I think culture is the key element in language. Sometimes I can catch the whole sentence. But I can't understand the true meaning of the words. Because I haven't the same culture as the speaker, I couldn't give the accurate response to it. When I couldn't understand the speaker's words, I give a smiling to response it. Maybe I look a little wooden, but I have no choice. If I always ask the speaker to say again, he or she'll feel too boring with me. (Wang Li)

I had dinner with a Japanese couple. We talked about wide-ranging general topics in a relaxed atmosphere. If I encounter some unknown words, I would ask my friend politely. Then he would explain it to me, or give an example. I think to improve my listening skill, I'd better talk with native speaker as much as possible. (Carmen)

Last Saturday, after having enjoyed an English discussion on TV for more than 20 minutes, I suddenly realized that I had been watching with almost complete understanding of every sentence and that I had not been forcing myself to concentrate as before. It was as if I was watching a Spanish programme. It was incredibly wonderful. Later, as I reflected upon the experience I assumed that it was because I had been caught by the topic that was being discussed. So next time, I will try to be an active listener instead of a passive one. (Xavier)

When I listened to the BBC I noticed that it was easy to understand the familiar news. If an event happens for a long period and has being reported continuously and I know the process and background, it will be easy to understand. And if I've read the news in the newspapers in Chinese or English, it is also easy to understand the same news in radio. (Ling)

Pre-reading Reflection

1.   What do these learners say about the demands of L2 listening?
2.   What do these learners recount about listening in different contexts?
3.   What seem to be the common listening difficulties reported by these learners? How might they be able to overcome these difficulties?
4.   To what degree do the listening experiences of these L2 learners resonate with your own L2 listening experiences or those of your students? Explain.

Introduction

The last chapter concluded that a more innovative approach to teaching listening is needed to help L2 listeners regulate their own learning. The first step is a good understanding of the listening process. How does L2 listening comprehension work? What are the cognitive processes that operate during listening? What are the most crucial knowledge sources on which listeners draw to process and interpret what they hear? What are the unique cognitive and affective demands of interactive listening, where listeners can intervene and alternate in the roles of both speaker and listener?

This chapter will discuss what we know about the listening skill to better understand what listeners do to comprehend what they hear. That is essential to determine how to teach learners to listen effectively. The examination of listening will focus on three components in order to understand what it means to be a competent listener in a broad range of contexts:

•   The cognitive processes involved in listening.
•   The knowledge sources used in listening.
•   The unique features of interactive listening.

Cognitive Processes in Listening

This section will discuss the cognitive processes that come into play during the process of L2 listening comprehension: (1) top-down and bottom-up processing; (2) controlled and automatic processing; (3) perception, parsing, and utilization; and (4) metacognition. These processes describe what listeners do during the act of listening, how they can do this efficiently, and how they regulate these processes. The interrelationships between the various cognitive processes in rapid, automatic listening comprehension are encapsulated in Figure 2.1.

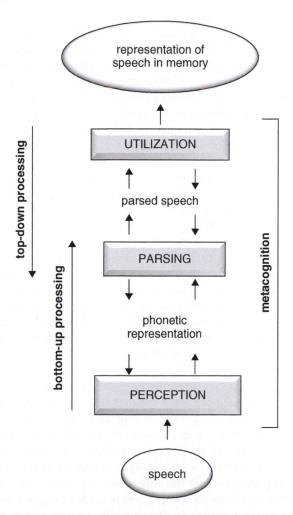

Figure 2.1. Cognitive Processes in L2 Listening and Their Interrelationships

Top-Down and Bottom-Up Processing

Fundamental to an understanding of comprehension processes are the distinction between bottom-up and top-down processing, the types of knowledge each process applies to the emerging interpretation of a message, and the interaction between these processes.

Bottom-up processing involves segmentation of the sound stream into meaningful units to interpret the message. It is a rather mechanical process in which listeners segment the sound stream and construct meaning by accretion, based on their knowledge of the segmentals (individual sounds or phonemes) and suprasegmentals (patterns of language intonation, such as stress, tone, and rhythm) of the target language. Listeners gradually build meaning from phonemes to words to increasingly larger units of meaning (full sentences and larger chunks of discourse).

This component of listening, seen as a decoding process, assumes that the comprehension process begins with information in the sound stream, with minimal contribution of information from the listener's prior knowledge of the world. Listeners draw primarily on linguistic knowledge, which includes phonological knowledge (phonemes, stress, intonation, and other sound adjustments made by speakers to facilitate speech production), lexical knowledge, and syntactic knowledge (grammar) of the target language. Used alone, this approach to comprehension is not adequate, because listeners cannot keep up with the sound stream.

Top-down processing, on the other hand, primarily involves the application of context and prior knowledge to interpret the message. Listeners who approach a comprehension task in a top-down manner use their knowledge of the context of the listening event or the topic of a listening text to activate a conceptual framework for understanding the message. Listeners can apply different types of knowledge to the task, including: prior (world or experiential) knowledge, pragmatic knowledge, cultural knowledge about the target language, and discourse knowledge (types of texts and how information is organized in these texts). These knowledge sources are stored in the listener's long-term memory in the form of schemata (complex mental structures that group all knowledge concerning a concept). This top-down component of listening, seen as an interpretation process, assumes that comprehension begins with listener expectations about information in the text and subsequent application of appropriate knowledge sources to comprehend the sound stream. Used alone, this approach to comprehension is not adequate either, because listeners may not have all the prior knowledge required, or share enough of the speaker's perspective on the subject matter to interpret accurately.

In reality, top-down and bottom-up processes rarely operate independently. Research in L1 speech perception provides evidence for the interactive nature of these processes, particularly regarding how information from top-down processing drives and constrains interpretation (Davis & Johnsrude, 2007). Linguistic information gleaned from the decoding process and prior knowledge applied during the interpretation are processed in parallel fashion as listeners create a mental representation of what they have heard (see the next chapter for a more complete description of this parallel processing).

The degree to which listeners may use one process more than another will depend on their purpose for listening. A listener who needs to verify a specific detail such as the price of an item or driving directions, for example, may engage in more bottom-up processing than a listener who is interested in obtaining an overview of what happened at a particular event. Research on these cognitive processes suggests that L2 listeners need to learn how to use both processes to their advantage, depending on the purpose for listening, learner characteristics (e.g., language proficiency, working memory capacity, age) and the context of the listening event.

Controlled and Automatic Processing

When listening is fluent, as in L1 listening, cognitive processing occurs extremely rapidly, moving back and forth between top-down and bottom-up processes as required to achieve comprehension. Successful L2 listening depends, obviously, on the degree to which listeners can efficiently coordinate these processes. L1 listeners do this automatically (particularly bottom-up processing), with little conscious attention to individual words. L2 listeners, on the other hand, usually have limited language knowledge; therefore, they are not able to automatically process everything that they hear. Depending on their level of L2 proficiency or their familiarity with the topic of the text, listeners may need to focus consciously on some aspects of the input or learn to selectively attend to basic elements of meaning, such as salient content words. Whatever listeners cannot process automatically is subject to controlled processing, time permitting.

Controlled (as opposed to automatic) processing involves conscious attention to and processing of elements in the speech stream. A cognitive skill, such as listening, becomes automatic with practice, like other skilled behaviors (Johnson, 1996). When we first begin riding a bicycle, for example, we need to pay deliberate attention to coordinate getting on the bike, maintaining balance, steering with the handle bars, and gaining momentum by moving the pedals with our feet. Eventually this becomes automatic and we no longer need to pay conscious attention to the coordination of these different elements of the skill. When processing spoken language requires conscious attention to different elements of the sound stream, due to the limitations of working memory and speed of the incoming input, comprehension will suffer. Controlled processing is not efficient because it cannot keep up with the incoming input; consequently, comprehension either breaks down or listeners resort to compensatory strategies, contextual factors, and other relevant information available to them, to guess at what they did not understand.

As suggested in our discussion so far, memory plays a crucial role in comprehension processing. Traditionally, the concept of memory has been divided into two components: long-term memory and working memory (formerly called short-term memory). Long-term memory, as noted in the discussion of top-down processing, is the bank of information that listeners access to interpret what they are trying to understand. This bank of information is comprised of accumulated prior knowledge and life experiences of the listener, organized as schemata. Appropriate schemata are activated when listening to a related topic. While long-term memory shapes the interpretation of what listeners hear, working memory influences the efficiency of the cognitive processing and allows the listener to think about an appropriate response, as in the case of interactive listening.

In contrast to long-term memory, working memory has limited capacity; listeners can only hold a limited number of units before this information fades and new information has to be processed (Call, 1985). Listeners hold the retained units of information in a phonological loop for a few seconds until the sounds can be segmented into words or larger chunks of meaningful speech through links with long-term memory. How much information a listener can hold in working memory will depend on their level of language proficiency. As their level of language proficiency increases, listeners are able to retain and process increasingly larger chunks of meaningful speech.

Cognitive activity in working memory is overseen and regulated by an executive control responsible for high-level activities such as planning, coordinating flow of information, and retrieving knowledge from long-term memory (Baddeley, 2003). The more familiar the units are to listeners, the more quickly long-term memory can supply previously acquired linguistic knowledge and prior knowledge for listeners to process. An example of this phenomenon is the difference we experience in processing a new telephone number, in contrast to processing a sentence with the same number of individual units. We process the sentence more efficiently because the links between the units are meaningful and easier to retain, owing to the rapid links with semantic and syntactic components of our linguistic knowledge store in long-term memory. The digits of the telephone number, on the other hand, need to be processed individually because the digits, although meaningful as individual numerals, are new information to long-term memory as a single, combined unit. Once we have more experience with this telephone number, it will be stored in long-term memory and processed in working memory as one meaningful unit: for example, the phone number of a newly discovered restaurant. Processing the telephone number as a single unit leaves more attentional resources (room in working memory) for additional information, thereby increasing the efficiency of cognitive processing.

The link between working memory and long-term memory plays a critical role in successful listening comprehension. The more listeners process information automatically, the more they can allocate the limited attentional resources of their working memory to processing new information. Increased working memory space also allows listeners to think about the content of what they are hearing, which is essential for critical listening.

Perception, Parsing, and Utilization

Another perspective on cognitive processes that can provide further insight into how listeners construct meaning is Anderson's (1995) differentiation of listening comprehension into three interconnected phases: perceptual processing (perception), parsing, and utilization. Although this model may suggest a sequence of phases (see Figure 2.1), the three phases have a two-way relationship with one another that, in fact, reflects the integrated nature of how bottom-up and top-down processing occurs.

During the perception phase, listeners use bottom-up processing to recognize sound categories (phonemes) of the language, pauses, and acoustic emphases, and hold these in memory. Listeners decode incoming speech by (1) attending to the text, to the exclusion of other sounds in the environment; (2) noting similarities, pauses, and acoustic emphases relevant to a particular language; and then (3) grouping these according to the categories of the identified language. This is the initial stage in the word segmentation process. A phonetic representation of what is retained is passed on for parsing.

Development of word segmentation skills is a major challenge for L2 listeners. Unlike readers, listeners do not have the luxury of spaces to help them determine word boundaries. Listeners must parse the sound stream into meaningful units when word boundaries are difficult to determine because of stress patterns, elisions, and reduced forms. Even if they can recognize individual words, when spoken in isolation or presented in written form, listeners may not always be able to recognize those same words in connected speech. Furthermore, word segmentation skills are language-specific and acquired early in life. They are so solidly engrained in the listener's processing system that these L1 segmentation strategies are involuntarily applied when listening to a non-native language. Difficulties reported by L2 listeners during the perception phase include (1) not recognizing words; (2) neglecting parts of speech that follow; (3)

not chunking the stream of speech; (4) missing the beginning of a sentence or message; and (5) concentration problems (Goh, 2000).

During the parsing phase, listeners parse the phonetic representation of what was retained in memory and begin to activate potential word candidates. Listeners use the parsed speech to retrieve potential word candidates from long-term memory, based on cues such as word onset, perceptual salience, or phonotactic conventions (rules that apply to the sequencing of phonemes). Using any one or more of these cues, listeners create propositions (abstract representations of an idea) in order to hold a meaning-based representation of these words in working memory as new input is processed. Meaning is often the principal clue in segmentation. As language proficiency develops, listeners can more quickly activate successful word candidates related to the context or topic, and hold meaning in increasingly larger chunks of propositional content. With regard to the identification of function and content words, L2 listeners appear to be more successful in identifying content words (Field, 2008b). This is not surprising, because content words carry meaning and the limitations of working memory require L2 listeners to be selective. Difficulties reported by listeners during this phase include (1) quickly forgetting what has been heard; (2) being unable to form a mental representation from words heard; and (3) not understanding subsequent parts because of what was missed earlier (Goh, 2000).

Finally, in the utilization phase, listeners relate the resulting meaningful units to information sources in long-term memory in order to interpret the intended or implied meanings. This phase primarily involves top-down processing of the parsed speech. An important characteristic of this phase is that listeners use information from outside the linguistic input to interpret what they have retained (the parsed speech). Using pragmatic and prior knowledge (stored as schemata in long-term memory) and any relevant information in the listening context, listeners elaborate on the newly parsed information and monitor this interpretation for congruency with their previous knowledge and the evolving representation of the text in memory, as often as necessary within the time available.

During this utilization phase, listeners generate a conceptual framework against which to match their emerging interpretation of the text or conversation and to go beyond the literal meaning of the input, when warranted. Fluent listeners then automatically reconcile linguistic input with their accumulated store of prior knowledge, in order to determine meaning. When the automatic processes break down because of a comprehension problem, listening becomes a problem-solving activity. Listeners, for example, may need to reconsider inferences made. Difficulties reported by listeners during this phase include (1) understanding the words but not the message, and (2) feeling confused because of seeming incongruencies in the message (Goh, 2000).

These processes work neither independently nor in a linear fashion, as can be seen in Figure 2.1. Arrows moving back and forth between the component processes suggest that cognitive processing at each level can influence and be influenced by the results of cognitive processing that precedes or follows. In fact, this occurs so rapidly in fully automatic, fluent listening that these processes take place in parallel fashion: that is, they occur simultaneously as new speech is processed.

Metacognition

How do listeners manage to control comprehension processes that occur at different levels with lightening speed? Proficient listeners are able to control or regulate these processes through their use of meta-cognitive knowledge. Metacognition refers to listener awareness of the cognitive processes involved in comprehension, and the capacity to oversee, regulate, and direct these processes (Goh, 2008). In addition to the ability to reflect on these processes, it includes knowledge about the factors relating to task, person, and strategy that come into play during any cognitive activity (Flavell, 1979). The control dimension of meta-cognition involves use of cognitive processes such as planning, monitoring, problem-solving, and evaluating to effectively regulate listening comprehension.

Application of metacognitive knowledge is a mental characteristic shared by successful learners; in fact, Vandergrift, Goh, Mareschal, and Tafaghodtari (2006) found that approximately 13 percent of variance in listening achievement could be explained by metacognition. In sum, listeners who can apply metacognitive knowledge about listening during the cognitive processes of comprehension are better able to regulate these processes and draw on the relevant knowledge sources in an efficient manner to build text comprehension.

The nature and role of metacognitive knowledge will be discussed in detail in Chapter 5. We now turn to the knowledge sources on which listeners must draw for comprehension purposes.

Knowledge Sources in Listening

As listeners engage in the cognitive processes described earlier, they draw on different knowledge sources: linguistic knowledge, pragmatic knowledge, prior knowledge, and discourse knowledge. Information retrieved from these "data banks" will influence the quality and the direction of the cognitive processing. In this section we will focus on the role of each of these knowledge sources in the listening process. These relationships are encapsulated in Figure 2.2 on page 27.

Linguistic Knowledge

Linguistic knowledge is fundamental to listening comprehension; vocabulary knowledge is a strong predictor of L2 listening success. In addition to vocabulary, or semantic knowledge, linguistic knowledge includes phonological knowledge (phonemes, stress, intonation, and speech modifications such as assimilation and elision) and syntactic knowledge (grammar) of the target language. Phonological and syntactic knowledge help listeners parse the sound stream for meaningful units of language and assign semantic roles to words. Application of all three elements of linguistic knowledge helps listeners assign meaning to word-level units and to the relationship between words at the discourse level.

Linguistic knowledge also means knowing how to use one's knowledge of a language in real time—that is, as rapid speech unfolds. Recognizing a word in its written form or hearing it in isolation does not necessarily mean that we will recognize that same word in the context of rapid speech. This is the real challenge of listening comprehension: L2 listeners need to be able to rapidly parse words out from a stream of sound. Some words are easily parsed and can be quickly mapped onto long-term memory. These include cognates for linguistically similar languages; sound effects and paralinguistics that are not culturally bound; and, increasingly, English words related to technology or the media (e.g., iPod) that are becoming universally understood. Other words will require deeper processing.

Pragmatic Knowledge

Listening comprehension involves far more than just understanding words. Listeners use pragmatic knowledge when they apply information that goes beyond the literal meaning of a word, message, or text to interpret the speaker's intended meaning. Listeners usually apply pragmatic knowledge during the utilization phase of the comprehension process. It is informed, for example, by interpretation of tone (e.g., sarcasm and questions). L2 pragmatic knowledge helps the listener to infer the speaker's intention, particularly if there is any ambiguity in the literal meaning of the utterance. Pragmatic knowledge is often culturally bound and, therefore, closely related to sociocultural and sociolinguistic knowledge (e.g., formal or informal registers, idioms, and slang), which listeners use to further interpret an utterance (Buck, 2001).

Recent work by Dipper, Black, and Bryan (2005) on "thinking for listening" may help to explain how listeners use pragmatic knowledge to enrich the linguistic input. During the utilization phase, they found that listeners generate familiar "conceptual events" or scenarios from long-term memory and match the emerging meaning of the text or utterance against them. In adapting this scenario, according to Dipper et al., listeners go beyond semantic meaning to consider the contextualized meaning intended by the speaker. A request such as "Do you have the salt?" at the dinner table likely suggests that the speaker would like someone to pass the salt, rather than reply affirmatively. This is the process underlying the cognitive strategy of elaboration.

Prior Knowledge

Listening comprehension is comparable to a problem-solving activity: listeners match what they hear (the linguistic input) with what they know about how things work in the world (their prior knowledge). The role of prior knowledge (also known as world, encyclopaedic, or experiential knowledge) in L2 listening comprehension is well established (e.g., Macaro, Vanderplank, & Graham, 2005). This knowledge source plays a critical role in the utilization phase of the listening process. For example, a discussion about experiences in renting an apartment, intended to activate vocabulary and types of scenarios, will greatly facilitate comprehension of a listening text where students listen to a phone conversation enquiring about rental space or watch a video about visiting the apartment and talking to the landlord. For this reason, it is important to provide listeners with the context of a listening text or event, before they begin listening. Contextualized listeners then have the necessary information to activate their prior knowledge on the topic and to develop a conceptual framework in order to parse the linguistic input for potential words and content. Contextual information can help listeners process the linguistic input more efficiently, freeing up working memory resources to process larger chunks of information.

Although prior knowledge is important for facilitating comprehension, it can also be misleading when used inflexibly. Listener use of prior knowledge can lead to inaccurate comprehension when it is not supported by corroborating evidence that matches the listener's expectations (Macaro et al., 2005). This underscores the importance of flexibility in the comprehension process. Using a combination of questioning and elaboration (activating prior knowledge), listeners must continually consider different possibilities and monitor the emerging interpretation for congruency with their expectations and prior knowledge (Vandergrift, 2003b).

Discourse Knowledge

Discourse (textual) knowledge involves comprehension at the level of text organization. Awareness of the kind of information (sometimes called script knowledge) found in certain texts and how that information is organized will facilitate the listener's ability to process this information. A restaurant advertisement, for example, is likely to include name, address, phone number, and the restaurant's specialty or current specials, in addition to other information. Listeners use discourse knowledge when they consider and apply knowledge of text types to the comprehension process.

Depending on the nature of the text, this category includes knowledge of and attention to discourse markers that signal the beginning (e.g., first of all) or conclusion (e.g., in sum) of a set of arguments, an opposing argument (e.g., on the other hand) or a hypothesis (e.g., if). Such signals give listeners some idea of what type of information they can expect to hear. Discourse knowledge can be used proactively by the listener to anticipate the kinds of information that might be found in a text. This kind of knowledge is often used in combination with prior knowledge. Listeners, for example, can use knowledge about how an interview with a soccer player might begin, what questions are asked, and how the interview will likely end, in order to anticipate what they will hear in a similar interview.

Discourse knowledge is very important in interactive listening. In these contexts, listeners use discourse knowledge to facilitate the processing of what they hear and how they may be asked to respond. For example, in an information exchange, such as purchasing shoes, listeners can use their knowledge of the script that is likely to unfold to anticipate the questions that will be asked and the answers they will need to provide for the exchange to be successful. Furthermore, in these contexts, listeners use discourse knowledge when they use appropriate back-channelling cues, determine when to take their turn in conversation, and decide when and how to ask clarification questions.

In sum, the different knowledge sources work together with the cognitive processes to help listeners arrive at a meaningful interpretation of a listening text. Some of these knowledge sources, such as prior knowledge, can be transferred from L1. In other cases, depending on the similarities between the languages (root language, script system, and cultural conventions), some elements of pragmatic, discourse, and linguistic knowledge may transfer. As L2 listeners gain more language experience and their language proficiency develops, they are able to process information more efficiently and access these knowledge sources more rapidly. A schematic representation of these knowledge sources and how they relate to the component processes underlying listening comprehension is illustrated in Figure 2.2.

Interactive Listening

Most classroom listening instruction uses non-participatory, one-way listening. This kind of listening is primarily transactional in nature:

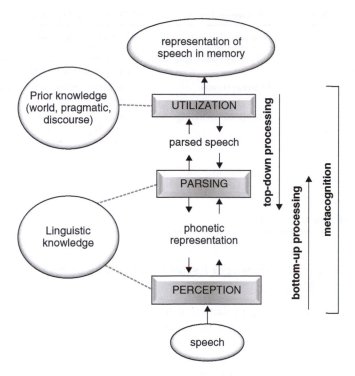

Figure 2.2. Cognitive Processes and Knowledge Sources in Listening Comprehension

the goal is to obtain information for some kind of communicative purpose and there is no opportunity to intervene for purposes of clarification. An important goal for many L2 learners, however, is competence in interactive listening, which is the ability to interact with speakers of the target language in social situations, such as conversations. The goal of this kind of listening can be transactional, interactional, or purely social, to foster social relationships. Learning how to handle the cognitive and social demands of these kinds of listening events is an important component of listening competence. For this reason, we include the unique features of interactive listening in our discussion of L2 listening competence. While the cognitive processes are common to both types of listening, there are also some important differences related to flow of communication, listening function, communication goal, strategy use, social demands, and cognitive demands, as can be seen in Table 2.1.

Table 2.1. Differences Between Interactive and One-Way Listening

Criterion	One-way listening	Interactive listening
Flow of communication	One-way: listening only	Two-way: listener alternates as speaker and listener
Function of language	Transactional	Transactional, interactional, and/or social
Goal of communication	Interpret meaning	Interpret meaning; negotiate meaning; respond and/or initiate; establish social relationships
Strategy use	Comprehension strategies	Comprehension and reception strategies
Social demands	Low	High
Cognitive demands	High	High

Similarities and Differences Between One-Way and Interactive Listening

Cognitive processing is fundamental to the listening process, regardless of context. Listeners engaged in one-way listening or interactive listening events use top-down and bottom-up processing and, concurrently, engage in perception, parsing, and utilization to understand what their interlocutor is saying. In both contexts they use metacognitive knowledge to control these processes as efficiently as possible.

While they are processing what their interlocutor is saying, listeners involved in interactive listening access the same knowledge sources as in one-way listening. They draw on their mental lexicon for the linguistic knowledge necessary to parse the input, and on their bank of prior, pragmatic, and discourse knowledge to interpret the overall intended meaning of their interlocutor within the context of the interaction.

Although one-way and interactive listening share many characteristics, they are also different in important ways. First, in interactive listening, speaker and listener share a common communicative goal, listening context, or life experience. Second, interactive listeners have the opportunity to act in the dual role of listener and speaker: they can clarify meaning or ask their interlocutor to slow down or repeat what was said. In this regard, a number of reception strategies are available to listeners to facilitate listening in these contexts. This makes interactive listening less demanding.

On the other hand, there are factors in interactive listening that can make it equally more demanding. First, listeners in these contexts are expected to reply: they must prepare and formulate a response as they process the speech of their interlocutor. This adds significantly to the cognitive load, because they must begin to formulate a response while at the same time attending to the speaker's message. Second, depending on the relationship betweena listener and interlocutor, the social and affective demands of the listening task may be very high, thereby constraining working memory resources. We will now consider separately the role of each of these factors in L2 listening competence.

Contextual Nature of Interactive Listening

Context plays a greater role in interactive listening than in one-way listening. Whether the context is formal or informal, listeners in interactive situations often have a common communicative goal that facilitates interpretation: e.g., the job description, the applicant's curriculum vitae, and the job interview protocol between the job applicant and the interviewer; the "script" for selling or buying shoes shared by the salesperson and the customer; or the common life experiences and assumptions shared by friends in conversation. In each of these situations, the context provides the backdrop against which (1) to predict information heard, question-types used, routines followed, or, in the case of conversation between friends, to assume common understandings without stating things explicitly, and (2) to monitor interpretation as the interaction unfolds. The highly contextualized nature of each of these interactive situations will facilitate perception and parsing, because potential word candidates will be more quickly activated and connections between words made more quickly, allowing listeners to process the interlocutor's utterances more efficiently. At the same time, listeners use their metacognitive knowledge to guide their predictions and to monitor their comprehension for congruence with their expectations. When they are confronted with something unexpected and are unable to resolve the comprehension problem internally, or simply do not understand, listeners can intervene and ask their interlocutor to clarify, repeat, or speak more slowly. The possibility to clarify and/or verify meaning is probably the greatest benefit for L2 listeners in interactive listening. They can be provided with strategies to become good listeners and to intervene appropriately.

Strategies for Interactive Listening

In a classroom study on interactive listening strategies used by students during seminar discussions, Lynch (1995) observed two broad categories. The first includes old information questions for clarification of an earlier comprehension difficulty—responses characterized by a backward orientation. The second includes new information questions or receipt tokens that carry the discourse forward or ask the interlocutor to elaborate further—responses characterized by a forward orientation. Table 2.2 highlights a number of interactive listening strategies identified through research with L2 listeners engaged in interactive tasks (Dörnyei & Kormos, 1998; Rost & Ross, 1991; Vandergrift, 1997b). Evidence for these strategies was corroborated in subsequent studies (Farrell & Mallard, 2006; Vandergriff, 2006).

Table 2.2. Interactive Listening Strategies: Definitions and Examples

	Strategy	*Definition*	*Examples*
Backward Orientation	1. Global reprise/ask for repetition/ convey non-understanding	Listeners either ask for outright repetition, rephrasing, or simplification of preceding utterance, or indicate non-understanding in non-verbal ways.	What was the question? Pardon? Confused looks, blank looks, furrowed eyebrows . . .
	2. Ask for clarification/ specific lexical reprise	Listeners ask a question referring to a specific word, term, or fragment that was not understood in the previous utterance.	Where? . . . le souper? Is that dinner? . . . he is going . . .?
	3. Hypothesis testing/ ask for confirmation	Listeners ask specific questions about facts in the preceding utterance to verify that they have understood and/or what they are expected to do.	. . . after finishing his homework? . . . the last book?
Forward Orientation	4. Uptaking/back-channelling	Listeners use kinesics and verbal or non-verbal signals to indicate to their interlocutor to continue and that they understand.	Nods, "uh-huh," "oui," "ah," "oh," laughing at the appropriate time
	5. Forward inference/ interpretive summary	Listeners overtly indicate current understanding by asking questions using previously understood information.	If he is chosen, do you think he will go?
	6. Faking/feigning understanding	Listeners send uptaking signals or non-committal responses in order to avoid seeking clarification and admitting to their interlocutor that they have not understood.	Comme ci, comme ça (so so) Yes (smile) Je pense (I think so).

Adapted from Vandergrift, 1997b

Strategies with a Backward Orientation

The first three strategies in Table 2.2 describe the efforts employed by listeners to clarify understanding of an earlier difficulty. When they do not understand, cannot hear, or are uncertain about what they have heard, listeners can use a global reprise such as "Pardon?" They can also ask their interlocutors to repeat what they have said, or they can convey non-comprehension through some voluntary or involuntary non-verbal signal such as a confused look. The first two signals are explicit requests for help, while the third, more subtle signal may or may not be picked up by the interlocutor. On a less global level of misunderstanding, when listeners have not understood a particular word or fragment that appears to be key to understanding the message, they can use a specific reprise: that is, ask for clarification by pointing out the word or fragment that is not understood. Finally, to ensure that they have understood correctly, listeners can seek clarification through a process of hypothesis testing. They can ask a specific question about what their interlocutor has just said to confirm that they have understood and/or know what they are expected to do. With the help of these kinds of strategies, listeners signal their need for confirmation or clarification, prompting their interlocutor to confirm or clarify comprehension and then move the interaction forward.

When listeners clarify or verify comprehension, they are engaged in meaning negotiation. By signalling comprehension difficulties to their interlocutor, listeners solicit further language input. The interlocutor responds by repeating or restating the message in a different way, thereby tailoring the language input to a level comprehensible to the listener. If the restated information is still not adequately understood for the interaction to move forward, both interlocutors can continue to negotiate meaning until an adequate level of comprehension has been realized. The importance of these interactive listening strategies cannot be underestimated. Besides allowing interaction to move forward between interlocutors at different levels of proficiency, reception strategies have the potential for providing comprehensible input to language learners, particularly the less proficient learner. When listeners have the opportunity to negotiate meaning, language input can be made comprehensible to them at their current level of understanding. This can have salutary effects on language acquisition (Lightbown & Spada, 2006; Pica, 1994).

Strategies with a Forward Orientation

Interactive listening involves more than comprehension clarification. Good listeners also do their part to move the interaction forward through culturally acceptable receipt tokens (uptakes or back-channels) or other acknowledgments of comprehension, as described in the last three strategies in Table 2.2. Before examining these strategies more closely, it is worth noting that although hypothesis testing, the third strategy, is included with clarification strategies, it is also a transition strategy. It allows listeners to clarify understanding, the interlocutor to affirm comprehension, and the interaction to move forward. Among the strategies used by listeners to move the interaction forward, however, the most common and natural response is uptaking or back-channelling. To signal to their interlocutor to continue, listeners use kinesics (nods), verbal (yes, really?), or other non-verbal signals (uh-huh) that convey their interest and their comprehension so far. The types of back-channelling cues, as well as when and how often to use them, are often culturally bound.

The forward inference is a useful, higher level of back-channelling. In this case, listeners overtly indicate their current understanding by asking questions that include an interpretive summary based on previously understood information. For example, in a conversation where a woman is explaining that her daughter will likely place high enough at the regional diving competition to go on to compete at the provincial level, the listener can demonstrate involvement in the interaction and move the conversation forward with a question such as "That's great. If she wins, where will she go?" In this case, the listener has helped her interlocutor move the interaction forward through active listening.

The final strategy, feigning understanding or faking, has mixed usefulness. Listeners may feign understanding in situations where their intervention may appear disruptive or discourteous, particularly if the interlocutor is not well known to them. In these contexts, listeners may hope that what was misunderstood will be clarified through contextual clues in the developing interaction or that an upcoming response on their part will not be related to what they did not understand. Listeners may initiate a global or specific reprise at that time, depending on their relationship to the interlocutor. Sometimes, however, interlocutors will continue to fake understanding, just to save face. For example, in a study by Foster and Ohta (2005), a qualitative analysis of negotiation of meaning revealed that interlocutors in each dyad, in order to save face, actively supported each other in accomplishing the task, even when meaning may not have been entirely clear.

Social Demands of Interactive Listening

An important variable in the success of interactive listening is the social dynamic between the interlocutors. When listeners face a comprehension problem, how they deal with it will depend on a number of affective variables such as willingness to take risks, fear of losing face, assertiveness, and motivation. The degree to which these variables will influence the interaction depends on the relationship between the interlocutors, because status relationships can affect comprehension and the freedom to negotiate meaning. Differences, for example, in age, gender, language proficiency, and power relationships (employer–employee) often make interactive listening a context where the disadvantaged listener feels powerless. This sense of inferiority can affect how much is understood (because of increased anxiety) and the degree to which listeners will dare to clarify comprehension, in order to save face. Furthermore, the face-to-face nature of these events also requires listeners to attend to non-verbal signals (e.g., furrowed eyebrows), body language, and culturally bound cues (e.g., certain gestures), which can add to or change the literal meaning of an utterance. This also increases the cognitive demands of interactive listening.

Finally, the obligation of listeners to respond to their interlocutor, an integral part of interactive listening, adds to the demands of the task. As listeners attend to their interlocutor, they must not only process the content of the message in real time: they also need to clarify their understanding when comprehension is uncertain, and respond appropriately. This increases the cognitive load significantly, because listeners must allocate their limited attentional resources to both comprehension and production in swift succession.

In sum, the unique features of interactive listening bring to light additional factors for a more comprehensive understanding of listening competence. For interactive listening, listeners must process linguistic input in real time (as in one-way listening) and respond appropriately. In this context, listeners can generally exert greater control by clarifying understanding, when comprehension is uncertain or incomplete, through the use of culturally appropriate interactive listening strategies. Interactive listening may be easier than one-way listening, particularly if the context is familiar and the interlocutors are comfortable with each other. On the other hand, social relationships can negatively affect comprehension and the freedom to negotiate meaning, particularly when one interlocutor is in a power relationship over the other.

Summary

This chapter has presented and discussed the factors that contribute to competence in L2 listening. We have seen that listening is a complex cognitive skill that must operate automatically for listeners to efficiently process what they hear. Listeners construct meaning by linking information from a listening text with knowledge stores in long-term memory, informed by their overall prior knowledge and life experiences. Top-down and bottom-up processes play a key role in all three phases of comprehension (perception, parsing, and utilization) and they are informed by knowledge sources such as linguistic, pragmatic, discourse, and prior knowledge. Competent listeners use metacognition to regulate these processes to achieve successful comprehension. Finally, we have examined the differences between interactive and one-way listening, noting the unique features of interactive listening that provide us with a more complete picture of listening competence in different contexts.

In the next chapter, we will examine a model of listening comprehension that integrates into one comprehensive system the interaction between these cognitive processes and knowledge sources for both one-way and interactive listening.

Discussion Questions and Tasks

1. How might learner characteristics such as language proficiency, L1 listening, and cultural background constrain the type of language processing used by listeners?
2. Buck (2001) suggests that listening is a very individual and personal process where there are often differences between listener interpretations of a text. Explain how this might be possible.
3. Looking back at the diary excerpts in the opening scenario of this chapter, what are the knowledge sources these students have identified?
4. Think back to the difficulties you experienced in listening to a new language. What was most difficult for you? Relate this to the listening processes described in this chapter. Based on your new awareness of the processes underlying listening comprehension, what might you do differently? Why?
5. Why is interactive listening a fertile environment for language acquisition? What are the ideal conditions of the task or context that can potentially foster language acquisition?

Suggestions for Further Reading

Buck, G. (2001). *Assessing listening* (Chapter 1: An overview of listening comprehension, pp. 1–30). Cambridge, UK: Cambridge University Press.
   Although the emphasis of this volume is on the assessment of listening, the overview of theory and research on listening in the first chapter is both comprehensive and accessible.
Eckerth, J. (2009). Negotiated interaction in the L2 classroom. *Language Teaching, 42,* 109–130.
   A classroom-based study on the negotiation of meaning, replicating an earlier, often-cited study by Foster (1998).
Farrell, T. C., & Mallard, C. (2006). The use of reception strategies by learners of French as a foreign language. *The Modern Language Journal, 90,* 338–352.
   A study of interactive listening involving language learners engaged in an information gap task, documenting the reception strategies used.

Goh, C. (2000). A cognitive perspective on language learners' listening comprehension problems. *System, 28,* 55–75.
A study on comprehension problems that identifies the real-time listening difficulties faced by a group of English as a Second Language (ESL) learners, examining and discussing these difficulties within the three-phase model of language comprehension proposed by Anderson (1995).

Chapter 3

A Model of Listening Comprehension

Scenario

Rose and Nina, English speakers in the same beginner-level French class, listen individually to a dialogue in which a talk-show host informs a woman that she has won a weekend ski trip for two. Their task is to "think aloud": that is, to reveal to the researcher, as closely as possible, all the thoughts in their mind as they attempt to understand. Working individually with each listener, the researcher stops the recording at pre-determined points to allow each one to relate what is going on in her mind, the emerging meaning of the text, any difficulties she is struggling with, and what she is doing to resolve these points of difficulty. In order to obtain a more complete picture of the comprehension process, each listener began "cold": that is, she was not given any preliminary information about the text.

As Rose listens and attempts to convey her understanding, she cites, verbatim, bits and pieces of the dialogue that relate to either the beginning or the end of the segment that she has just heard. She continues in this same pattern, sometimes providing an individual word that she has understood. After a second listen to the text, her understanding remains rudimentary: she understands that a man is calling a girl about a ski weekend and that her sister is involved.

Nina, on the other hand, begins by noting that this is a phone conversation where the two speakers do not know each other and she thinks it may have something to do with advertising. She translates the word "news" as "new" and then speculates about how this might have something to do with advertising. She uses her understanding of the word "surprise" to suggest that this might be a radio talk show. She also thinks that she heard the word for "win" but she's not sure about that. In the next segment, she confirms the idea of winning something related to skiing. In her second listen to the entire text, Nina confirms her understanding of "news" and "winning a draw," and comments again on the surprise and excitement she hears in the woman's voice.[1]

Pre-reading Reflection

1. Describe the difference in approach to comprehension between the two listeners.
2. Why is Rose less successful in her approach?
3. What does Nina do that makes her approach more successful?
4. Besides a difference in approach, might there be other differences between the two listeners that could explain the disparity in comprehension success?

Introduction

Listening is a complex cognitive skill. That is clear from our discussion of the cognitive concepts and processing skills involved in listening comprehension in the previous chapter. Listeners must be able to process what they hear in real time and, concurrently, attend to new input. Processing of rapid speech in our first language is mostly implicit, effortless, and automatic, with little conscious attention to what we are doing as we comprehend. Only when we encounter unknown words, an unfamiliar accent, an unknown topic, or some interference in the listening environment (e.g., noise or a poor phone connection) do we think about the process more consciously. For most of us, the first real confrontation with the complexities of listening comes when we learn a new language and have to identify and remember something meaningful in a largely incomprehensible speech stream.

In this chapter, we will continue to examine the cognitive architecture for comprehension with the help of a theoretical model of L2 listening comprehension (see Figure 3.1 on p. 39). We will describe the model and demonstrate how it represents a synthesis of the cognitive skills, discussed in the previous chapter, encapsulated into one coherent system. After demonstrating how this model captures what we currently know about listening, we will illustrate how the various processing components in this model might operate during listening, for both one-way and interactive listening. As we have already seen, listening is anything but a passive activity; we will continue to discover how listeners are actively engaged on many levels as they build comprehension.

---

1 See Vandergrift (2003a) for the complete think-aloud transcripts.

A Cognitive Model of Listening Comprehension

In contrast to L2 reading comprehension research, very few theoretical models have been elaborated for L2 listening comprehension. A theoretical model could help to clarify our understanding of the cognitive processing and processing components involved in L2 listening comprehension. For this reason, we will attempt to synthesize into one coherent model what we know listeners need to do to comprehend speech.

Models are helpful to account for what we know about a construct, provide a coherent explanation for how the parts work together, and provide a springboard for further research on the construct. Given our interest in synthesizing information and establishing some central claims about L2 listening, we are opting for a descriptive model, whose goal is to "synthesize the most important evidence in order to explain, in accessible terms, how a cognitive process works" (Grabe, 2009, p. 84). A descriptive model that can explain "how a cognitive process works" will be helpful for teachers. When teachers better understand the nature of listening comprehension, suggests Buck (1995), they can better provide optimum listening practice for their learners.

We are proposing a model for listening comprehension that builds on a model of speech production, mirrored by a comprehension processing side, developed by Levelt (1989, 1993, 1995). Developed to describe the unilingual speaker, this "blueprint" outlines how communicative intentions are formulated into actual speech by passing through a number of processing components that tap into different knowledge sources.

There are several good reasons for adopting and fleshing out the Levelt model. First, the speaking side of the model is based on several decades of psycholinguistic research, a wealth of empirical data obtained through experimental research, and the observation of speech errors (e.g., Levelt, 1995), and neural research (e.g., Hagoort & Levelt, 2009). Second, it is not restricted to parts of the production process: its strength lies in the integration of the different parts (de Bot, 1992). Third, the speaking side is mirrored by a comprehension side (to account for self-monitoring of speech), and thereby integrates production and reception of speech into one comprehensive system (Dörnyei & Kormos, 1998). This makes the model particularly useful to describe listening in both one-way and two-way (interactive) listening contexts. This is only a working model because, currently, there is no comprehensive theory that fully explains either the production or comprehension sides. Furthermore, this model is limited to the cognitive dimension of listening. There are also a number of important affective factors (e.g., motivation) that affect cognitive processing as listeners attempt to understand messages in various social contexts. A fully comprehensive model of L2 listening, therefore, will also have to account for the affective dimension of listening. In the interim, the Levelt model is a useful heuristic for visualizing and describing the cognitive processing components involved in listening comprehension, the knowledge sources, and their interactions.

Our explanation of listening comprehension begins with a brief overview of the production side of the model. We will then elaborate the comprehension side to incorporate the information about cognitive processing and knowledge sources discussed in the previous chapter. The processing components and their interactions will be further elaborated, using the cognitive framework posited by Anderson (1995) and the construct of metacognition.

In schematic representation (see Figure 3.1), the boxes represent the processing components, and the circles and ellipses represent knowledge sources. The vertical lines moving either up or down between the processing components portray the recursiveness of the processing between the

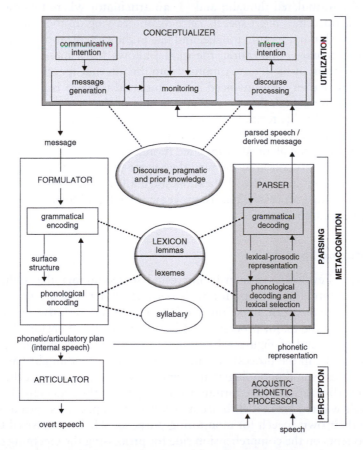

Figure 3.1. Schematic Representation of the Processing Components Involved in Speech Production and Comprehension

Based on Levelt, 1993

components. The dashed lines between the knowledge sources and the processing components indicate the knowledge sources upon which these components draw.

Producing Speech

As seen on the left side of Figure 3.1, three processing components are involved in the production of speech: (1) a conceptualizer where speakers decide what to say and the order in which their thoughts will be expressed, drawing on their world and discourse knowledge; (2) a formulator where thoughts are put into words by drawing on a lexicon (linguistic knowledge) for the required content and function words, ordering these grammatically while drawing on the syllabary (a mental store of articulatory gestures for each phonological syllable) to plan the actual articulation of this grammatically formulated thought; and (3) an articulator where this thought is transformed into overt speech, once again drawing on the syllabary to coordinate larynx, mouth, tongue, and lips in the verbalization process.

Before actual verbalization, the model allows for a monitoring loop (at the bottom of the figure, running from the internal speech to the bottom of the parser). An unvoiced but formulated thought is processed as inner speech through the comprehension side of the model, allowing the speaker to edit this formulated thought for appropriate intentional and grammatical speech. In other words, through inner speech, speakers can verify whether the planned formulated thought is, indeed, what they want to say and is structured in the way they want to say it. This capacity to monitor output at a pre-verbalization stage allows for the recursiveness of the cognitive processes: that is, movement back and forth between the processing components.

Monitoring Speech

Although Levelt was primarily interested in explaining the ability to speak, the monitoring loops, for purposes of checking both pre-verbalized and verbalized speech, make this model useful as a descriptive model for synthesizing the major processes in L2 listening comprehension. As seen at the lower end of Figure 3.1, speakers can monitor their own speech at two points in the process: as inner speech, after the thought has been grammatically and phonologically formulated, and as overt speech, after actual verbalization of the formulated thought (via the articulator).

Levelt wanted his model to account for what happens as speakers listen to their own speech for monitoring purposes. He hypothesized three components on the comprehension side for processing the emerging communicative intention: an acoustic-phonetic processor, a parser, and a conceptualizer. These processing components mirror those on the production side and tap into the same knowledge sources as those accessed by speakers (except for the syllabary because this is involved only in speech). We will examine these processing components and their interactions in greater detail, relating them to the cognitive processes posited by Anderson (1995). These cognitive processes, perception, parsing, and utilization have been inserted into the schematic representation on the right side of the corresponding processing component.

Perception

Perception in listening involves the recognition of sound signals by the listener as words or meaningful chunks of language (Anderson, 1995). Comprehension of spoken language, the inverse of speech production, begins with perception of sound signals by the acoustic-phonetic processor (see bottom right side of Figure 3.1). The perceived information is active for a very short time in working memory and processed for meaning. Some sounds are retained for processing (the number will depend on the listener's language proficiency) and are quickly displaced by other incoming sounds.

At this point, analysis of speech from an interlocutor or an aural text begins. Initially, listeners separate speech sounds from other sounds in the input. Depending on the context, listeners will recognize some or all sounds, individual or in combination, as language relevant or not. For L2 listeners at the beginning stages of language learning, what the acoustic-phonetic processor is capable of perceiving will depend very much on their L1. At this point, for example, the initial inability of English speakers to distinguish tones in Cantonese or of Spanish speakers to differentiate between "b" and "v" in English can become problematic. The degree of perception at all levels can depend on other factors, such as speed of the sound stream, dialect, or a dense text on a topic unfamiliar to the listener. Sound effects (e.g., a car crash) in an aural text can often be helpful to beginning listeners, if these sounds are similar in L1 and the target language.

The perception phase of listening involves bottom-up processing and becomes increasingly automatic with practice. L2 listeners make more rapid progress once they overcome the natural compulsion to listen using the sound categories of their L1 and when they acquire greater phonological knowledge of the sounds in their L2.

In the next stage, the phonetic representation of what was perceived and retained in working memory is parsed for meaning.

Parsing

Parsing in listening involves the segmentation of an utterance according to syntactic structures or semantic cues to create a mental representation of the combined meaning of the words. The comprehension process now continues with the parser in charge of the analysis of the phonetic representation output from the acoustic-phonetic processor. Using bottom-up processing, informed by top-down processing from the conceptualizer, the parser attempts to segment the sound stream into meaningful units, through phonological analysis and word retrieval from the listener's mental lexicon. This lexicon consists of lemmas, which specify the meaning and properties of a word (e.g., form, gender) and lexemes, which carry the morphophonological form (e.g., tense or plural markers that may slightly change the pronunciation) of a word. On a very rudimentary level, for example, when listeners segment the lexeme "flaʊr" (flower) from the sounds in the phonetic representation that they have retained, a number of possible lemmas present themselves: (1) semantic: "flour" versus "flower," which can usually be resolved by context, and (2) syntactic: "flower" (verb) versus "flower" (noun), which can be resolved by its syntactic feature: that is, its role in the sentence. Depending on the information activated, through grammatical parsing, the listener assigns to the lemma the syntactic role of either verb or noun.

Processing activity between the different model components is not linear. The two comprehension processes (perception and parsing) continue to inform each other within the available time, until a plausible mental representation emerges. The product of parsing is typically monitored in the conceptualizer for congruency with the listener's prior knowledge stored in long-term memory and/or current understanding of the whole text.

Utilization

Utilization in listening involves creating a mental representation of what is retained by the perception and parsing processes and linking this to existing knowledge stored in long-term memory (Anderson, 1995). This cognitive activity occurs in the conceptualizer, the processing component (top of Figure 3.1) shared by both the production and comprehension processes. Utilization is top-down in nature. During this phase of processing, the derived meaning from the parsed speech is monitored against the context of the message, what the listener knows about the speaker, the tone used to convey the message, and any other relevant information available to the listener, in order to interpret the intended meaning of the speaker or text. Elaboration of the intended meaning, described by Levelt as discourse processing, is similar to what Anderson calls utilization. It can occur at a micro level (at the level of the utterance or a part of that utterance) or at a macro level (the meaning of an entire text or the ensemble of utterances that form a conversation). By applying prior, pragmatic, and discourse knowledge, for example, listeners enrich the meaning of the text or the utterances of their interlocutor. Interpretation adds to the emerging representation of the aural text or co-text (see below) in memory, based on everything that has been comprehended so far. Levelt calls this product the "inferred intention" to parallel the "communicative intention" of the speaker or text.

Metacognition

As listeners process incoming input, they regulate the cognitive processes by using their metacognitive knowledge. The degree of conscious control of the process will vary with listener language proficiency. Metacognition involves planning (e.g., anticipating), monitoring (e.g., checking the accuracy of anticipations), problem-solving (e.g., repairing inaccurate comprehension), and evaluating (e.g., verifying overall comprehension, ideas, and performance). When listeners exercise metacognitive awareness and knowledge about L2 listening, they are able to orchestrate the cognitive processes more efficiently and effectively.

In Figure 3.1, metacognition is portrayed by the bracketed line on the far right. The regulatory role of metacognition will be further elaborated in Chapter 5.

Parallel Processing

The cognitive processes described earlier do not occur in a linear fashion. As output from each component of the model is passed on for processing or sent back for further processing, new incoming aural input is processed and informed by the results of earlier and ongoing cognitive processing. In Figure 3.1, the continued exchange of information, through top-down and bottom-up processing, is suggested by the bi-directional lines between the processing components (parser and conceptualizer) of the model.

The emerging meaning of the text, or mental model, in the conceptualizer serves as a context for further interpretation. Identification of the phonetic representations in the acoustic-phonetic processor becomes easier, because the co-text (what the listener has understood so far) will be activating potential word candidates, making subsequent word identification more rapid. Marslen-Wilson and Tyler (1980) proposed that various knowledge sources (lexical, structural, and world) interact during processing in an optimally efficient and accurate manner, such that information processed at one level will constrain and guide simultaneous processing at other levels. Eysenck (1993) suggested that one type of processing may take precedence over others in particular comprehension tasks. This, he noted, would usually depend on the amount of practice an individual had had with a particular task.

Parallel processing can be illustrated through the following example. Hearing a news item on the Olympic men's hockey final game, listeners will have activated a number of word candidates to complete the following sentence: "The game will take place on . . ." Upon hearing the phoneme "m," the word "Monday" will likely be activated (because, in this context, a day of the week would likely follow) without having to actively parse the remaining phonemes of the word. In this way, the different components of the model operate almost simultaneously and draw on the lexicon and world knowledge sources to inform these processes. In connected, real-time speech these processes occur so rapidly that listeners must automatically process different elements of the input in parallel fashion. Through frequent exposure to large doses of language input, fluent listeners implicitly learn that certain patterns and categories in the target language are more possible than others (Hulstijn, 2003). This makes processing easier, faster, and more accurate.

Mental Representation of Comprehension

The comprehension process operates in inverse order to the production process. The production process begins in the conceptualizer with a mental representation of what the speaker wishes to say and it is converted to words through the formulator. In comprehension, understood words are passed from the parser to the conceptualizer, drawing on appropriate knowledge sources through the process of utilization along the way. Through this process, listeners construct a mental representation of their understanding of the message in the conceptualizer, with the end product retained in long-term memory.

The mental representation is more than just a simple replica of text in memory: we likely do not retain the actual words but are left with a representation of those words in memory. This representation can be referred to as either a text representation or a situation representation of comprehension, depending on the amount of interpretation that listeners bring to the emerging representation.[2] A situation representation incorporates information from the text (message) in addition to the listener's interpretation of those words, whereas a text representation involves more of a literal understanding of the text.

These two accounts of comprehension are helpful for explaining the different levels of interpretation possible in response to a text, depending on the listener's world knowledge, life experience, and listening goals

2   In cognitive psychology, these are referred to as discourse comprehension models (Grabe, 2009). However, given that the goal of this chapter is to elucidate a descriptive model of listening comprehension, we have chosen to use the word "representation" instead of "model," so as not to confuse readers.

(Grabe, 2009). Different texts and purposes for listening will determine whether the listener builds more of a text representation or situation representation of the message (Kintsch, 1998). Some texts leave little room for individual interpretation: for example, passengers listening to a safety message on an airplane are expected to interpret the text in only one way if they wish to survive a potential forced landing. On the other hand, the lyrics of a song usually allow for a range of interpretations by different listeners, depending on their circumstances.

Returning to our working model of listening comprehension in Figure 3.1, when speakers monitor their formulated utterances, either as inner or overt speech, they are creating a text representation of comprehension, because it should correspond very closely to what they intend(ed) to say and be interpreted as such. On the other hand, other listeners listening to this same speaker, based on their own background knowledge and other contextual factors, may well interpret the utterances or speech differently, creating more of a situation representation of the utterances (and larger conversation) or speech.

As suggested earlier, these two accounts of comprehension are useful for explaining differences in the development of comprehension. This is particularly useful for understanding differences in listening comprehension among L2 learners who lack the linguistic knowledge to develop an adequate text representation and, consequently, create a situation representation, heavily influenced by their own interpretations and expectations, in order to compensate for what they were not able to understand. We will illustrate how this can occur, using the think-aloud protocols of an L2 listener attempting to comprehend an aural text.

Illustrations of Listening Processes at Work

One-way Listening

Beginning-level listeners sometimes make misconnections between linguistic input and world knowledge because of limited linguistic knowledge, and still make plausible but incorrect interpretations of the text. John, in his first year of studying French, is listening to a text that announces a hockey game between the Soviets and the Canadians and includes information about purchasing tickets. The English translation appears immediately below the French excerpts from the text.

John is "thinking aloud": that is, he is verbalizing what he is thinking as he attempts to comprehend the text, which is delivered in clear, naturally paced speech. The presiding researcher stopped the tape recorder at pre-determined discourse boundaries in the text while another tape recorder recorded John's comments. When he stopped the recording, the researcher used only non-cueing probes to avoid directing John in any way. John approached the text "cold": before he began listening, he had no idea what the text was going to be. This was done deliberately so that construction of meaning could be observed from inception.

We will analyze the think-aloud protocols for insights they can give us into the workings of the comprehension model represented in Figure 3.1 and the mental representation of the text that John is developing. Given that we do not know much about John, and that processing in the perception and parsing phases is largely covert, we can only speculate about what is happening, based on the limited information revealed by John as he grapples with the text.

> *Écoutez bien, tous les amateurs de hockey.*
> *Listen up, hockey fans.*

> *John:*   Sounded like "arcade" something.

The speech stream passes through the acoustic-phonetic processor and a phonetic representation is parsed for anything meaningful. John can only use bottom-up processing because he has not been given a context for interpretation; therefore, the conceptualizer, with the support of prior knowledge sources, cannot activate the appropriate schema to interpret what is heard. This likely prompts John to translate on a word by word basis, which, because of the constraints of working memory and/or the fact that he has an extremely limited mental lexicon in French, leaves him with just the last two phonemes that are meaningful to him as the word "arcade" (from "hockey," pronounced, in French, like the English word "arcade"). He is likely using the categories for word segmentation from his first language (English) which, as well as drawing on his English lexicon, leaves him with a word that sounds like something meaningful in his first language. Given that he is a 15-year-old boy, John is likely very familiar with arcades, prompting the conceptualizer and prior knowledge source bank to accept this word as a plausible interpretation of what he has just heard. It is not clear whether John has accepted this framework for interpreting the remainder of the text, based on his activation of the word "arcade."

> *Au Forum, c'est un match de hockey extraordinaire entre les Étoiles soviétiques et les Canadiens! Retenez la date! C'est vendredi, le 31 décembre, à 19h au Forum de Montréal!*
> *(Russian national anthem is playing.) There will be an amazing hockey game between the Soviet Stars and the Canadians at the Forum. Remember the date: Friday, December 31 at 7:00 p.m. at the Montreal Forum!*

> *John:*   Okay, it sounded like the Olympics or something, I got Olympics and it's saying Canada is in the Olympics. Can't

> remember all the countries but they're saying several countries are in these Olympics, could be one event and it says it was on vendredi, I can't remember.
>
> *Int.:* How do you know that?
>
> *John:* It sounded like they were going versus each other, like with each other, and it sounded like and they were going just with two people. They were going countries type of thing and I would have countries go against each other. You're thinking of something big and then just because of the music, it sounded like there is something like Olympics or something.

The acoustic-phonetic processor recognizes the opening sounds immediately as music, not language-specific sounds. John uses this non-linguistic cue, which he can map directly on to his world knowledge store in long-term memory without analysis by the parser or lexicon in working memory, to begin top-down processing and activate a framework for interpretation. Any schema associated with "arcade," if ever activated, appears to have faded. John also (incorrectly) segments "Olympics" from the sound stream (likely from "soviétique"), presumably in the same way as hypothesized for segmentation of the word "arcade" in the previous segment. In all probability, he activates the word "Canada" (from "Canadiens") in the same way. It is not clear, however, whether the music and/or the segmented words have triggered the Olympics schema. There was, most likely, some top-down and bottom-up processing between the conceptualizer and parser, in interaction with the lexicon and prior knowledge sources that resulted in the activation of this particular schema. His schema is reinforced by the sense of "they were going versus each other" and "something big" that may have been activated by the announcer's tone of voice and description of the event, coupled with the rousing music, all mapped directly to long-term memory with little analysis by the parser and no need to access the lexicon. Capitalizing on his world knowledge and the discourse processing in the conceptualizer, these cues all contribute to John's coherent (but incorrect) interpretation of the text so far. Bringing coherence to his interpretation is likely due to the monitoring carried out by the conceptualizer.

Interestingly, John is able to parse out one French word: "vendredi" (Friday). He does not link it with the rest of the text, other than to say it "could be one event," which suggests that he briefly questioned, through monitoring in the conceptualizer and drawing on prior knowledge, how this could fit in with a multi-day event such as the Olympics.

La vente des billets commence lundi à 9h du matin.Voici les prix des billets:

Ticket sales will begin on Monday at 9:00 a.m. Here are the ticket prices:

John: I didn't catch anything.
Int.:   What are you thinking?
John: Sounded like introducing something—like it says here is some-thing but I can't figure out what it is, it could be like . . . one of the athletes, like introducing some person or something.

Parsing the sound stream yields nothing in terms of words that are mean-ingful to John, not even the time of day nor day of the week. Once again, he uses non-linguistic cues such as voice intonation and prosody, which he can process directly in the conceptualizer. Drawing on his prior knowl-edge store and the co-text (what he has understood so far), and informed by his interpretative framework (Olympics), he suggests that an athlete is perhaps being introduced.

Blancs—treize dollars cinquante (White [seats]) $13.50)
Bleus—huit dollars (Blue [seats] $8)
Bleus du centre—onze dollars cinquante (Center blue [seats] $11.50)
Places debout—huit dollars (Standing room $8)

John: Sounds like they're saying like these people can get second or third or something, I think.
Int.:   Okay . . .
John: Sounds like they're ordering something, this person is first, this person is second.
John: It said "cinquante." I didn't catch very much of that.

Parsing the sound stream, John continues to be incapable of segmenting many words, even though most of them (numbers and colors) should have been familiar to him. However, given the rapid, concatenated speech, he is only able to recognize "cinquante" (50, repeated twice). He suggests that he has heard numbers ("second or third or something") and fits that in with his interpretive schema through the same processes of monitoring and discourse processing carried out in the conceptualizer, while draw-ing on his prior knowledge store. Presumably, prosody and intonation (a useful knowledge source when relying on an impoverished L2 lexicon) lead him to suggest that "they're ordering something." John continues to develop a coherent representation of the text, in spite of the fact that it is incorrect.

On peut les acheter aux guichets du Forum et à tous les comptoirs Ticketron.

A ne pas oublier—il y a une limite de six billets par personne.
You can buy them at the Forum and at all Ticketron outlets.
Don't forget, there's a limit of six tickets per person.

John: CBA or something; it sounded like it's being broadcasted on a TV station and CBA is probably a TV station there or something.

As John parses this final segment of the text, the only meaningful word he appears to be left with is "CBA" (an exact phonemic equivalent of "six billets"). He perceives this word, as suggested earlier, using the word segmentation categories of his first language. Because of his limited L2 linguistic knowledge and his apparent L1 word segmentation strategies, John uses the few items that he is able to parse from the rapid sound stream (strings of L2 phonemes that resemble L1 words, sound effects, intonation, and prosody) to activate and embellish a schema for interpretation. The comment "it sounded like it's being broadcasted on a TV station" suggests that John may be bringing text awareness (an advertisement) to bear on his interpretation. Whether this awareness comes as a justification for his interpretation of "CBA" or it was there earlier is not clear. In other words, in the rapid top-down and bottom-up processing that occurs between the parser and conceptualizer, with the help of the prior knowledge store, the outcome of one process informs the other, making it difficult to determine which came first. One thing appears certain: through monitoring and discourse processing (in the conceptualizer), John continues to work at a coherent representation of the text, slotting anything he does understand to fit the framework he activated and strengthened as he listened. What would have happened if John had understood "hockey" correctly when he first began listening?

These protocols also provide an interesting insight into building a coherent situation representation of text comprehension, even though this mental representation is totally inaccurate. Given that the text is too difficult for John because of his limited L2 vocabulary, he cannot possibly create a text representation. He resorts to strategies such as interpreting strings of L2 phonemes that resemble L1 words, sound effects, intonation, and prosody to build a situation representation of comprehension. As he works through the text, in spite of difficulties, he continues to impose a degree of coherence to what he hears and understands. In the end, he has built a coherent situation representation of the text that is totally "off the mark." As noted by Grabe (2009), the situation representation of text comprehension provides L2 learners with an opportunity to respond to a comprehension task in a coherent way, but not necessarily in a way that indicates comprehension of the task.

Interactive Listening

In interactive listening, L2 listeners alternate as listener and speaker. They are obliged to understand their interlocutor, clarify meaning if necessary, and move the interaction forward through an appropriate response, clarification request or back-channelling cue. The dialogue below between Vikram, a native speaker (NS), and Sam, a non-native speaker (NNS), illustrates many of these strategies in the responses of Sam as listener/respondent in the exchange. The dialogue is an adaptation of a dialogue in Anderson and Lynch (1988).

We will analyze the exchanges between the two speakers, focusing primarily on the responses of Sam, the less proficient partner. We will examine his responses for any insights they can provide into the workings of the comprehension and production processing model illustrated in Figure 3.1 and the mental representation of the text (directions for making curry) that Sam is developing. Once again, given that we do not know much about the interlocutors, and that processing at the perception and parsing phases is largely covert, we can only speculate about what may be going on in the mind of the listener, with reference to the processing model.

(1) Vikram (NS):	Now, the important thing about making curry is the spices. They must be fresh, not out of tins in your cupboard.
(2) Sam (NNS):	Tins?
(3) Vikram:	Yeah, you know those horrible little tins, those little containers of spices you've had at the back of your cupboard for ages.
(4) Sam:	Uhuh.
(5) Vikram:	Then you must fry the spices in oil, before you add the meat.
(6) Sam:	In oil, oh.
(7) Vikram:	Yes. Then you brown the meat in the spices . . .
(8) Sam:	What? Brown the meat?
(9) Vikram:	. . . yes, you brown the meat . . . you fry it until it is all brown on the outside and then you add any liquid . . . chicken stock or water or . . .
(10) Sam:	. . . I must remember that. Have you tried that Indian restaurant by the market? It's really good. (Based on Anderson and Lynch, 1988, p. 8)

Before beginning our analysis, we need to highlight two important features of this exchange that will influence the evolution of the mental representation of comprehension developed by Sam. First of all, the context has clearly been established. What has motivated the exchange is not clear. However, Sam knows that Vikram is explaining how to make curry. Second, the interlocutors are likely friends and comfortable enough with each other for Sam not to feel intimidated when he needs to seek clarification. In other words, he should not have to fake comprehension to save face in front of his friend.

Exchanges (1) and (2)

Given that the context is clearly established, Sam can activate what he knows about curry (prior knowledge) and any scripts (discourse knowledge) he may have for explaining how to cook something. Whether he has done so yet is not clear, however.

Vikram's opening speech stream passes through Sam's acoustic-phonetic processor and a phonetic representation is forwarded to the parser for grammatical and phonological analysis, and lexical selection. This analysis is likely informed by top-down processing from any activated schema that interacts with bottom-up processing and segmenting activity by the parser. Although it is not clear whether Sam has fully understood, we do know that the word "tin" (not closely related to the activated schema) apparently was not understood. It appears that Sam makes a decision, based on cognitive activity in the conceptualizer and any pressing affective influences, to signal a problem with this word/phoneme.

When monitoring in the conceptualizer prompts him to signal difficulty with the word "tin," Sam chooses to intervene, now in the role of speaker. Based on his world, pragmatic, and discourse knowledge, Sam chooses, from a repertoire of possible clarification strategies, a specific reprise (see Table 2.2 in the previous chapter): that is, he repeats, with rising intonation, the one-word phoneme he does not understand. The conceptualizer sends this pre-verbal message (on the production side of Figure 3.1) to the formulator for phonological and grammatical encoding where the retained word (still in working memory) is phonologically encoded for production purposes, drawing on the syllabary, with a rise in intonation to signal a question, as dictated by the conceptualizer. This phonetic plan is then forwarded to the articulator where lips, tongue, and larynx work together to reproduce, with rising intonation, the problem word/phoneme (tins?).

This hypothetical account of the covert processes on both the comprehension and production sides of the processing model demonstrates how the Levelt model works particularly well as a comprehensive and coherent system for describing cognitive processing in interactive listening, where the listener also alternates in a speaker role. In our analysis of this initial exchange between Sam and Vikram, we have chosen to demonstrate how cognitive processing on the production side flowed from the comprehension product, in the common conceptualizer, to verbalization on the production side. Analysis of the remaining exchanges, however, will focus on the comprehension side of the model only, unless additional information relevant to the production process emerges.

Exchanges (3) and (4)

Sam's response to Vikram's elaboration on the word "tin" would suggest that he does not understand. He signals neither that he understands nor that he wants more information. After parsing this lengthy utterance (and we cannot be certain that he has even been attentive to it), Sam presumably draws on his knowledge stores (world, discourse, and pragmatic), in concert with his lexicon, to send a neutral back-channelling cue "uhuh" to his interlocutor. What this signals is not certain; Sam may just want to get on with the directions (without really understanding what "tin" means), he may be signalling comprehension without explicit confirmation, or he may be signalling an increased sense of confusion. Information on the intonation of this cue would likely be helpful in interpreting Sam's response in this case.

Exchanges (5) and (6)

Sam parses the next utterance and chooses to send an uptaking forward inference by repeating "in oil," to signal comprehension and move the dialogue forward. Alternatively, he was only able to parse "in oil" from the sound stream and offers this as confirmation of comprehension. Sam adds the interjection "oh," which, in addition to signalling comprehension, may suggest an unanticipated step in the directions for making curry. On the other hand, it may signal feigned engagement with the speaker and serve as a back-channelling cue for Vikram to get on with the directions. As in the earlier exchanges, Sam presumably draws on his knowledge stores (world, discourse, and pragmatic) to parse Vikram's utterance. He prepares his ambiguous response, consulting the repertoire of back-channelling cues in his lexicon.

Exchanges (7) and (8)

In this exchange, Sam chooses to interrupt, breaking the respectful turn-taking behavior established up to this point. Sam uses top-down and bottom-up processing between parser and conceptualizer, and he draws on his lexicon and prior knowledge stores. The parser recognizes the word "brown" but, presumably, cannot reconcile the syntactic property (lemma) of the word as color with the same word as verb, as in the case of this utterance. This seeming incongruence prompts Sam to break the established turn-taking behavior with an abrupt "What?", a less polite clarification request than alternatives such as "Pardon" or "I'm sorry," to suggest that he does not understand the concept of "browning meat." Using the same knowledge sources as mentioned earlier, he opts for a more informal intervention, presumably acceptable because of his relationship with Vikram. Given the immediacy of the intervention, Sam's utterance hints that he might well be more engaged in the interaction than earlier exchanges have suggested.

Exchanges (9) and (10)

A number of details become clear in these final utterances. First of all, given the length and quality of Sam's utterance, his language proficiency appears to be more advanced than earlier responses might have suggested. Although we cannot be fully certain, ostensibly Sam was likely able to process Vikram's utterances relatively fluently, except when he encountered unfamiliar words. Second, it may be that Sam likes curry, but he may not be interested in putting in the effort to prepare it, as suggested by his final utterance.

In these circumstances, although Sam was likely able to process and comprehend Vikram's last utterance, he may not have been attentive to it. The first utterance, "I must remember that," may be a polite way of "shutting down" the exchange about *making* a good curry. Given the details of what he has just heard and the paucity of confirmation checks that usually follow a systematic description, such as a recipe, Sam was likely not paying attention. He may not have been really interested in learning how to make a good curry in the first place, or he may have lost interest once he realized how much work was involved. His last utterance suggests that he would rather go out to eat curry. Drawing on his knowledge stores (world, discourse, and pragmatic) as well as his lexicon, Sam finds an indirect way to end the exchange and move the interaction into a direction that he would prefer to take. This line of interpretation may also explain the minimalism of Sam's earlier utterances.

Sam's utterances also provide insight into building a mental representation of text comprehension during interactive listening. In these exchanges, the overall communicative intent conceptualized by Vikram has resulted in a very fuzzy mental representation of comprehension (inferred intent) in Sam's conceptualizer. In fact, even though the nature of this exchange would require building a text representation of comprehension, with very little room for inference if the curry is going to be successful, Sam did not appear to be interested in building such a representation. In order to be polite, he likely played along with Vikram's goal until it was acceptable for him to intimate his more tacit goal. All of this is speculation, of course, given that we know nothing about how and why the exchange began. It appears that, because of his listening goal, Sam has some fuzzy situation representation of text comprehension.

To sum up, our analysis of this exchange illustrates not only the complexity of the underlying cognitive processes but the powerful influence of equally complex social and affective factors that can shape the outcome.

Summary

Listening comprehension is an active process. Listeners analyze what they hear and interpret it on the basis of their linguistic knowledge and their knowledge of the topic. Meaning-building is largely a covert process, not easily open to inspection and empirical verification. Nevertheless, in this chapter we have attempted to present a synthesis of the processing components that underlie and support L2 listening comprehension, and to explain how these comprehension processes work together as one comprehensive, coherent system for both one-way and interactional listening. We did this through the use of a theoretical working model. We then attempted to illustrate the workings of this model in a more concrete way by analyzing (1) the think-aloud protocols of a listener engaged in a one-way listening task, and (2) the exchanges between two interlocutors, with a particular focus on the listening behavior of the less proficient participant as each one attempted to construct a representation of the text in memory.

Discussion Questions and Tasks

1. Take another look at the depictions of Rose and Nina's listening behavior as described in the opening scenario. Based on what you have read in this chapter, and making reference to the model outlined, describe the differences in cognitive processing between the two listeners.
2. What are the unique insights into the process of L2 listening revealed by Wendy in the following listening diary excerpt:

> Day after day I feel myself improve my listening a little, but I still cannot understand nearly half. I did not want to identify every sentence and every word. I just tried to catch the main idea and the most important word of the news. This is an interesting but true description of the course of my listening skill. "I'm not listening, but only hear." At the moment I can pick up the meaning of words here and there. But it isn't a process of understanding. After a short while, even just as the material is over, I have forgotten the valuable words, phrases and main sentences. Only some vague ideas remain. (Wendy)

3. What is turn-taking behavior? Why is this knowledge important for the listener in interactive listening?
4. With a partner, develop a script that outlines the probable exchange in reporting a stolen bicycle to the police.
5. Record or find a short recording of (1) friends interacting, and (2) two people in a differential power relationship interacting (work site, interview, etc.). Analyze each excerpt for the cognitive, linguistic, and social demands being placed on the listener, with reference to the model presented in this chapter.

Suggestions for Further Reading

Goh, C. (2002). Exploring listening comprehension tactics and their interaction patterns. *System, 30*, 185–206.

This paper examines how broad listening strategies were realized through different mental techniques (tactics) by a group of ESL learners. It describes the way these tactics interacted in the processing sequences of two learners. A comparison of their retrospective protocols shows that even though they used many similar strategies, the higher ability listener demonstrated more effective integration of both cognitive and metacognitive strategies in parallel processing.

Grabe, W. (2009). *Reading in a second language: Moving from theory to practice.* (Chapter 3: How Reading Works: Comprehension Processes, pp. 39–58). Cambridge, UK: Cambridge University Press.

Although this book deals with reading, given that listening and reading build on the same cognitive architecture for comprehension, this chapter gives an excellent cognitive perspective on comprehension processes.

Hulstijn, J. H. (2003). Connectionist models of language processing and the training of listening skills with the aid of multimedia software. *Computer Assisted Language Learning, 16*, 413–425.

A cognitive perspective on two views of how the brain processes sounds automatically and efficiently to recognize words in speech, and how this knowledge might be used in computer-assisted language learning to develop proficient listening skills.

Vandergrift, L. (2003). Orchestrating strategy use: Toward a model of the skilled second language listener. *Language Learning, 53*, 463–496.

This study examines differences between more skilled and less skilled listeners. Quantitative and qualitative data show how more skilled listeners can systematically orchestrate a cycle of cognitive and metacognitive strategies to remedy gaps in comprehension. This study provides the complete think-aloud transcripts for Rose and Nina.

Chapter 4

Factors That Influence Listening Success

Scenario (excerpts from learner listening diaries)

I listened to a story about an elephant. It sounded familiar, but after I listened to the story for one time, I hardly got anything. I was very depressed, but I knew I must listen again even though maybe the second try would give me a greater shock. However, from the second try I got a spark of hope. I was glad that I could get about half the story. It was an incentive for me. (Mae)

I found the big barrier to my listening is inefficient memory. When I heard the new words, I forget the contents mentioned before. So if I listened to a long sentence, I seldom catch the whole sentence's meaning, although sometimes I could hear every word clearly. My listening memory is a big problem for me. (Ronald)

After class I spend a lot of time picking up vocabulary. I think it's important. I try my best to catch the crucial words of the talking. After getting these words, I can understand the content on the whole. (Yang)

Everyday I listen to BBC and the news. But only when I totally concentrate on the broadcast, I can catch what it says. There are also some intervals when I ponder upon the specific meaning of one word and lose the following words, which hinder me from coherent understanding. Mind-absent is the most dangerous and frequent barrier in my listening practice. (Wendy)

I listened to BBC news. I think my problem lies in the correction of pronunciation and the speakers' accent. Many of the words they spoke I couldn't hear clearly. Even though I could understand what they were talking about. (Boris)

This week, I kept listening to FM 90.5. Though its English is not so good as BBC, it is more interesting. Many of these lectures are close to our life, so when I listen to it, I feel I can concentrate and also understand it better because of the existing idea about that. I think the improving is really helpful and it always makes me be more confident. (Stuart)

Pre-reading Reflection

1. What do these learner reflections on their listening experiences tell you about the factors that affect L2 listening competence? Name the factor(s) that each listener is evoking? Why are these factors important for listening success?
2. To what degree do these learner experiences resonate with your own experience with L2 listening? Do you have similar or different experiences to add?
3. Based on your earlier reading of Chapter 2 and your own language learning and teaching experiences, what are the most important factors that affect L2 listening success? Explain.
4. To what degree might the social context for learning (formal or informal) influence these factors and affect listening success? How would this affect the development of good listening skills?

Introduction

Teachers often wonder why learners achieve different levels of success in L2 learning. Given two learners who have gone through the same classroom learning experiences with the same teacher and the same curriculum, why does one learner become more successful than the other?

This chapter will build on the overview of cognitive processing presented in the last two chapters by examining the factors that can influence the quality of that processing and lead to different results for different learners. Knowledge of these factors and how they hinder or facilitate successful comprehension is important for informed teaching of L2 listening. Many factors are assumed to influence L2 listening, but there is still very little research to provide empirical evidence for a causal relationship. This chapter will discuss this incipient but informative body of research.

Imhof and Janusik (2006) framed the process of aural information processing and listening by adapting a systems model of study processes (Biggs, 1999). It identifies three interdependent stages: person- and context-related factors, process, and results. This is a useful heuristic for further understanding the listening construct; it helps us more clearly visualize the interrelationships between individual factors, listening context, and different processes. As seen in Figure 4.1, it is an integrated system in which person factors and listening context can affect the process (quality of the processing) and the results (comprehension, learning, or

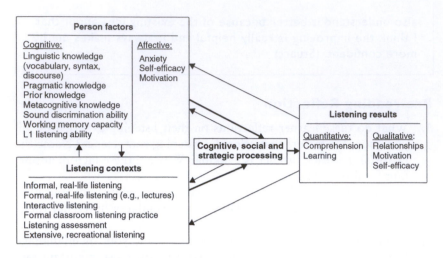

Figure 4.1. Systems Model of Listening
Adapted from Imhof & Janusik, 2006

affective factors such as self-efficacy). Vice versa, the result (e.g., comprehension or miscomprehension) can affect the factors that affect the listening process (e.g., feelings of self-efficacy) and the listener's further efforts
at processing subsequent input. Qualitative dimensions of the listening
results (e.g., developing relationship with a sympathetic native speaker or
motivation) can determine the levels of attention and effort the listener
puts into understanding a speaker (strategies deployed).

The person factors are important to listening success on both a macro
and a micro level. As explained by Imhof and Janusik, on a macro level
these factors affect the overall self-regulation of listening by the listener
(monitoring, effort expended, and motivation). On a micro level, these
factors affect the quality and quantity of processing resources available for and allocated to the task, such as working memory capacity.
As seen in Figure 4.1, person factors are both cognitive and affective.
Cognitive factors include linguistic knowledge (vocabulary and syntactic
knowledge), discourse knowledge, pragmatic knowledge, metacognitive
knowledge, prior knowledge, first language listening ability, sound discrimination ability, and working memory capacity. Affective factors
include factors such as anxiety, motivation, and self-efficacy. Listening
context factors include informal real-life listening outside the classroom
(listening to television or radio), formal real-life listening in the classroom
such as lectures, formal classroom listening practice, interactive listening,
and listening assessment. Each of these contexts places different cognitive
and affective demands on the listener.

This chapter will examine what we currently know about the factors related to L2 listening. We will begin by examining research into the cognitive factors that are known to affect listening success. Then the affective factors that play an important role in listening will be explored. Finally, the chapter will conclude with an examination of some of the contextual factors that can affect listening success.

Cognitive Factors

Vocabulary Knowledge

When L2 learners are asked what they consider to be the most important element for L2 listening success, they almost unanimously identify vocabulary knowledge as key. Anecdotally, language learners most often respond with comments such as "learn more words." Very few studies, however, have attempted to verify this claim empirically. The first attempts to do so were studies that examined the potential difference in comprehension processes for listening and reading.

Working with learners of German, Lund (1991) found that readers at lower levels of proficiency were able to recall more details than listeners who were able to recall more main ideas. In the absence of linguistic knowledge, listeners created plausible constructions to fill in the details that they were not able to either comprehend or retain. Lund argues that the listening mode forces listeners to approach the listening task differently, to compensate for the ephemeral nature of the text.

In a significantly larger study, Mecartty (2000) worked with fourth semester learners of Spanish to examine the degree to which vocabulary knowledge and syntactic knowledge contribute to listening and reading comprehension. She found that vocabulary knowledge emerged as a significant predictor for both reading and listening, explaining about 25 percent of L2 reading ability and 14 percent of L2 listening ability. Based on her research, Mecartty concluded that (1) comprehension processes in listening and reading may share similar characteristics; (2) L2 vocabulary knowledge appears to be less important in the comprehension process underlying L2 listening compared to reading; and (3) it is important to identify the factors that can explain the remaining variance in L2 listening.

An investigation by Bonk (2000) of Japanese learners of English is one of few studies focusing exclusively on the relationship between vocabulary knowledge and L2 listening comprehension. Similar to the Lund (1991) study, learners listened to texts and demonstrated comprehension using free written recall protocols (learners write from memory, usually in L1, what they recall after listening to an aural text). Learners listened to four texts of increasing lexical complexity, wrote recalls, and then took dictation of the text. Overall, high comprehension scores were associated with greater lexical knowledge; there was a greater dispersion of recall scores as vocabulary texts increased in difficulty. Some listeners, however, obtained high comprehension scores even though they demonstrated knowledge of only 75 percent or fewer of the targeted words in a text. In all likelihood, these listeners were able to use productive strategies, such as inferencing, to compensate for what they did not know (even though texts were created so that world knowledge would not be a confounding factor). Interestingly, overall, higher dictation scores were associated with better comprehension.

A more recent study with a much larger sample of advanced-level Danish learners of English found even more impressive evidence of the relationship between L2 vocabulary knowledge and listening comprehension (Staehr, 2009). Correlations between the listening test score and measures of vocabulary size and depth of vocabulary knowledge demonstrated their relationship to listening to be .70 and .65 respectively. Based on further analysis through regression analysis, Staehr observed that over one half—51 percent—of listening variance could be explained by L2 vocabulary; 49 percent could be attributed to vocabulary size (breadth of vocabulary); and depth of vocabulary contributed only 2 percent more (quality of knowledge related to different aspects of a word and other words associated with it). A further analysis of the listening scores demonstrated that 27 of the 56 participants who scored below the 5000 word level on the vocabulary measure were still able to achieve a listening test score of 60 percent or higher. This echoes the findings of Bonk (2000) and of a more qualitative study by Graham, Santos, and Vanderplank (2010), who observe that listeners can overcome a weaker linguistic base. Presumably they do this by inferencing what was not understood, based on what was understood. However, as noted by Graham and colleagues, a certain threshold of accurate linguistic recognition needs to be attained before listeners can successfully use inferencing strategies to compensate for gaps in understanding. Although a threshold for reading has been investigated (see Lee & Schallert, 1997), evidence for a threshold for listening remains to be explored.

In sum, research does corroborate the anecdotal evidence from L2 learners that L2 vocabulary size (particularly breadth of knowledge) is important for listening success. However, the existing studies suggest that a very high percentage of variance remains to be explained in order to account for L2 listening comprehension success. In addition, these studies also indicate that some L2 listeners are able to compensate for a weaker linguistic base, suggesting that these listeners are very strategic in their approach to the listening task.

Syntactic Knowledge

Syntactic or grammatical knowledge plays an important role in L2 learning and is hypothesized to contribute to comprehension success. In the Mecartty (2000) study, cited earlier, the potential contribution of syntactic knowledge to L2 reading and listening comprehension was also examined. Although syntactic knowledge did correlate significantly with both reading and listening comprehension, multiple regression analyses demonstrated that this relationship was not strong enough for syntactic knowledge to be a significant predictor of L2 listening success. Mecartty concluded that, although syntactic knowledge is perceived as essential in overall language learning, its precise role in comprehension, both listening and reading, remains to be determined.

Conrad (1985) hypothesized that beginner-level listeners would pay more attention to syntactic cues and that higher proficiency listeners would increasingly pay greater attention to semantic cues. After listening to a text (a recorded lecture), an intermediate-level L2 group, an advanced-level L2 group, and a native speaker group completed a cloze exercise, using the same text in print form with some of the words missing. Similar control groups did not engage in the listening component. Conrad found that listening to the passage first was beneficial to all experimental groups and, with increased proficiency, each group paid more attention to semantic cues than syntactic cues as the basis for their cloze responses. With increased proficiency, listeners processed information using primarily semantic units. In other words, the more advanced the listeners, the more they paid attention to global meaning, processing language more deeply, and paying greater attention to semantic cues. On the other hand, listeners at lower levels of proficiency tended to process what they heard at a more surface level, paying greater attention to syntactic cues instead of meaning-laden semantic cues.

A later study by Field (2008b) produced different results. Field wanted to determine which type of words listeners rely on most: content words (semantic) or function words (syntactic). He asked listeners to write down the last four or five words they heard when a recording of a listening text was paused. Native language listeners outperformed L2 listeners in correctly identifying both function and content words. All L2 learners of English recognized a greater percentage of content words, compared with function words. One of the native language groups (a group of highly successful learners of French) was able to identify almost all words accurately, with no disparity in recognition between form and content words. Field attributes these results to the limitations of working memory: L2 learners need to choose where to direct their attention. Given these constraints, L2 listeners will opt to focus on the content words, often identifiable by stressed syllables, which are very dependable for identifying meaning-bearing items in the sound stream.

How do we reconcile the difference in results between the two studies? The methodology used might explain the difference. Participants in the Conrad study completed a cloze test in which they had to insert every fifth word; this allowed them to process the text in a reading mode at their own pace. This activated their expectancy grammar (the ability to anticipate words by using one's knowledge of the structure of language and the topic [Oller, 1979]) and helped them to more accurately identify the function words (generally easier words) without actually understanding the meaning of the text (which would require them to identify more content words). On the other hand, in the Field study, participants had to identify words without any written support. Given that these listeners were likely processing the text for meaning, they were better able to retain the content words that were meaning-bearing.

Based on the studies available to date, syntactic knowledge does not appear to play a strong role in listening comprehension. This might be explained, as suggested by Field (2008a, 2008b), by the cognitive demands of listening and the depth at which listeners are able to process the text. This is also consistent with the literature on word segmentation, which finds that meaning is often the principal clue in segmenting the sound stream. If listeners pay too much attention to syntactic cues (function words), this may actually interfere with comprehension by limiting how much attention they can allocate to semantic cues that carry more meaning and are easier to retain in memory. As we will see later in our discussion of metacognitive knowledge, skilled listeners appear to be more successful because they are able to focus more on the semantic cues and not get hung up on processing syntactic cues that contribute less to the overall meaning of a text.

Discourse Knowledge

Discourse knowledge, sometimes called script knowledge (Dunkel, 1986), refers to awareness of the type of information found in listening texts, how that information might be organized, and how listeners can use the information to facilitate comprehension. Discourse knowledge has mostly been researched in the context of academic listening, where discourse signaling cues such as previews ("First, let's look at"), summarizers ("To sum up so far"), emphasis markers ("and, to repeat, this is why preparation is so important"), and logical connectives ("first, " "second, " etc.) play an important role in facilitating lecture comprehension. Recent research by Jung (2003) concluded that listeners who had the benefit of these cues accurately recalled more high-level information units (main ideas) and low-level information units (supporting or exemplifying the main ideas). Jung suggests that listeners may benefit more from discourse signaling cues when (1) the text structure is not evident; (2) the text type is known to the listener; (3) the listener has the required background knowledge for the text topic; and (4) the text is unscripted.

Although recognition of discourse signaling cues has received some research attention, there has been little research on the role of discourse structure knowledge. In one study, language learners were found to use text-type identification as a prominent strategy (Wolff, 1989). Young (1994) argues that the best way for teachers to help L2 learners improve lecture comprehension is to acquaint them with the general schematic structure of lectures by providing systematic instruction in the macro and micro features of lectures. In addition, specific knowledge about variations in the discourse patterns of lectures in different disciplines would be beneficial (Dudley-Evans, 1994).

In sum, research on the role of discourse knowledge in successful L2 listening has been limited up to now to academic listening where discourse signaling cues can help call learner attention to the organization of information and the important information to note.

Pragmatic Knowledge

Pragmatic knowledge involves the application of information regarding a speaker's intention that goes beyond the literal meaning of an utterance (Rose & Kasper, 2001). Listeners generally apply pragmatic knowledge to determine a speaker's intention by elaborating on what they heard, using linguistic, cultural, and contextual information.

Most research on the use of pragmatic knowledge has been conducted with reference to the production of speech acts; research on the application of pragmatic knowledge to L2 listening comprehension remains limited. One of the main outcomes of research related to this factor is that the ability to activate pragmatic knowledge during comprehension appears to depend on language proficiency: lower proficiency listeners have greater difficulty processing both contextual and linguistic information and, therefore, are less able to activate their pragmatic knowledge.

Cook and Liddicoat (2002) examined listener comprehension of request strategies. Native speakers, high-proficiency, and low-proficiency L2 learners listened to scenarios illustrating direct ("What time is it?"), indirect ("Do you have the time?"), and unconventional indirect ("Is it getting late?") questions. Learner interpretations varied by levels of proficiency. Native speakers had no difficulty with any of the questions; high-proficiency learners had more difficulty interpreting the unconventional indirect questions; and the low-proficiency learners had difficulty with both types of indirect questions. The researchers attribute these differences to (1) the processing demands of more indirect information, which requires processing both linguistic and contextual information, and (2) the limitations of working memory for lower proficiency

L2 learners. The comprehension processes are not sufficiently automatic for these learners to attend to both contextual and linguistic information at the same time.

Garcia (2004) arrived at similar conclusions concerning the comprehension of conversational implicatures (inferring the attitude and intentions underlying indirect requests) and speech acts (comprehending requests and corrections). Higher proficiency learners of English outperformed lower proficiency learners on all measures that assessed linguistic ability and pragmatic appropriacy. More importantly, Garcia determined that linguistic ability is distinct from pragmatic ability, suggesting that development in linguistic ability is not necessarily accompanied by development of pragmatic knowledge. She concludes that L2 learners can benefit from a targeted focus on pragmatic comprehension.

Speed and accuracy in the comprehension of implied meaning were examined by Taguchi in a number of studies. In a study of Japanese learners of English, she found that more conventional implicatures (indirect requests and refusals) appear to be less difficult and take less time to interpret than less conventional ones (indirect opinions). In addition, she found a strong proficiency effect for accuracy of both types of implied meaning, but not for speed of interpretation (Taguchi, 2005). She also investigated the role of context in the development of pragmatic competence (Taguchi, 2008). Over time, both ESL learners in the US and English as a Foreign Language (EFL) learners in Japan improved in speed and accuracy of implied meanings; however, the magnitude of improvement for speed was much greater for the ESL learners and the magnitude of increase for accuracy was much greater for the EFL learners. Taguchi speculated that the intensity of the EFL learning experience fostered the development of pragmatic competence, an expertise often associated with "real-life learning" in the context of the target culture.

In sum, pragmatic knowledge appears to be distinct from linguistic knowledge and, therefore, worthy of targeted classroom practice. The ability to process both pragmatic information and linguistic information simultaneously, however, appears to be related to language proficiency, suggesting that the use of listening texts requiring L2 pragmatic knowledge for comprehension be reserved for intermediate-level classes and higher, or that learners be provided with this information as part of pre-listening activities. Targeted instruction in pragmatic competence for L2 listening, similar to studies on the role of prior knowledge (described later), has not yet been investigated.

Metacognition

The importance of metacognition in comprehension, particularly for L1 reading, has long been acknowledged and continues to be widely researched (see, for example, Block & Pressley, 2002; Hacker, Dunlosky, & Graesser, 2009). Although the role of metacognition in successful L2 reading comprehension has received some research attention (see Hulstijn, 2011, for example), research activity on the role of metacognition in L2 listening has been minimal.

Much of what we know about the relationship between metacognition and successful L2 listening comes from research into the strategies of skilled listeners. Using a think-aloud methodology (tapping the thought processes of listeners while they are actually engaged in the listening event), researchers record, transcribe, and analyze the "think-alouds" of skilled and less skilled listeners for evidence of strategy use (Goh, 2002a; O'Malley & Chamot, 1990; O'Malley, Chamot, & Küpper, 1989; Vandergrift, 1998, 2003a). Skilled listeners reveal using about twice as many metacognitive strategies as their less skilled counterparts, primarily comprehension monitoring. A qualitative analysis of the think-aloud protocols has further revealed that successful L2 listening appears to involve a skillful orchestration of strategies to regulate listening processes and achieve comprehension (Vandergrift, 2003a). This finding was also observed by Graham and Macaro (2008) in a recent listening strategy instruction study; they attributed the positive results to listener "clustering" of strategies. Finally, in their validation of the Metacognitive Awareness Listening Questionnaire (MALQ), Vandergrift et al. (2006) determined that metacognitive knowledge, as tapped by participant questionnaire responses, was able to explain about 13 percent of the variance in L2 listening performance of university-level language learners.

Although the evidence is only preliminary, it is clear that a certain amount of variance in listening success can be explained by metacognition: that is, learner knowledge and control of their listening processes. This finding echoes the research findings in L2 reading and writing for the substantial impact of metacognitive knowledge on success in these skills (Hulstijn, 2011).

Prior Knowledge

Prior knowledge refers to all the conceptual knowledge and life experiences that language learners have acquired and are available for comprehension purposes. It plays an important role in listening. Prior knowledge is organized in the form of schemata (networks of abstract mental structures) that listeners use as a conceptual framework to fill in missing information as they listen. The influential role of prior knowledge in L2 listening comprehension has been empirically established in a number of studies carried out in different contexts, as noted in a recent systematic review by Macaro et al. (2005).

An important study by Long (1990) provides empirical evidence for the powerful role of prior knowledge in L2 listening. A large group (188) of American university learners of Spanish listened to two texts deemed to be similar on a number of important characteristics except topic. The first text dealt with the Ecuador gold rush and the second text was about the rock group U2. In each case, before listening to the text, participants completed a background questionnaire on their knowledge of the topic and then listened to the text twice. After the second listen, they summarized what they had understood of the text content. Finally, they completed a checklist consisting of a number of paraphrased statements in English of the text content, along with plausible distracters. Identical procedures were followed for the second text. As hypothesized, the participants possessed significantly less prior knowledge related to the gold rush (69 percent) compared with U2 (90 percent), and this influenced how much information they were able to recall after listening to the text. With regard to the results for the written summary (recall of information), Long observed an average of 53 percent for the gold rush text and 68 percent for the U2 text, for a modest difference of 15 percent. However, with regard to the checklist (recognition of information), the average score for the U2 text was 28 percent higher than for the gold rush text. Similar results for prior knowledge were observed in a subsequent study by Chiang and Dunkel (1992) on knowledge of different religions.

Although prior knowledge is important for facilitating comprehension, it can also be misleading when used inflexibly, as demonstrated in the think-aloud protocols by John in Chapter 2. Long (1990) noted similar infelicities in the recall summaries of her research participants. For example, some of the listeners who "possessed very good linguistic knowledge" overextended their knowledge of the California gold rush to the Ecuador gold rush text, even though this information was clearly incongruent with information in the text. Indeed, imprudent use of prior knowledge can misinform comprehension efforts when listeners do continue to seek corroborating evidence as the text unfolds (Macaro et al., 2005). This caveat underscores the importance of flexibility in the comprehension process and the need for listeners to continually elaborate, through a combination of questioning and prior knowledge, and monitor for congruency in the interpretation process (Vandergrift, 2003a).

Another important study on the role of prior knowledge by Tsui and Fullilove (1998) is worth mentioning here since it took place within the context of a widely used, standardized high-stakes examination. This study considered the responses of a huge sample of learners to questions on listening comprehension passages. Two types of short listening texts were presented: (1) "non-matching schema type" texts where initial linguistic information was not congruent with subsequent linguistic information, and (2) "matching schema type" texts where subsequent information was congruent with the initial linguistic input. Processing these types of texts required listeners to carefully monitor the input and revise their initial schema if there was a mismatch. Two types of questions were also used: (1) global-type questions requiring overall comprehension and the ability to draw conclusions or inferences, and (2) local-type questions requiring comprehension of specific details. The researchers determined that skilled listeners were able to outperform less skilled listeners on both question types on the non-matching schema-type texts. This outcome is not surprising, considering the flexibility of skilled listeners noted by Vandergrift (2003a). Less skilled listeners are able to perform better on "matching schema type" texts (in contrast to "non-matching schema type" texts) because they can use their prior knowledge to compensate for what they were not able to understand.

The role of prior knowledge in facilitating listening comprehension prompts the current methodological principle of providing listeners with a context. Contextualization through pre-listening activities can provide listeners with an advance organizer to help them predict and monitor their comprehension efforts. Research into pre-listening activities has documented positive effects on listening performance for visuals (e.g., Ginther, 2002), advance organizers and captions (e.g., Chung, 2002), and questions (e.g., Flowerdew & Miller, 2005). Contextualized listeners have the resources to activate prior knowledge and to develop a conceptual framework for inferencing (top-down processing). This allows them to process the linguistic input more efficiently, freeing up working memory resources. As observed by Tyler (2001), when listeners had access to the topic through an advance organizer, there were no differences in working memory consumption between L1 and L2 listeners; however, when advance information on the topic was not available, working memory consumption was much higher in L2 listeners.

The research on prior knowledge in comprehension provides ample evidence for its crucial role in listening comprehension. Activating this vital resource is particularly important when teaching adults. Because of their life experiences, they bring to their language learning a great deal and a wide range of prior knowledge on which they can draw to facilitate comprehension. On the other hand, younger language learners, because of their more limited life experience, may need to be provided with more information during pre-listening activities.

LI Listening Ability

L2 listeners already possess an acquired listening competence in their first language (L1). The degree to which this ability might contribute to L2 listening ability has only recently been examined. The role of L1 in L2 comprehension has received significant research attention in L2 reading (see, for example,

Schoonen, Hulstijn, & Bossers, 1998). Results of a recent study on this question for L2 listening with adolescent learners of French (Vandergrift, 2006) indicated that L1 listening ability and L2 proficiency together could explain about 39 percent of the common variance in L2 listening ability. L2 proficiency explained about 25 percent and L1 listening ability about 14 percent. The close links between literacy in L1 and L2 have also been observed by Hulstijn and colleagues in a number of studies related to L2 reading and L2 writing. They note that for Dutch learners of English (languages similar typologically and using the same alphabetic writing system) the relationships between L1 and L2 literacy appear to be a function of vocabulary and grammar knowledge, processing speed, metacognitive knowledge, and other general, language-independent skills (Hulstijn, 2011).

Determining the potential contribution of L1 listening to L2 listening ability is important because we may be inadvertently measuring L1 listening ability in our assessment of L2 listening and erroneously calling it L2 listening ability (Bernhardt & Kamil, 1995). This is important information because language learners may be weak listeners in L2 because they are also weak listeners in their L1.

Sound Discrimination Ability

One explanation for an overall weakness in listening ability that may transfer from L1 to L2 is sound discrimination ability. There is some evidence that phonological memory skill contributes to growth in listening ability and vocabulary learning, particularly with children at a beginning level of language proficiency (French, 2003). The actual role of sound discrimination ability in L2 listening, however, has not been investigated until very recently.

Additional Factors: A Recent Study

Current research by Vandergrift (2010) seeks to obtain empirical evidence for a number of factors and their relative contribution to the listening success of learners in the first year of French immersion, an academic context where listening comprehension is the foundation for L2 acquisition. The results include additional information on some of the factors reported earlier (L1 listening ability and metacognition) and other, yet unexplored factors (sound discrimination ability, L2 vocabulary, L1 vocabulary, and working memory capacity). Initial findings are promising, as can be seen in Table 4.1.

Data were collected from three different cohorts for a total of 157 participants. They showed a relatively consistent pattern of correlations between L2 listening ability and the factors under investigation. Earlier findings on the important role of L2 vocabulary in listening success are

Table 4.1 Relationship between L2 Listening Comprehension and Listening Factors for Grade 7 French Immersion Students

Variable	Cohort 2008	Cohort 2009	Cohort 2010	Combined cohorts
French vocabulary	.42**	.47**	.54**	.51**
English vocabulary	.47**	.30*	.15	.23**
English listening ability	—	.40**	.14	.16
Sound discrimination ability	.36*	.42**	.07	.22**
Working memory	.37*	.27	.07	.20
Metacognition (global)	.15	.25	.21	.23**

* $p<.05$; ** $p<.01$

confirmed in strong correlations for all three groups. English vocabulary also appears to play a strong role, although less so for the third cohort. English listening ability is confirmed for the 2009 cohort but appears to play a lesser role for the 2010 group. Hypotheses about the influential role of sound discrimination appear to be confirmed for the first two cohorts, but not the third. Findings for working memory appear to be related but not strongly enough to obtain significant results. Finally, the role of metacognition is also confirmed. Although the relationship with L2 listening for each individual cohort is not significant, taken together, the result for metacognition is significant. As in the earlier findings by Vandergrift et al. (2006), this significance is largely accounted for by the person knowledge factor: that is, learner perceptions of the difficulty of listening compared with the other skills and the associated anxiety.

A regression analysis on the results of the full cohort indicated that L2 vocabulary and L1 listening ability together could explain about 29 percent of the common variance in L2 listening ability. L2 vocabulary explained about 25 percent and L1 listening ability about 4 percent. These results contribute to a deeper understanding of the range of cognitive factors that can potentially predict L2 listening success. Obviously, further research is needed with different populations of language learners.

Cognitive Factors: Summary

In sum, the discussion of cognitive factors highlights the different aspects of cognition that appear to be related to L2 listening ability. Some of these are factors that listeners bring to their language learning, such as sound discrimination ability, working memory capacity, L1 listening ability, metacognition, and prior knowledge. Other factors, such as L2 vocabulary and syntactic, discourse, and pragmatic knowledge are developed as a result of the language learning process. The latter factors may also develop differentially as a function of the former.

Affective Factors

L2 listening involves more than paying attention to linguistic input and understanding the different cognitive demands made on the listener. In fact, listener ability to maximize comprehension efforts can be influenced by a number of affective factors. These emotionally relevant learner characteristics will shape how listeners respond to a listening task and thereby influence the outcome and listening success. This section of the chapter will discuss the role of three affective factors that have been researched in the context of L2 listening: anxiety, motivation, and self-efficacy.

Anxiety

L2 learner perceptions that listening is the most difficult skill (Graham, 2006), coupled with a classroom practice that often associates listening with evaluation (Mendelsohn, 1994), contribute to a high degree of anxiety. Extensive work over the last two decades by Horwitz (e.g., Horwitz, 1986; Horwitz & Young, 1991; Horwitz, Tallon, & Luo, 2009) on cause and effect in L2 anxiety and on development of a scale to measure language learning anxiety has recently been pursued by Elkhafaifi (2005), more specifically for L2 listening in Arabic. Using existing scales and adapting them for listening, Elkhafaifi was able to distinguish L2 listening anxiety from general L2 classroom anxiety. He also observed, not surprisingly, negative correlations between anxiety and final course grades. A later study by Mills, Pajares, and Herron (2006) with L2 learners of French also determined that the relationship between listening proficiency and listening anxiety (as measured from a scale adapted from mathematics) was negative and significant: that is, the higher the level of listening ability, the lower the level of reported anxiety.

When learners were asked to report on the causes of listening anxiety in their Spanish classes (Vogely, 1999), they most often cited factors related to L2 input (speed, clarity, lack of visual support), followed by process factors such as use of inappropriate strategies. When asked what could be done to alleviate listening comprehension anxiety, the bulk of responses fell into two categories: making input comprehensible and improving instructional factors such as increased time for listening and combining listening with other skills. Although 24 percent of the participants cited inappropriate strategy use as a problem, only a small number (3 percent) cited a focus on strategies as desirable for alleviating listening anxiety. In her discussion of the results, Vogely suggests that teachers begin by increasing self-confidence in the classroom.

Much of the research in L2 listening anxiety has been done in the context of testing, which is understandable given the high stakes associated with test outcomes. Arnold (2000), for example, used relaxation (breathing exercises) and visualization exercises (mental imagery to induce a more positive self-image as a listener) to reduce the level of anxiety before participants took a listening test each week over a period of eight weeks. The experimental group outperformed the control group on the listening test at the end of the study. Differences in a pre- and post-experiment questionnaire reflected a "highly positive" attitude towards the exercises in increasing self-confidence and reducing anxiety. As noted by Arnold, changing attitudes and beliefs about a skill such as listening is crucial to changing the effort learners are willing to put into listening.

Given the widespread report of anxiety among language learners, surprisingly little research has been done on what teachers can do to alleviate anxiety. Not all anxiety is detrimental, however. As noted by Horwitz (2010), anxiety is multi-faceted and can be so high as to be debilitating; however, a certain level of anxiety can be facilitating, giving learners the "edge" to concentrate harder and be more successful.

Self-Efficacy

High levels of anxiety often lead to low levels of confidence and self-efficacy because L2 listeners attribute L2 listening success to factors outside their control (Graham, 2006). Self-efficacy, the basis for self-confidence and motivation, refers to learners' beliefs about their ability to successfully participate in learning activities. Listeners with high self-efficacy feel confident about their ability to handle listening situations because they have learned to manage these challenges, based on past experience. They attribute their success mainly to their own efforts. On the other hand, listeners with low self-efficacy lack confidence in their listening ability and will hesitate to participate in listening activities for fear of revealing their inadequacies. They often feel incapable of improving their abilities because they attribute their listening ability to factors beyond their control. According to self-efficacy theory, when learners attribute success to factors within their control they will be more motivated to attempt future tasks (Bandura, 1993). This suggests that teaching L2 learners to better regulate their comprehension processes could help them perceive listening success as something within their control. Self-efficacy beliefs regarding listening will improve and, consequently, motivation to be more successful will grow. Graham and Macaro (2008) did indeed demonstrate that listening strategy instruction improved comprehension and had salutary effects on listener self-efficacy.

The Mills et al. (2006) study reported earlier also examined the role of self-efficacy in L2 listening proficiency. When effects for anxiety were controlled for, results showed that L2 learner judgments of their self-efficacy influenced their approach to listening tasks and performance;

however, this was true for females only. The researchers attribute this difference to the voluntary nature of the study, which the males may not have taken seriously since their listening test scores were considerably lower than their actual classroom listening performance and the listening scores for the female participants.

Motivation

The role of motivation in L2 learning has been investigated extensively; however, there is very little research on the relationship between L2 listening and language learning motivation. Anecdotally, there is some evidence that language learners engaged in tasks that develop metacognitive knowledge about listening become more confident and motivated as a result (Goh & Taib, 2006; Vandergrift, 2002, 2003b). A later study by Vandergrift (2005) provides some supporting empirical evidence for the potential relationship between motivation, metacognitive control of listening processes, and comprehension outcomes. Scores on a listening test were correlated with responses on a motivation questionnaire (Noels, Pelletier, Clément, & Vallerand, 2000), grounded in self-determination theory (Deci & Ryan, 1995), and a metacognitive awareness of listening strategy use questionnaire. Listening comprehension correlated negatively with amotivation (−.34); however, correlations with extrinsic motivation (for personal gain such as a passing grade) and intrinsic motivation (for enjoyment only, or a desire to know speakers of the language) were only modest at .21 and .34, respectively. Only the relationships for amotivation and intrinsic motivation were significant.

As hypothesized, a greater awareness of listening processes (as reported in the questionnaire) was related to greater levels of motivational intensity. An interesting pattern of increasingly higher correlations between the three levels of motivation (from amotivation to extrinsic to intrinsic motivation) and metacognitive awareness of listening strategies emerged. Participants who scored low on motivation, perhaps because of a lack of self-confidence and self-efficacy, demonstrated a passive attitude towards L2 learning, and also reported using less effective listening strategies. On the other hand, those who indicated high levels of motivation appeared to engage in listening behaviors that were increasingly metacognitive in nature. Vandergrift suggests that this study provides some empirical support for the hypothesized links between self-determination theory, self-regulated learning, learner autonomy, and metacognition.

In sum, the three affective factors discussed here greatly affect how language learners perceive a listening task, apply themselves to the task, and experience success in listening comprehension. These factors are also very much interrelated. Confident L2 listeners are likely more motivated, less anxious and to possess higher levels of self-efficacy, and this has important implications for the teaching of L2 listening.

As suggested earlier, a metacognitive approach can help language learners become more aware of listening processes and the demands of listening tasks, so that they can better regulate their listening. This will help them develop key listening skills and a range of strategies to apply and adapt to the needs of specific contexts. More listening practice without the threat of evaluation, as well as opportunities to reflect and become aware of listening processes, can go a long way to make L2 listeners more proactive in their approach to listening tasks, reduce anxiety, and, ultimately, achieve greater success in comprehension. This will have repercussions for both motivation and learner self-efficacy. These relationships are illustrated in the interaction between the various components presented earlier in Figure 4.1.

Contextual Factors

Our discussion of contextual factors will consider research related to three of the contexts highlighted in Figure 4.1: interactive listening, listening in informal learning contexts, and listening in formal learning contexts. As for the other two contexts, formal classroom listening practice underlies most of the research described earlier, and listening assessment will be discussed in Chapter 12.

Interactive Listening

Interactive listening is an important part of listening competence. It most often takes place in more informal contexts for language learning and reflects the type of listening language learners would like to develop in order to interact with L2 speakers. However, there are constraints on interactive listening that can affect the process and product of the listening event. The listener's ability to deal with a comprehension problem in an interactive context will depend on a number of affective factors, such as willingness to take risks, fear of losing face, assertiveness, and motivation. The degree to which these factors influence the interaction will depend on the relationship between the interlocutors, because status relationships can affect comprehension and the freedom listeners feel to negotiate meaning. Differences, for example, in age, gender, language proficiency, and power relationships (employer–employee) often make interactive listening a context where the disadvantaged listener feels powerless. This sense of inferiority often affects how much is understood (because of increased anxiety) and the degree to which listeners will dare to clarify comprehension, in order to save face.

Listening in Informal Learning Contexts

Informal contexts are another factor for consideration. The study abroad program is an informal context of particular interest for the development of listening comprehension. In one research study, participants in a five-week study abroad experience were compared with a peer group taking a similar intermediate-level Spanish course on campus (Cubillos, Chieffo, & Fan, 2008). Participants completed a pre- and post-listening test, strategy questionnaire, and self-assessment of Spanish skills. Contrary to expectations, the study abroad group did not outperform the on-campus group on the listening test. The researchers suggest that this unanticipated finding may be due to the nature of the test, which was not sensitive to gains in interactive listening ability. At the same time, the higher level proficiency members of the study abroad group made more significant gains than their lower proficiency counterparts. This may suggest evidence for a listening threshold (Graham et al., 2010), a necessary level of L2 competence before L1 listening strategies can be effectively activated in informal listening contexts. Questionnaire responses indicated that the study abroad group demonstrated more confidence in interacting in Spanish.

In the same vein, Moyer (2006) examined the listening development of advanced-level L2 speakers of German who maintained contact with native speakers living in an English-speaking setting. Results from a listening test and a language contact questionnaire showed that both quality and quantity of language contact were significantly related to listening ability and greater confidence in listening.

Listening in Formal Learning Contexts

Academic listening refers to listening to learn subject matter content in formal classroom contexts. Research in academic listening has focused on the specific characteristics of lectures and how these can be made more comprehensible to L2 learners. Working within this context, Flowerdew and colleagues conducted a series of studies to investigate the perceptions, problems, and strategies for lecture comprehension from the perspective of learners (Flowerdew & Miller, 1992), native-speaking lecturers (Flowerdew & Miller, 1996), and non-native speaking lecturers (Flowerdew, Miller, & Li, 2000). Common problems identified in these studies were speed of delivery of the lecture, difficulty with course-specific terminology, cultural differences, and note-taking skills. More recently, Miller (2009) explored the features of lectures that facilitated comprehension by L2 engineering students. Research participants identified linguistic features such as uncomplicated language and accent, as well as pedagogical features such as examples, visuals, humor, advance preparation, and organization of the lecture. The results of these studies have enormous implications for lecturers, suggesting many important teaching strategies to help non-native students in their classes improve lecture comprehension. A lecturer sensitive to the needs of these learners will make the necessary changes and accommodations.

What can learners themselves do to enhance lecture comprehension? In the current research base on academic listening, the implications rarely focus on the implications for learners. Even the study that focused on learners in particular (Flowerdew & Miller, 1992) gave very few suggestions: (1) read course material before or after the lecture; (2) ask peers for help; (3) ask questions in class; (4) concentrate harder; and (5) add notes to handout or readings during the lecture. Although well intentioned, some of these suggestions are not very helpful given the context of huge classes, increased alienation of students (particularly L2 students), and the wide range of lecture styles. In order for L2 students to be more successful in academic listening, they need to take charge of their own learning. Future research needs to focus on providing L2 students in academic settings with the metacognitive tools to help them better regulate their listening efforts in contexts where the objective is understanding subject matter in the target language.

Kinesics is an important factor in each of the three listening contexts delineated earlier, or any context where the listener can observe the speaker (e.g., video, television). Kinesic behavior includes all body movements related to communication, such as gesture, head movements, lip movements, facial expressions, gaze, posture, and interpersonal distance (Kellerman, 1992). Kinesic behavior such as gesture can play an important role for comprehension of input in L2 classrooms (see, for example, Gullberg & McAfferty, 2008). It also plays a more subtle but important role in informal learning contexts outside of the classroom. Kinesic cues are often culturally bound and can add to, or change the literal meaning of an utterance (Harris, 2003).

Summary

This chapter has provided evidence that person and contextual factors play an important role in successful L2 listening comprehension. As depicted in Figure 4.1, these factors can affect the quality of cognitive processing and impact the listening outcome. With regard to cognitive factors, it appears that L2 vocabulary plays a significant role in successful listening outcome and that L1 listening ability also has an impact. Our discussion of the affective factors demonstrates the important role played by these factors in listener engagement with a speaker or the listening/learning environment. It is important to emphasize, once again, the interrelatedness of the three stages: the person and context factors will influence the quality of the processing and strategies a listener may deploy, which will affect the quality and nature of the outcome. The quality of this outcome will, in turn, affect some of the person factors, the affective factors that will have an effect on the strength of continued efforts to listen to the message, for example, or a more concerted effort to recall prior knowledge to interpret the message.

We have discussed some of the cognitive, affective, and contextual factors that can have an impact on L2 listening ability. Although positive or negative correlations may point to interesting relationships between a given factor and listening success, it is not necessarily possible to claim definitive causality between that factor and listening success, unless a regression analysis can explain the direction of the relationship. Uncovering the nature of the relationship between the factor and listening success requires careful interpretation and may be elucidated by more qualitative research methodologies such as interviews or stimulated recalls that explore the listening process.

Discussion Questions and Tasks

1. This chapter has discussed existing research on the factors related to L2 listening. What other cognitive or affective factors, not yet investigated, might also affect L2 listening performance? Given what you now know about L2 listening, why and how would these factors be relevant?

2. Two important studies on the "good language learner" by Rubin (1975) and Stern (1975) appeared in the 1970s. Rubin, for example, suggests that good language learners are open and willing to (1) guess and do so accurately; (2) communicate and express a strong desire to do so; (3) try, in spite of weaknesses in L2; (4) take risks, in that they are less inhibited; (5) pay attention to form; (6) monitor their speech and compare it with the native norm; (7) practice; and (8) attend to meaning in its social context. How many of these characteristics apply to listening? How so? What do these characteristics tell you about the relationship between listening success and language learning?

3. In the introduction to his edited volume on individual differences, Robinson (2002) states that the relative success of learning is a result of the interaction between learner characteristics and learning contexts. Explain how this would be true for the development of listening for:

   (a) a child in a language immersion classroom;
   (b) an international student living abroad and attending lectures in the target language; and
   (c) an immigrant mother with young children negotiating everyday language tasks outside the home.

4. How might the purpose for listening interact with the factors discussed in this chapter? Discuss how these factors might affect listening in the following tasks:

   (a) listening for changes in flight information as you are waiting in the airport;
   (b) conducting an interview with a school principal in order to write a report in the school newspaper about a controversial administrative decision; and
   (c) listening to a short video on the life cycle of the frog for a report to your study group.

Suggestions for Further Reading

Harley, B. & Hart, D. (2002). Age, aptitude and second language learning on a bilingual exchange. In P. Robinson (Ed.), *Individual differences and instructed language learning* (pp. 301–330). Amsterdam: Benjamins.
A good chapter on the questions of aptitude and age in language learning. Although the study touches on all the language skills, the results reported for growth in listening comprehension are noteworthy.

MacIntyre, P. (2002). Motivation, anxiety and emotion in second language acquisition. In P. Robinson (Ed.), *Individual differences and instructed language learning* (pp. 45–68). Amsterdam: Benjamins.
A good chapter on the affective factors related to language learning in general, discussed within the framework of Gardner's socio-educational model (Gardner & MacIntyre, 1992).

Vandergrift, L. (2006). Second language listening: Listening ability or language proficiency? *The Modern Language Journal*, *90*, 6–18.
This exploratory study, the first to examine the relationship between L1 and L2 listening ability, provides an overview of the literature on the same question for L2 reading and outlines an agenda for further research on this question in L2 listening. It also examines the issue of the type of vocabulary important to listening success.

Part II

A Metacognitive Approach to Listening

Chapter 5

A Metacognitive Approach to Listening Instruction

Scenario

Mr. Yasuo greets his class of college English learners. He asks them to take out their listening diaries and discuss their most recent L2 listening event with the person sitting next to them. The learners refer to their last entry to explain the strategies they used to assist their comprehension and what they plan to do to improve their listening in the future.

After the learners have finished, Mr. Yasuo tells them that they will watch a video on YouTube and use the information from the video to write a report. He tells them the title of the video and instructs them to just watch it to get a general idea first. After they have watched it, Mr. Yasuo flashes guiding questions on the screen and asks listeners to discuss in small groups of three. The questions are: What is the main idea in this video? Do you like what you watched? Was it difficult to understand what the people in the video said? Which part was the easiest to understand and which part was the hardest? The learners make individual notes, based on the discussion, and watch the video again. They are told to make notes about the content of the video during the second viewing.

After the learners finish watching the video, they pool their notes to write a detailed description of the video, which they submit to their teacher. Mr. Yasuo then asks them to discuss what they think made the video easy or difficult to understand and report to the rest of the class. When they have finished, Mr. Yasuo discusses some of their points and offers his feedback. He stops 10 minutes before the end of the class, as is his usual practice, and tells his learners to take out their listening diaries to write down some thoughts about the lesson. This time he tells them to recall one main idea from the video and explain how they understood it. He encourages them to write in English but permits them to write in Japanese if they find it difficult to express some of their thoughts in English.

Pre-reading Reflection

1. Identify two things Mr. Yasuo does that are different from the lesson described in the scenario of Chapter 1. Comment on the differences.
2. Consider the guiding questions that Mr. Yasuo gives to his class. Do you think they help the learners? Why? What other guiding questions would you give?
3. "Learners listen best when they know what to listen to and why they have to listen." What is your response to this statement? How does Mr. Yasuo help his learners to listen in the scenario described? Try to relate your response to knowledge you gained from earlier chapters in the book.

Introduction

In Chapter 1 we highlighted three main orientations in the teaching of L2 listening over the last five decades. These are text-oriented listening instruction, communication-oriented listening instruction, and, most recently, learner-oriented listening instruction. We noted that there is indeed much to be gained from adopting a learner-oriented approach to listening instruction. At present, it is mainly focused on strategy instruction in the classroom and learners having opportunities to use strategies outside the classroom.

Learning to listen remains mainly an individual affair, however. Learners do not benefit significantly from the knowledge and experiences of their peers and teachers. More importantly, many language programs still lack curricular support for overall listening development during and beyond the formal classroom. Learner-oriented listening instruction, therefore, needs to take advantage of the whole gamut of learning processes that learners experience in order to develop different aspects of their listening competence. Teachers need to nurture self-regulated learning and promote peer dialogue so that learners can learn to listen in a holistic manner (Goh, 1997, 2008; Vandergrift, 2004, 2007). In addition to the practice of listening, learners should know how to put metacognition into action. They can learn to use strategies appropriately during real-time listening and to direct their own learning though planning, monitoring, and evaluation, so that they continuously improve their listening abilities over months and years.

In this chapter we discuss the role of metacognition, which lies at the heart of learner-oriented listening instruction. We also explain why a metacognitive approach is crucial to helping learners engage more effectively with input and guide their overall listening development in and out of the classroom. The goal of a metacognitive approach to listening is to develop learners who:

- understand the challenges of listening in a second language;
- think about their learning development individually and collaboratively with others;
- habitually make plans to self-direct and manage their progress in listening;
- use listening strategies appropriately;
- have greater self-efficacy and motivation; and, last but not least,
- can improve their listening proficiency to process aural input and engage effectively in oral interaction.

In other words, these L2 listeners are self-regulated learners, who are aware of their own learning processes and the demands of their learning tasks. They have also developed key listening skills and a range of strategies to meet their listening needs in various contexts.

Metacognition has been shown to be one of the most reliable predictors of learning (Wang, Haertel, & Walberg, 1990). In fact, many education scholars consider it central to the learning process and key to its success (Alexander, 2008; Borkowski, 1996). The benefits of metacognitive instruction have been reported in different subject domains, such as mathematics and reading. More recently, the positive outcomes of different kinds of metacognitive interventions for L2 listening have also been reported (see for example, Cross, 2009b; Goh & Taib, 2006; Graham & Macaro, 2008; Mareschal, 2007; Vandergrift & Tafaghodtari, 2010; Zeng, 2007).

In this chapter we will explain a metacognitive framework that underpins the teaching of listening, as conceptualized in this book. Grounded in metacognitive theory, the framework and the specific activities in subsequent chapters also draw on the understanding of listening processes discussed in previous chapters. We will show how this comprehensive framework can help to improve L2 listening competence by enhancing the learner's cognitive processes, utilization of knowledge sources, and strategies for successful one-way and interactive listening, and at the same time help them manage different cognitive and affective variables that can influence listening success.

What is Metacognition?

Metacognition has been defined and applied in different ways, but the different conceptualizations all share a common basic understanding. Metacognition is our ability to think about our own thinking or "cognition," and, by extension, to think about how we process information for a range of purposes and manage the way we do it. It is the ability to step back, as it were, from what occupies our mind at a particular moment in time to analyze and evaluate what we are thinking. Much of our current understanding of metacognition can be traced back to the work of Flavell (1976, p. 232), who described it as "one's knowledge concerning one's own cognitive processes and . . . active monitoring and consequent regulation and orchestration of these processes in relation to the cognitive objects or data on which they bear, usually in the service of some concrete goal or objective."

Metacognition enables us to be agents of our own thinking—individuals who can construct an understanding of themselves and the world around them, control their thoughts and behaviors, and monitor the consequences of these thoughts and behaviors (Kluwe, 1982, cited in Hacker et al., 2009). Learners who engage at the metacognitive level acquire a sense of agency as they gradually gain more control of their learning through effective steps in problem-solving and understand more of what is being learned. This sense of agency can develop the learners' self-concept, motivating them toward greater success (Hacker et al., 2009).

What does managing or taking charge entail? According to Hacker et al. (2009, p. 1), "At the minimum, taking charge requires learners to be aware of their learning, to evaluate their learning needs, to generate strategies to meet their needs, and to implement these strategies." Metacognition has been referred to as the "seventh sense" in learning (Nisbet & Shucksmith, 1986).

The concept of metacognition was first applied to language learning by Wenden (1987) who articulated its role in developing learner autonomy and differentiating cognitive processes between learners. Wenden (1991) added a new dimension to the discussion of the good language learner by arguing that learners who are metacognitively aware are self-directed and can take charge of their own learning processes. Since Wenden's pioneering work, other scholars have further examined the role of metacognition in the development of language skills, particularly reading and listening.

Metacognitive awareness refers to a state of consciousness of our own thoughts as we focus on a particular cognitive or learning situation. According to Flavell (1979), it is demonstrated in at least two ways. The learner may experience a distinct thought or feeling apart from the regular train of thought, or the learner may retrieve something from stored knowledge in relation to the train of thought. A third way of demonstrating metacognitive awareness is the use of strategies for problem-solving, comprehension, and learning. Considering strategy use as part of metacognition is consistent with current discussions about metacognition in the field of education (Hacker et al., 2009). Much of the literature on strategy use in language learning, however, tends to discuss strategies with little direct reference to metacognition, except for the strategies that regulate learning. Metacognition is often seen as a process in the service of strategy use, rather than an overarching process that manages learning. Strategies are metacognitive in that they enable learners to purposefully change the way they learn and use language. Wenden's (1991, 1998) understanding of learner autonomy attempted to bring together the constructs of metacognition and strategy use.

The metacognitive framework that we propose serves two important functions in language learning: (1) self-appraisal or knowledge about cognitive states and processes, and (2) self-management or control of cognition (Paris & Winograd, 1990). Self-appraisal occurs through personal reflections about one's ability and means to meet the demands of a cognitive goal. Self-management is executive in nature and "helps to orchestrate cognitive aspects of problem solving" (Paris & Winograd, 1990, p. 18). This is consistent with the concept of executive functions of human cognition—the way we think and control our thinking (Baddeley, 2000). These two functions of metacognition have continued to find support within current scholarly efforts to develop a unified understanding of the concept of metacognition (Nelson, 1996; Veenman, Van Hout-Wolters, & Afflerbach, 2006).

To address these functions, the metacognitive framework draws on three components: experience, knowledge, and strategies (see Figure 5.1). As a description of a learner, one can say that metacognitive awareness helps learners become self-knowing, self-directed, and self-managed in their learning. Further exploration of the three components fleshes out what the concept means.

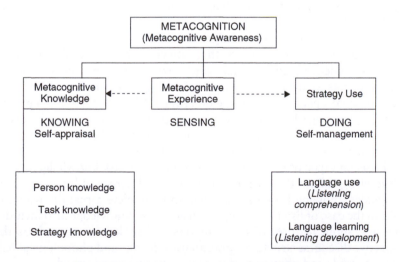

Figure 5.1. A Metacognitive Framework for Listening Instruction

Metacognitive Experience

According to Flavell (1979, p. 906), thinking and learning are accompanied by other "conscious cognitive and affective experiences." If one thinks of experience as the main activity or train of thought, then a metacognitive experience is a thought or feeling that occurs to a person during and about the main thought. An example of metacognitive experience during listening is when learners realize that they do not recognize the words they hear but remember a similar situation where they managed to solve a word recognition problem. Listeners, confronted with an unknown sound, may recall a strategy that they used before and use it again to manage the new problem. This is metacognitive experience.

Some metacognitive experiences are fleeting and do not have any lasting impact. An example of this is when listeners notice an unfamiliar sounding word, ignore it, and soon forget the sounds that they perceived momentarily. Metacognitive experience is useful to learners if it leads to some productive application of strategies or further understanding about the task, themselves, and/or the world around them. The two arrows in Figure 5.1, pointing from metacognitive experience to the other two components, show that it can influence the development of metacognitive knowledge, and the selection and use of strategies.

Metacognitive Knowledge

Learners store three kinds of knowledge about cognition: person, task, and strategy (Flavell, 1979). This knowledge is "similar in structure and function to other kinds of knowledge in long-term memory" (Borkowski, 1996, p. 392).

Person knowledge is knowledge about how a particular individual learns and the various factors that affect that individual's learning. Person knowledge includes what we know about ourselves as learners and the beliefs we have about what leads to success or failure in learning. An individual's person knowledge determines his or her self-concept. For example, language learners who often experience listening problems in interactive listening may develop a strong belief that they are poor listeners and may therefore try to avoid such situations.

The second type of metacognitive knowledge is task knowledge, which is knowledge about the purpose, demands, and nature of learning tasks. It includes knowing how to approach and complete a real-life listening task. In the case of listening comprehension, task knowledge also includes knowing about features of different types of spoken texts, such as the respective discourse structures, grammatical forms, and phonological features of words and phrases as they appear in connected speech.

The third type of metacognitive knowledge is strategy knowledge: that is, knowing which strategies can be used to accomplish a specific goal, be it achieving comprehension in a specific communicative context or improving one's listening ability after one term of study. Strategy knowledge can be distinguished from strategy use in that the former is limited to knowing about strategies. Figure 5.2 illustrates the different types of metacognitive knowledge about listening.

Type	Examples for L2 listening
Person Knowledge Knowledge of the cognitive and affective factors that facilitate one's own listening comprehension and listening development.	Self-concept and self-efficacy about listening • I am an anxious listener. • I can improve my listening if I try harder. • I dare to take risks. • My ability to relate to the content of the text determined the accuracy of my anticipations which in turn affected the quality of my listening. Specific listening problems, causes, and possible solutions. • I have problems catching the beginning of what other people say. • English sounds and pronunciation are too different from Korean. • I can "psycho" myself, talk, and comfort myself to get rid of negative feelings.
Task Knowledge Knowledge of purpose and nature of the listening task, knowledge of task demands and knowledge of when deliberate effort is required.	Mental, affective, and social processes involved in listening • You need to concentrate very hard if you are not strong in the language. • You need to stay calm to hear clearly. • Listening is difficult because people expect you to respond to them when they talk to you. • Pay attention to the exercise in front of us and the oral at the same time because if we get lost, we can't catch up. Skills for completing listening tasks • When you listen to a talk, you need to get only the general idea. • Since I now can anticipate, I am more aware of what to listen to and can pick up more of the conversations. • I find I have slow reaction to numbers. So I want to do more practice like listen more to business news or anything that contains a lot of numbers.

	Factors that influence listening • That speaker's accent is different from the one my teacher has and it makes listening challenging for me. • News reports are more difficult to follow than stories. • I need to look for key words and not let myself mire in the dialogue . . . I really need to work on this. Ways of improving listening outside class • I should try to talk to English speakers more. • Mobile devices are excellent for my listening development. • I think I should listen to news and watch some documentaries too . . . not just listen to songs I like.
Strategy Knowledge Knowledge about effective strategies for listening tasks and knowledge about how best to approach listening tasks.	General and specific strategies to facilitate comprehension and manage learning • If you don't understand what you hear, just guess. • Watching English movies can help my listening, but I should try not to read the Chinese subtitles. • Predicting may not always be correct but it helps. Strategies appropriate for specific types of listening tasks • To get the information on train time, you need to listen to all the details carefully. • When somebody is speaking too fast, we can ask them to slow down or repeat. • During the second listen, I can keep my ears open for the things I missed but my partner caught. Ineffective strategies • I shall make my reaction as quickly as possible as I can. The less translation the better. • Try not to focus too hard on the text, it will only make you anxious. • My listening depends on guessing too much. If I couldn't guess the topic correctly, what would I do?

Figure 5.2. Types of Metacognitive Knowledge About L2 Listening and Examples from Learners

Based on Flavell, 1979; Goh, 2002a; Goh & Taib, 2006; Vandergrift, 2002, 2003b; Wenden, 1991

Before we end this discussion about metacognitive knowledge, it is useful to clarify the relationship between this construct and learner beliefs. The latter, which are value related views, are considered a sub-set of metacognitive knowledge (Wenden, 2001) and are subsumed in our discussion of metacognitive knowledge. For example, a learner's person knowledge—"I'm always anxious and slow to respond during conversations"—is also a belief about oneself as an L2 listener; it can be something that the learner holds so firmly that it takes a great deal of time and effort to change.

Strategy Use

The third component of metacognition is an individual's ability to use appropriate strategies to achieve cognitive, social, and affective goals. Strategy use is the deployment of specific procedures or actions to make learning easier, faster, more enjoyable, more self-regulated, more effective, or more transferable to new situations. Strategy use builds on strategy knowledge; it includes awareness of when and how to use specific strategies (see Figure 5.3).

On the whole, learners who have good strategic knowledge are also more likely to use strategies (Zhang & Goh, 2006). Strategies contribute directly to language learning as well as language use (Cohen, 1998; Cohen & Macaro, 2007). Learners use strategies to achieve comprehension goals, particularly when they have limited ability to understand what they hear. Strategies help them improve comprehension, retention, and recall of information; and, at the same time, they assist in planning for overall listening development as part of their language learning effort.

Some key characteristics of learner strategies (Cohen, 2007), which also apply to listening strategies, are listed as follows:

(a) Strategies are conscious behaviors involving cognitive, social, and affective processes.

Figure 5.3. The Relationship Between Strategy Knowledge and Strategy Use

(b) The use of strategies is managed by metacognition.

(c) The amount of attention learners give to strategies they employ varies according to different factors.

(d) Strategies are mainly employed in an interactive and orchestrated manner to form a network of processes for achieving better comprehension or learning outcomes, but sometimes individual strategies are used.

(e) Some strategies contribute to language development directly while others may not.

(f) The quality and use of strategies by individual learners is influenced by internal and external factors.

(g) At the macro-level, strategies are viewed as a general strategic approach to a task, and at the micro-level as specific strategies for realizing that approach.

(h) Knowledge about and use of strategies can be jointly constructed and managed by learners working together.

In a critical review of studies on listening strategies, Macaro et al. (2007) identified some common strategies that proficient listeners use more than less proficient listeners. This is particularly true for a group of strategies popularly referred to as metacognitive strategies, such as planning for, monitoring, and evaluating comprehension. Proficient listeners also have better understanding of the strategies they can use to facilitate their comprehension and interaction efforts. This fact supports the link between metacognitive knowledge and strategy use mentioned earlier. Metacognitive knowledge about strategies and the use of strategies such as monitoring can contribute powerfully to multiple-intelligent behavior (Perkins, 1995). Strategies help learners control their thinking and learning while listening, as well as manage their overall learning process, to become skillful L2 listeners. Good metacognitive control over appropriate strategy use is an essential aspect for long-term listening success (Graham & Macaro, 2008).

Appendix A presents a list of listening strategies derived from several key sources (Goh, 1998, 2002b; O'Malley & Chamot, 1990; Vandergrift, 1997a, 2003a; Young, 1997). Rather than group them according to commonly used distinctions such as cognitive and metacognitive, we have organized them according to the role they play to facilitate listening comprehension and overall listening development. These include:

- helping to process and interpret information by manipulating and transforming the aural input;
- observing the way information is processed or learned;
- taking appropriate steps to manage and regulate these cognitive processes;
- managing emotions; and,

- involving other people or exploiting learning resources to assist in comprehension and learning.

Some of the strategies are more relevant for real-time listening comprehension while others help to enhance learner efforts to improve listening over time. Listeners with heightened metacognitive awareness are able to orchestrate the deployment of various strategies according to task and learner variables.

A clarification of the relationship between listening strategies and listening skills may be in order here. In the literature on L2 listening, the terms "skill" and "enabling skill" are often used to describe what skilled or proficient listeners do to listen efficiently. Many of these skills—for example, listen for gist, monitor comprehension, and ask for clarifications—appear to be indistinguishable from listening strategies. An individual can engage in these processes without giving much thought to them when the listening text is easy and the task is simple. However, when faced with a challenging text and a complex task, the same individual may have to consciously deploy the strategy of listening for gist and deliberately ignore details that cannot be recognized. What is the difference, if any, between skill and strategy? In clarifying this, we follow Afflerbach, Pearson, and Paris (2008) who make the following distinction for processes in reading, the other receptive language skill:

> It is important that the terms *skill* and *strategy* be used to distinguish automatic processes from deliberately controlled processes. At the heart of accomplished reading is a balance of both—automatic application and use of reading skills, and intentional, effortful employment of reading strategies—accompanied by the ability to shift seamlessly between the two when the situation calls for it. The difficulty of the reading, influenced by text, task, reader, and contextual variables, will determine the shifting balance. (p. 371, italics in original)

This distinction underscores one of the key features of strategy use in L2 listening—listening strategies are conscious and goal-directed behaviors, cognitive and social in nature, which learners use to assist their comprehension and learning. Unlike skills, which are automatic processes that make little or no demand on processing capacity, strategies are controlled processes that require conscious attention in their deployment, modification, and orchestration.

Strategies and skills share the common characteristic of goal-directedness. The active use of strategies and skills is triggered by comprehension goals, which include achieving the purpose for listening to a particular text, establishing a coherent meaning of the text or discourse, and utilizing information and knowledge gained from listening. Goal-directedness is consistent with the view that listening is a purposeful process, that "people listen for a purpose and it is this purpose that drives the understanding process" (Rost, 1990, p. 7).

Metacognition in Action

It is clear that metacognitive processes are by definition active because they involve conscious attention to one's thoughts. For learning to be effective, however, learners must do more than just think about their cognition and learning. They must also act on the thoughts they have. This is metacognition in action. The main characteristics of this phenomenon include:

- conscious attention to one's knowledge, experience, and strategic behaviors;
- reflection on thoughts and actions and recording for sharing, analysis, and feedback;
- planning for future learning, based on reflections;
- follow-up actions may be immediate or delayed;
- changes occur in thinking and action in response to changes in the task environment;
- plans and follow-up action may involve two or more individuals; and,
- knowledge or experience is not exclusive to an individual: it can be jointly constructed by two or more individuals.

Metacognitive experience, awareness at a particular moment, can be fleeting; for this reason, immediate follow-up is important. Learners need to reflect more deeply on their feelings in a particular context in order to construct a deeper understanding of themselves as learners and the nature of the task at hand. Learners who are aware of learning needs or problems can either choose to do nothing differently or they can select appropriate strategies to improve their learning. We see metacognition in action when learners show awareness of gaps in comprehension and take immediate action, such as orchestrating the use of selected strategies to bridge the gap.

Learners may also involve other participants in an interaction to help out when they experience difficulty in oral communication. For example, a learner senses that he or she does not understand what is being said and asks the speaker to repeat or clarify. A learner may also learn to use back-channelling or response tokens (e.g., "Yes," "That's really interesting," etc.) as strategies to keep the conversation going for as long as possible. Metacognition in action is also demonstrated when learners critically reflect on their knowledge about learning, before, during, or after a particular listening experience or task, or when they actively involve other agents in their environment to facilitate their learning as a result of these reflections (e.g., classmates, computers).

Metacognition, as a concept, has common elements with other concepts used in language learning. The concept of self-regulation, for example, is used by some scholars to describe an individual's ability to change cognitive processes in response to new or changing task demands (Borkowski, 1996). While the two concepts are similar, metacognition has "a clear cognitive orientation," and self-regulation focuses more on the "human action than the thinking that engendered it." The construct of self-regulation also draws attention to the role of environmental factors as a stimulant for self-awareness and a trigger for regulatory responses (Dinsmore, Alexander, & Loughlin, 2008).

The metacognitive approach in this book integrates these two emphases in learning: learning as an individual cognitive enterprise and learning as a social enterprise. It accounts for both cognitive and social processes in language learning and it reflects both cognitive and socio-cultural theories of learning (Firth & Wagner, 1997, 2007; Lantolf, 2000; Lantolf & Thorne, 2006).

Following Bruer (1998) it recognizes predictable paths in each learning domain, guided by learners' awareness and control of their mental processes. It is facilitated by collaborative settings that value self-directed student dialogue, in which learners use conversation to achieve a better understanding of their world and more efficient ways to organize their learning. This framework emphasizes the constructive nature of learning and the important role that L2 learners play in the process of learning to listen (O'Malley & Chamot, 1990). It also takes into account paths of development that learners take as they become more skilled at listening.

The framework is informed by socio-cultural perspectives on learning. Dialogic interaction and the activity learners participate in during that interaction contribute to the overall learning of each individual in the interaction (Atkinson, 2002). Clearly, they derive many cognitive and affective benefits from working and talking together to explore ways of learning (Hancock, 2004). The learning and increase in metacognitive knowledge for each learner can be bigger than the sum of each of the individual parts. The pedagogical sequence in the next chapter illustrates this. Many of the metacognitive activities proposed in other chapters also provide learners with opportunities to enrich individual learning though peer dialogue and cooperation.

Cross's (2010) listening study, situated within a socio-cultural paradigm, demonstrates the important role of peer dialogue in metacognitive instruction and the impact it has on developing learners' metacognitive awareness about listening text, listening comprehension, and listening strategy. Cross meticulously cross-matched three sets of data from transcripts of dialogues and listening diaries. He was able to show that learners' metacognitive knowledge had indeed increased as a result of the dialogic interaction, through individual knowledge construction and peer joint-construction. The way learners engaged in the process of learning to listen during dialogues at various points in their activities and their post-listening diary reflections clearly illustrated metacognition in action. This study also demonstrates how the pedagogical sequence, presented in the next chapter, can be utilized for planning lessons that have an explicit focus on "sharing, selecting, and reflecting on listening strategies by learners as a mechanism for stimulating their metacognitive awareness" (Cross, 2010, p. 285).

L2 Listener Metacognitive Knowledge

Language learners demonstrate various degrees of metacognitive knowledge about themselves as L2 listeners and the listening process (Goh, 1997; Graham, 2006). This is also true of younger learners (Goh & Taib, 2006; Gu, Hu & Zhang, 2009; Vandergrift, 2002). Several recent studies have shown that metacognitive knowledge can be increased through classroom instruction (Cross, 2009b; Liu & Goh, 2006; Mareschal, 2007; Nathan, 2008; Vandergrift, 2002, 2003b), and that weak listeners stand to benefit the most in terms of proficiency improvement.

How does metacognitive awareness influence the outcome of listening comprehension? One way is that it influences the manner in which learners approach the tasks of listening and learning to listen. Learners who have appropriate task knowledge better plan, monitor, and evaluate what they do, compared with those who approach listening in a random or incidental manner. What language learners know about their learning often directly affects the process and the outcome of their learning. For example, learners' perceptions of the demands of listening tasks and strategies, as well as their own abilities and interests, can lead them to select, evaluate, modify or even abandon plans, goals, tasks, and strategies.

Teachers and learners can find out more about metacognitive knowledge by using a questionnaire or a checklist on which learners track their progress over time. The Metacognitive Awareness Listening Questionnaire (MALQ) by Vandergrift et al. (2006) can be used to assess L2 listeners' metacognitive awareness and perceived use of strategies. The MALQ, based on the model of metacognitive knowledge in this chapter, aims to elicit L2 listeners' perceived use of strategies while listening to spoken texts. The 21-item instrument assesses five distinct factors in listening: problem-solving; planning and evaluation; (no) mental translation; person knowledge; and directed attention. It has high reliability and factorial validity, based on statistical tests that used data from a large sample of over 900 respondents from a number of countries.

Although the MALQ was intended to be a research instrument, it can be used to provide useful insights for both teaching and learning. Learners can use it for self-assessment to chart their changes in strategy use. It helps learners increase their metacognitive knowledge about the task of listening, preparing them to take effective measures to improve comprehension over time. The MALQ is also an awareness-raising tool for metacognitive instruction: it helps learners understand the processes that take place during listening. Teachers can use it for diagnostic purposes to find out the extent to which learners are aware of the strategies for listening. A copy of the MALQ, along with the factor that each item taps, is presented in Figure 5.4. A reproducible form of the questionnaire is found in Appendix B.

Circle the number which best shows your level of agreement with the statement at the present time.

	Strongly disagree 1	Disagree 2	Slightly disagree 3	Partly agree 4	Agree 5	Strongly agree 6
Factor	**Strategy or Belief/Perception**					
Planning/ Evaluation	1. Before I start to listen, I have a plan in my head for how I am going to listen.			1 2 3 4 5 6		
Directed Attention	2. I focus harder on the text when I have trouble understanding.			1 2 3 4 5 6		
Person Knowledge	3. I find that listening in English is more difficult than reading, speaking, or writing in English.			1 2 3 4 5 6		
Mental Translation	4. I translate in my head as I listen.			1 2 3 4 5 6		
Problem Solving	5. I use the words I understand to guess the meaning of the words I don't understand.			1 2 3 4 5 6		
Directed Attention	6. When my mind wanders, I recover my concentration right away.			1 2 3 4 5 6		
Problem Solving	7. As I listen, I compare what I understand with what I know about the topic.			1 2 3 4 5 6		

Person Knowledge	8.	I feel that listening comprehension in English is a challenge for me.	1	2	3	4	5	6
Problem Solving	9.	I use my experience and knowledge to help me understand.	1	2	3	4	5	6
Planning/ Evaluation	10.	Before listening, I think of similar texts that I may have listened to.	1	2	3	4	5	6
Mental Translation	11.	I translate key words as I listen.	1	2	3	4	5	6
Directed Attention	12.	I try to get back on track when I lose concentration.	1	2	3	4	5	6
Problem Solving	13.	As I listen, I quickly adjust my interpretation if I realize that it is not correct.	1	2	3	4	5	6
Planning/ Evaluation	14.	After listening, I think back to how I listened, and about what I might do differently next time.	1	2	3	4	5	6
Person Knowledge	15.	I don't feel nervous when I listen to English.	1	2	3	4	5	6
Directed Attention	16.	When I have difficulty understanding what I hear, I give up and stop listening.	1	2	3	4	5	6
Problem Solving	17.	I use the general idea of the text to help me guess the meaning of the words that I don't understand.	1	2	3	4	5	6
Mental Translation	18.	I translate word by word, as I listen.	1	2	3	4	5	6
Problem Solving	19.	When I guess the meaning of a word, I think back to everything else that I have heard, to see if my guess makes sense.	1	2	3	4	5	6
Planning/ Evaluation	20.	As I listen, I periodically ask myself if I am satisfied with my level of comprehension.	1	2	3	4	5	6
Planning/ Evaluation	21.	I have a goal in mind as I listen.	1	2	3	4	5	6

Figure 5.4. Metacognitive Awareness Listening Questionnaire (MALQ) Items and Corresponding Factors

Source: Vandergrift et al. (2006)

Metacognitive Instruction

Discussion of the metacognitive approach to listening instruction so far has focused on theoretical principles and research findings that inform the approach. In this section, we will focus on the application of these perspectives in listening instruction.

Metacognitive instruction refers to pedagogical procedures that enable learners to increase awareness of the listening process by developing richer metacognitive knowledge about themselves as listeners, the nature and demands of listening, and strategies for listening. At the same time, learners also learn to plan, monitor, and evaluate their comprehension efforts and the progress of their overall listening development. Metacognitive instruction will enable learners to become better learners of listening as they take positive action to self-regulate their learning. When integrated with well-planned listening tasks, metacognitive activities can be an effective way to improve listening proficiency and learner motivation.

Why is metacognitive instruction useful? Text-oriented and communication-oriented instruction focuses mainly on the product of comprehension, and learner-oriented listening instruction tends to focus narrowly on cognitive strategy instruction in the classroom. Metacognitive instruction is learner-oriented and addresses more aspects of learning by focusing on both cognitive and social variables and processes that affect listening success. It increases awareness of variables and processes that may seem a mystery to learners, who are often left to figure out how to learn to listen on their own. While some learners become successful listeners, others are less successful. Those who could achieve greater success are unable to reach their goals because of a lack of scaffolding and feedback from their teachers. Scaffolding refers to support in performing a task provided by teachers or more proficient peers. Metacognitive instruction ensures that learners develop greater metacognitive knowledge and more effective strategy use through systematic and principled planning of learning activities. In other words, it enables learners to engage in self-appraisal and self-management activities that are supported and guided by teachers (Goh, 2010).

This cognitive, social, and affective engagement with learning is a very important aspect of L2 learning; in a sense it is more crucial for learning to listen than any of the other language skills because listening is a largely unseen process that makes it a difficult skill to teach. This probably explains why, for such a long time, listening was done in the language classroom but not systematically taught. Metacognitive instruction offers teachers and learners a means to examine the hidden processes while working on tasks that improve learners' ability to process aural information. It also provides teachers with a perspective on their learners' individual learning styles, goals, and abilities.

Metacognitive instruction can be delivered during formal listening lessons and it can continue to provide structure and support to learners after they leave the classroom and work on their listening without a teacher present. Veenman et al. (2006) offer three principles for planning effective metacognitive instruction:

1. Embed metacognitive instruction in the subject matter to ensure connectivity.
2. Encourage learners to put in extra effort by showing them the usefulness of metacognitive activities.
3. Sustain training to ensure that metacognitive activity is maintained.

As Figure 5.5 shows, metacognitive instruction creates a continuous cycle of learning. It typically begins in the classroom where listening lessons are conducted. Through carefully designed tasks, the teacher engages learners in thinking and learning about how to listen. The pedagogical sequence presented in Chapter 6 is one way to integrate metacognitive activities with conventional listening activities in a lesson.

Another way is to integrate listening practice and metacognitive activities through the use of communicative listening tasks and awareness raising, planning, and reflective activities. We can also introduce similar activities that learners can engage in after class. This increases their listening practice time and provides the much needed scaffolding that is often absent in extensive listening. Through a continuous cycle of learning to listen in and out of class, learners are able to develop their listening ability more quickly and effectively. This is based on the simple yet valuable "time-on-task" principle for learning—for an individual to learn something well, they must spend enough time on it.

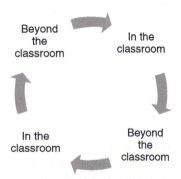

Figure 5.5. Metacognitive Instruction for Learning to Listen

Objectives of Metacognitive Instruction

Like all instruction, metacognitive instruction will only be relevant and useful to learners if teachers have clear objectives. Figures 5.6 and 5.7 identify objectives that teachers can use to plan activities that integrate with listening or as stand-alone metacognitive tasks.

Metacognitive activities enable learners to enjoy scaffolded learning experiences in which novices receive guidance, support, and feedback from their teachers, who are the experts. When learners make their mental processes explicit in discussion with a peer, and then track, monitor,

---

Person Knowledge

Aim: Develop better knowledge of self as L2 listener.
Objectives:
1. Examine personal beliefs about self-efficacy and self-concepts with regard to listening in a second language.
2. Identify listening problems, causes, and possible solutions.

Task Knowledge

Aim: Understand nature of L2 listening and demands of learning to listen.
Objectives:
1. Experience mental, affective, and social processes involved in listening.
2. Differentiate different types of listening skill (e.g., listening for details, listening for global understanding, listening to infer information).
3. Analyze factors that influence listening performance (e.g., speaker, text, interlocutor, strategy).
4. Compare and evaluate ways to improve listening abilities outside formal instruction.
5. Examine phonological features of spoken texts that influence perceptual processing.

Strategy Knowledge

Aim: Understand roles of cognitive, metacognitive, and social-affective strategies.
Objectives:
1. Identify strategies that are appropriate for specific types of listening tasks and problems.
2. Demonstrate use of strategies.
3. Identify strategies that may not be appropriate for learning style or culture.

Figure 5.6. Aims and Objectives for Developing Metacognitive Knowledge About L2 Listening

Planning	
Aim: Determine goals and means by which goals can be achieved.	
Listening comprehension	• Preview task demands and prepare for listening. • Rehearse language (pronunciation of key words and phrases) needed for the task. • Consider strategies for coping with potential challenges.
Overall listening development	• Set personal goals for listening development. • Seek appropriate opportunities for listening practice. • Make plans and preparations to address challenges in learning to listen.
Monitoring	
Aim: Check progress of efforts during listening and in learning to listen.	
Listening comprehension	• Check understanding of message by drawing on appropriate sources of knowledge (e.g., context, factual, linguistic). • Check appropriateness and accuracy of understanding against old and new information.
Overall listening development	• Consider progress of listening development in light of what has been planned. • Assess chances of achieving learning goals.
Evaluation	
Aim: Judge progress and success of efforts at listening and learning to listen.	
Listening comprehension	• Determine overall acceptability of understanding and interpretation of message/information. • Check appropriateness and accuracy of understanding against old and new information. • Assess the effectiveness of strategies for learning and practice.
Overall listening development	• Assess effectiveness of overall plan to improve listening. • Assess appropriateness of learning goals.

Figure 5.7. Aims and Objectives for Developing Strategies for Listening Comprehension and Overall Listening Development

and evaluate their own listening development, they will see the benefits of engaging in these metacognitive processes and be more motivated to continue using them.

An important expected outcome of metacognitive instruction for learners is the ability to self-regulate learning. In the process, they are also better able to perceive, parse, and utilize the aural input they receive, strengthening their abilities to engage in parallel processing, including both bottom-up and top-down processes. Self-regulated learning is described as "an active, constructive process whereby learners set goals for their learning and then attempt to monitor, regulate, and control their cognition, motivation, and behavior, guided and constrained by their goals and the contextual features in the environment" (Pintrich, 2000, p. 453). It is often considered to be part of the overarching construct of self-regulation, which involves "*cognitive, affective, motivational* and *behavioral* components that provide the individual with the capacity to adjust his or her actions and goals to achieve the desired results in light of changing environmental conditions" (Zeidner, Boekaerts, & Pintrich, 2000, p. 751, italics in original).

Self-regulated second language listeners will have the ability to do two things. First, they can manage the process and outcome of specific listening tasks in order to maximize opportunities for comprehending and using the information they have processed. Second, they can select, manage, and evaluate their own listening development activities outside of formal class time, an activity sometimes referred to as self-directed learning. Language learners who are aware of the benefits of specific listening strategies may also deliberately use these strategies to improve their listening comprehension. Learners who are conscious of their own listening problems may also be motivated to find ways of addressing them. Those who have engaged with good metacognitive processes can also teach their peers about them.

Summary

This chapter highlights the role of metacognition for learning to listen and identifies features of learning that show metacognition in action. It explains the theoretical bases for a metacognitive approach to L2 instruction and offers principles for metacognitive instruction that foster learner self-regulation of listening. The framework for metacognition contains three key components: experience, knowledge, and strategy. Of the three, experience is an involuntary response. The other two components, metacognitive knowledge and strategy use, are amenable to instruction and can contribute to more effective listening, confidence, and motivation. Even though perception, heeding, and recording of mental processes are done individually, metacognitive activities are not confined to the cognitive domains of an individual. Metacognition in action can and should involve peer cooperation and peer dialogue. Individual learners learn as much, if not more, when they interact with other learners in acknowledging, analyzing, and evaluating their experiences than when they construct this knowledge on their own.

Discussion Questions and Tasks

1. Based on your reading of this chapter, what is your understanding of a metacognitive approach to teaching listening? Discuss what you see as the relationship between metacognitive awareness raising and strategy use.

2. Select a language teaching course book along with all its accompanying resources for listening. Examine the activities in two units of the book. Are any features of metacognitive instruction described in these chapters? How can you incorporate some features of metacognitive instruction into the unit, if they are not present? What added benefits do you think learners will get from the new activities you have included?

3. How important is a language learner's self-concept? Do you think self-concept can change with time? If so, what do you think will lead to changes and development in a learner's self-concept as an L2 listener? You might want to refer to Chapter 4 to review the cognitive and social variables that could influence listening, motivation, and self-concept.

4. Consider the list of strategies in the table in Appendix A. Which of these strategies might be easy to teach and learn? Which might be more difficult? Explain why.

Suggestions for Further Reading

Cross, J. (2010). Raising L2 listeners' metacognitive awareness: A socio-cultural theory perspective. *Language Awareness*, 19(4), 281–297.
This study provides empirical evidence on how peer–peer dialogue during a pedagogical sequence of listening tasks helped a group of Japanese EFL learners develop their metacognitive awareness. Of particular interest is the clear and concise background on a socio-cultural view of metacognition and how knowledge is constructed through dialogue.

Goh, C. (2008). Metacognitive instruction for second language listening development: Theory, practice and research implications. *RELC Journal*, 39(2), 188–213.
This paper discusses a metacognitive approach, drawing on understandings from educational research as well as L2 listening studies, and outlines general instructional objectives and learning activities for metacognitive instruction.

Vandergrift, L., Goh, C., Mareschal, C., & Tafaghodtari, M. H. (2006). The Metacognitive Awareness Listening Questionnaire (MALQ): Development and validation. *Language Learning*, 56(3), 431–462.

This article describes the development and validation of a listening question-naire designed to assess L2 listeners' metacognitive awareness and perceived use of strategies while listening, and discusses potential uses of the question-naire for research and pedagogical purposes.

Wenden, A. (2001). Metacognitive knowledge in SLA: The neglected variable. In M. P. Breen (Ed.), *Learner contributions to language learning: New directions in research* (pp. 44–64). Harlow, U.K: Pearson Education.

This chapter reviews selected research studies on the metacognitive knowledge of L2 learners, explains the role of metacognitive knowledge in self-regulation of language learning, and discusses the implications for theory, research, and practice.

Chapter 6

A Metacognitive Pedagogical Sequence

Scenario

M. Aubert tells his class that they will listen to an interview with a university student about his summer job as a calèche[1] driver in Québec City. He asks them to think about the nature of this kind of aural text—an interview with someone about his/her work—and to anticipate the types of questions the interviewer might ask. He writes the key words of all the suggested questions on the board. Once the learners have exhausted all question possibilities, he invites them to anticipate possible responses based on their knowledge of Québec City and the nature of summer jobs. Learners jot down key words of possible responses alongside the questions in their notes.

Learners now listen to the text for the first time, placing a checkmark beside the questions and answers that they recognize in the text. Once they have listened to the text, the learners write down any other information they understood. In pairs, they share with each other what they understood, discuss discrepancies in understanding, and then decide where to pay particular attention during the second listen. After the second listen, they make necessary revisions to earlier notes and add any new information. Once again, they compare notes with their partners and make necessary additions and revisions.

M. Aubert now leads the class in discussion and learners share what they have understood. When he determines that the main points and important supporting details have been stated, M. Aubert asks them to listen for a third time to verify any of the main points and details they did not recognize earlier. Today, this final listen will also include following along with a transcript

---

1 A horse-drawn carriage popular with tourists for a guided tour of the old part of Québec City.

of the text, so that learners can match sound with written form. The activity concludes with a class discussion of what learners did to resolve difficulties and the effectiveness of their approach to the activity. Based on this discussion, learners then write goals for the next listening activity.

Pre-reading Reflection

1. How does the opening of this listening activity resemble the opening of a traditional listening lesson? How is it different?
2. Do you think this activity reflects real-life listening? Give your reasons.
3. How does M. Aubert develop student metacognitive awareness of L2 listening?
4. What do these learners discover about the process of listening?
5. How does M. Aubert verify comprehension? Do you think he does so adequately?

Introduction

In this chapter we will further build on the concept of metacognition and demonstrate concretely how to practice it in L2 listening comprehension. We will begin by discussing the development of metacognitive processes, such as planning, monitoring, problem-solving, and evaluation, for listening in real-life listening contexts. We will then demonstrate how these processes can be incorporated into a pedagogical sequence that teachers can use to nurture their development and guide learners through the process of L2 listening. To illustrate the pedagogical sequence in action, we will present a number of different listening activities that focus on the development of the metacognitive processes in a deliberate manner.

Finally, we will discuss research studies related to the use of this approach to metacognitive instruction. First, we discuss three studies that illustrate its impact on growth in metacognitive knowledge about L2 listening. Then we discuss a number of studies that provide evidence for the impact of this approach on improved L2 listening performance.

Metacognitive Processes

Metacognitive instruction in L2 listening refers to pedagogical methods that increase learner awareness about the listening process. In particular, it develops richer metacognitive knowledge about the nature and demands of listening and strategies for listening. Through metacognitive instruction, learners become more skilled in using the following processes: (1) planning for the activity; (2) monitoring comprehension; (3) solving

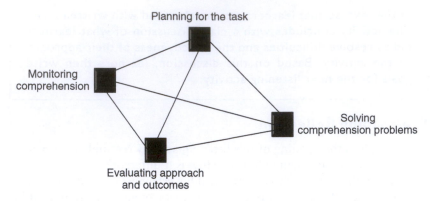

Figure 6.1. Metacognitive Listening Processes and Their Interaction

comprehension problems; and (4) evaluating the approach and outcomes. The result is improvement in overall ability to listen. These processes and their interaction are illustrated in Figure 6.1. However, before describing how these processes are developed in the pedagogical sequence, we will describe what listeners do as they engage in these processes.

Planning for the Listening Activity

The planning phase prepares listeners to be proactive in their listening efforts. Proactive listeners decide what to listen for and establish the necessary conditions for successful listening, in order to pay close attention to meaning while listening. During the critical planning phase, listeners prepare themselves for what they will hear and what they are expected to do, instead of barrelling into the activity without thinking. To plan for successful completion of the activity, listeners can:

- bring to consciousness their knowledge of the topic and any relevant cultural information;
- analyze the text genre and recall how information might be organized in it;
- anticipate words and/or ideas that they may hear;
- determine where to pay attention and decide on how much detail to find, based on their purpose for listening, in order to direct listening efforts;
- predict what they will hear, based on information brought to consciousness and any relevant contextual information; and,
- prepare the conditions for listening by clearing their minds of distractions and focusing their attention.

Monitoring Comprehension

While listening to the text, listeners monitor their comprehension in light of their predictions and make adjustments, as necessary. Listeners can:

- evaluate continually what they understand;
- check for consistency with their predictions, for appropriateness with world knowledge and for internal consistency: that is, the ongoing interpretation of the co-text;
- verify predictions and accept the fact that they do not need to understand every word;
- assess their level of comprehension;
- verify progress in their comprehension of the desired information and necessary details; and
- determine whether the approach to understanding the text is working or not.

Solving Comprehension Problems

As they monitor their comprehension and confront difficulties, listeners must adjust their approach to the text or activate specific strategies. Listeners can:

- adjust their approach by activating more appropriate strategies as required: for example, revise predictions or adjust their inferences to reflect new possibilities;
- make inferences about the meaning of a chunk of text they did not understand by deducing from the information they are confident they have understood; or
- ask for clarification, if the listening context allows for this.

Evaluating the Approach and Outcomes

Listeners need to evaluate the effectiveness of the approach adopted and/or decisions made during the listening process after completion of the activity. Listeners can:

- reflect on difficulties encountered, what went wrong, and why;
- confirm comprehension with a transcription of parts or all of the text; or
- reflect on the success of problem-solving efforts, such as the success of an inference or modification of a particular strategy (if the listening context allows for this).

These processes do not necessarily operate in a linear or circular manner. They interact in multiple ways as listeners trigger different processes to construct meaning—illustrated by the bi-directional lines in Figure 6.1. The paths to build meaning can be quite idiosyncratic, depending on the cues picked up by listeners, the quality of their planning efforts, their metacognitive knowledge about L2 listening, and other variables (e.g., prior knowledge). Listeners may go back to a modified form of planning when monitoring suggests that previous predictions were not fruitful. Before making that decision, however, they may make several attempts to problem-solve in response to difficulties encountered, and to monitor the emerging interpretation. Growing difficulties may suggest a return to planning. All of this occurs automatically, or in a more limited, controlled manner, depending on the level of listening proficiency.

The next section will illustrate how these processes can be developed by using a metacognitive pedagogical sequence in some specific listening activities, and then become more automatic over time. This kind of guided listening practice will enable learners to better understand how to listen and to regulate these metacognitive processes.

Metacognitive Pedagogical Sequence

The metacognitive pedagogical sequence (Vandergrift, 1999, 2004, 2007) can develop awareness of the process of one-way listening, and help listeners acquire the metacognitive knowledge critical to success in comprehension and in becoming self-regulated listeners. It builds on knowledge about skilled L2 listeners (e.g., Bacon, 1992; Goh, 1997, 2000; O'Malley, Chamot, & Küpper, 1989; Vandergrift, 1997, 2003a), comprehension instruction in cognitive psychology (e.g., Baker, 2002; Block & Pressley, 2002; Paris & Winograd, 1990), and the development of self-regulated language learners (e.g., Chamot, Barnhardt, El-Dinary, & Robbins, 1999; Eilam & Aharon, 2003; Wenden, 1998, 2002). This sequence involves the orchestration of metacognitive processes and other pertinent comprehension strategies, most notably inferencing and elaboration.

Metacognitive instruction adopts a process-based approach to instil in learners (1) knowledge about themselves as listeners (person knowledge); (2) the inherent complexities of L2 listening in relationship to task demands (task knowledge); and (3) effective listening strategies (strategy knowledge). The goal is to open up avenues to regulate listening comprehension and, ultimately, achieve greater success in L2 listening. We will illustrate this pedagogical sequence in three different listening activities; the first two are generic in that they can be used with any text and the last one is text-specific. Each activity leads listeners through the process of listening as illustrated in Figure 6.2.

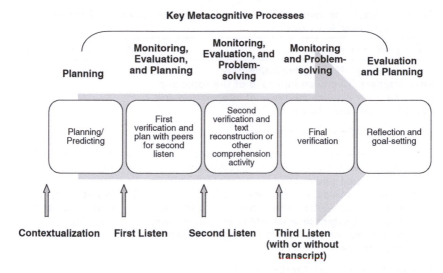

Figure 6.2. Stages in the Metacognitive Pedagogical Sequence for Listening Instruction

Activity I

The first activity is summarized in the opening scenario of this chapter. The phases of instruction, along with the metacognitive processes involved in each phase, are outlined below and summarized in Table 6.1.

The teacher opens the listening activity by providing context for the learners through information about topic, text genre, and any relevant cultural information, using statements such as:

- you will listen to an interview with a baker about his job in France;
- you will listen to a local weather report for tomorrow; or,
- you will listen to a dialogue between two friends on Monday morning in the school hallway before class begins.

In each case, learners can use (1) text knowledge (interview, weather report, dialogue) to predict organization of the information, and (2) topic knowledge (work life of a baker, types of weather for the season in the region, what teens might discuss on a Monday morning) to predict information they will hear. Learners should have the necessary background knowledge to help them make logical predictions: in other words, the text must be appropriate to their age level and life experience.

Table 6.1 Stages of Instruction and Underlying Metacognitive Processes for Generic Listening Activities

Pedagogical Stages	*Metacognitive Processes*
1. *Pre-listening—Planning/predicting stage* After learners have been informed of the topic and text type, they predict the types of information and possible words they may hear.	1. Planning
2. *First listen—First verification stage*	
a. Learners verify their initial hypotheses, correct as required, and note additional information understood.	2a. Monitoring and evaluation
b. Learners compare what they have understood/written with a partner, modify as required, establish what still needs resolution, and decide on the important details that still require special attention.	2b. Monitoring, evaluation, and planning
3. *Second listen—Second verification stage*	
a. Learners verify points of earlier disagreement, make corrections, and write down additional details understood.	3a. Monitoring, evaluation, and problem-solving
b. Class discussion in which all class members contribute to the reconstruction of the text's main points and most pertinent details, interspersed with reflections on how learners arrived at the meaning of certain words or parts of the text.	3b. Monitoring, evaluation, and problem-solving
4. *Third listen—Final verification stage* Learners listen specifically for the information revealed in the class discussion which they were not able to make out earlier. This listen may also be accompanied by the transcript of all or part of the text.	4. Monitoring and problem-solving
5. *Reflection and goal-setting stage* Based on the earlier discussion of strategies used to compensate for what was not understood, learners write goals for the next listening activity.	5. Evaluation and planning

From Vandergrift, 2004

Pre-Listening—Planning/Predicting Stage

The pre-listening, prediction phase, initially led by the teacher, begins as a whole class brainstorming activity; all suggestions are considered valid, written on the board by the teacher, and recorded by the learners on paper. The paper can be blank or a worksheet with separate columns for (1) initial predictions; (2) first listen; and (3) second listen. The important thing is that learners write down key words that itemize potential information that they will hear. These serve as reference points as they listen and verify predictions.

The role of the teacher in this phase is gradually relinquished in favour of discussion of predictions between learning partners only, in the interest of developing learner autonomy for real-life listening. Discussion between partners, in turn, is gradually withdrawn so that learners learn to regulate these processes on their own, automatically.

First Verification Stage

The goal of the first verification phase is to note information learners have successfully predicted and to add new information. A further goal of this phase is to set learners up for the second listen. When learners compare listening results with a partner and discuss discrepancies in their understanding, they prepare themselves to monitor more carefully during the second listen and to determine the parts of the text that need most careful attention. In fact, the greater the level of disagreement, the more actively learners will monitor during the second listen.

Second Verification Stage

After the second listen, learners begin by revising and adding new information to their notes, as required. Further discussion between the same partners is used to make any additional revisions to the interpretation of the text. Once learners have updated their understanding of the text, the teacher leads a class discussion to reconstruct the main points and most salient details of the text.

Final Verification Stage

The final verification stage begins with a third listen to the text. This allows learners to listen for information revealed during discussion that they may not have understood earlier. The teacher may also introduce all or part of the text transcript at this point so that learners can follow along for purposes of verifying sound–symbol relationships, particularly for points in the text where the sound stream seemed impossible to understand.

Reflection and Goal-Setting Stage

During the last step of this listening activity, the teacher encourages learners to evaluate their approach to the activity, the difficulties they confronted, and how they were or were not successful in coping with these difficulties. Setting goals for future listening efforts may also take place at this time.

Activity 2

The guide for listening (see Figure 6.3) is a worksheet that can be used with any listening text. This guide leads listeners through the process of listening in much the same way as the first activity; consequently, the phases of instruction and the metacognitive processes in each phase parallel those summarized in Table 6.1.

As in the first activity, the teacher begins with a contextualization stage by informing learners of the topic and type of text: for example, a short documentary on violence in schools. A class discussion on the topic or a reading activity on the same theme may also precede listening. This ensures that all learners have a basic knowledge of the issues and any necessary cultural information to predict possible content in the listening text. The activity then unfolds in much the same way as the first activity, with learners following the prompts on the worksheet.

Activity 3

The third activity is designed to help learners understand a listening text that would be too difficult without some written support because of unfamiliar vocabulary and rapid speech. The activity is structured to focus on understanding the sequence of events in the story. To prepare a worksheet for this activity (see Figure 6.4), the listening text is condensed and rewritten into a number of sequential simple sentences that summarize the events in the story. These sentences are then put in random order. Learners read these sentences before listening, with the goal of reordering the sentences according to the actual story sequence, after they have listened to the text. The stages of instruction, along with the metacognitive processes in each stage, are summarized in Table 6.2.

Pre-Listening—Planning/Predicting Stage

The teacher initiates the pre-listening, predicting stage by distributing the worksheet and reviewing the directions with the learners. When it is clear that everyone understands what to do, the teacher asks learners to read the randomized sentences on their own, to independently make a decision on the anticipated order of events, and to enter their predicted sequence of events in the column, "My Predictions."

First Verification Stage

The first verification stage begins with the first listen to the text. After listening, learners compare what they heard with their predicted sequence

A. Write down five main ideas that you think will be mentioned in the text:

1. _____ _____
2. _____ _____
3. _____ _____
4. _____ _____
5. _____ _____

B. Discuss your predictions with a partner and then write down at least two more ideas that your partner included in his/her list of predictions and that you consider logical possibilities:

6. _____
7. _____

C. Listen to the text. Place a check mark beside the ideas that you (A) and your partner (B) predicted and that were in fact mentioned in the text, and write down any other ideas that you had not predicted but were mentioned.

8. _____ _____
9. _____ _____
10. _____ _____

D. After verifying your predictions and discussing your listening results with your partner, listen to the text again to check your results and to resolve any discrepancies in comprehension between you and your partner. Add any further points and important details that you may not have understood during the first listen:

1. _____ _____
2. _____ _____
3. _____ _____
4. _____ _____
5. _____ _____

E. Listen to the text a third time to verify comprehension after a class discussion of the content of the text or a reading of the text transcript.

- -

Reflection and Goal-Setting

I was successful in anticipating _____ ideas.

What surprised me:

What I will do next time:

Figure 6.3. Guide for Listening

Strange but True!

You will hear a ghost story. Below you will find a number of sentences that summarize the events of this story. Organize the sentences in the most logical order in which you think the story will unfold. Place the letters of the sentences in the appropriate order under the column "My Predictions." To help you begin, the opening sentence has been marked with an asterisk (*). After the first listen to the text, place in the column "First Listen" the letters of the statements in the order in which you thought you heard them. Compare your order of events with a partner and then, collaboratively, decide on an order of events that you will enter in the column "Our predictions." After the second listen to the text, verify your predictions and make any changes, if necessary, in the column "Correct Sequence."

a.   The priest came to the ship and prayed that the sailor would find peace.
b.   The ship was bought by Jimmy O'Donnell for purposes of fishing.*
c.   One man was caught in the net, dragged overboard and drowned.
d.   Things always went wrong with the ship and it was always cold.
e.   He looked up but no one was there.
f.   The priest said that the spirit wandered around because the sailor had not been buried.
g.   Jimmy O'Donnell lost his taste for fishing and sold the ship.
h.   When he was going to sleep, the captain saw the mattress above him pulled down.
i.   The captain asked a priest to help.
j.   The next captain of the ship was Mick Laws.
k.   The crew said they kept seeing a shadowy figure on deck.
l.   The ship had no more problems.
m.   One freezing day, three crew members pulled in the nets.

	My Predictions	First Listen	Our Predictions	Second Listen	Correct Sequence
1.	b	b	b	b	b
2.					
3.					
4.					
5.					
6.					
7.					
8.					
9.					
10.					
11.					
12.					
13.					

Reflection/goal-setting: What made this task easy or difficult:

What I will do differently next time:

Figure 6.4. Activity 3 (Strange but True!)
Source: White, 1998, p. 20

Table 6.2 Stages of Instruction and Underlying Metacognitive Processes for Text-Specific Listening Activities

Pedagogical Stages	Metacognitive Processes
1. Pre-listening—Planning/predicting stage Learners predict the correct sequence or the correct answer based on the choices provided.	1. Planning
2. First listen—First verification stage	
a. Learners verify their initial predictions and make corrections as required.	2a. Monitoring and evaluation
b. Learners compare their answers with a partner, modify as required, establish what still needs resolution, and decide on what will require special attention.	2b. Monitoring, evaluation, and planning
3. Second listen—Second verification stage	
a. Learners verify points of earlier disagreement and make any required corrections.	3a. Monitoring, evaluation, and problem-solving
b. Verification of the correct sequence or correct answers.	3b. Monitoring, evaluation, and problem-solving
4. Third listen—Final verification stage Learners listen specifically for the information they were not able to decipher earlier. Depending on the difficulty of the text or task, this stage may be optional.	4. Monitoring and problem-solving
5. Reflection and goal-setting stage Class discussion of strategies used to determine the correct sequence of answers and reflection on goals for the next listening activity.	5. Evaluation, planning

Based on Vandergrift, 2004

of events and record their understanding of the sequence in the second column, "First Listen." Learners then work with a partner to compare the results of their first listen. After discussion, they identify parts of the text that will require more careful attention during the second listen. They decide on a revised order of events and record these in the third column, "Our Predictions," in preparation for the second listen.

Second Verification Stage

During the second verification stage, learners listen to the text again to resolve difficulties and verify their understanding of the sequence of events. The teacher then confirms the correct sequence by providing the correct answers or reviewing the story in a class discussion. The discussion may include a reflection on the strategies used to predict and to understand. At this time, the teacher may also provide learners with a transcript of the text to read, although this activity has already provided students with much of the actual text in summary form.

Final Verification Stage

A third verification stage is optional. The teacher can decide whether a third listen would be helpful for learners to verify information revealed in the class discussion or to follow along with the transcript.

Reflection and Goal-Setting Stage

Reflection can occur at this point if it did not happen at the end of the second verification stage. The teacher may also ask learners to complete a "reflection" section on the sheet (such as the example in Figure 6.4) and then engage in a class discussion on difficulties encountered and approach to similar activities in the future.

Alternatively, work with a partner could already begin at the planning/prediction stage of this activity by having learners compare and discuss predictions before the first listen. In this case, learners would enter their agreed-upon sequence in the third column before listening to the text for the first time.

Listening Activities: Concluding Comments

In all three activities, learners are encouraged to predict and then compare what they understand with their predictions. Learners are guided in predicting, monitoring, problem-solving, and evaluating as they work through a listening activity. This can be done without prompts, with generic guides to the process, or text-based worksheets, depending on the teaching context.

Because they are tied to a specific listening text, listening activities of the third type require more preparatory work by teachers; however, once created, they can be used again in the future. The third activity is offered as a template to guide teachers in creating their own text-based activities. It is also important to provide variety in the use of this particular metacognitive pedagogical sequence.

The pedagogical sequence underlying these activities, used in the context of regular listening practice, can facilitate the acquisition of L2 listening skills and gradually lead L2 listeners to take control of their own listening development. The listening practice afforded by these activities will be most fruitful, however, when the outcome is not associated with testing comprehension. The goal is formative assessment (see Chapter 12): that is, learners carry out these activities to learn how to listen and to improve their ability to control listening processes and listening performance. If learners know that the final product will be evaluated for purposes of a mark, their level of anxiety will increase considerably. A high level of anxiety, concomitantly, decreases the ability of working memory to process information. Practice without the threat of evaluation allows learners to use working memory to full capacity.

These types of activities develop both top-down and bottom-up listening ability. The bottom-up component is most often incorporated through the introduction of the text transcript at the end of the second verification stage. Matching all or parts of the listening text with the written text helps listeners develop awareness of form-meaning relationships and word recognition skills. It is crucial, however, that the transcript not be introduced before this point. Learners must first activate the metacognitive processes related to real-life listening to interpret the text, drawing on all knowledge sources available to them. Only after they have activated the appropriate cognitive processes can learners benefit from an examination of the written form of the text to discover words and phrases initially indistinguishable in the sound stream. Introducing the transcript too early in the process will only encourage word-by-word translation, an unproductive strategy that needs to be discouraged as much as possible.

In sum, leading learners through the process of listening so that they learn to control these processes on their own requires careful planning and guidance by the teacher. The teacher initially plays a major role in guiding learners, but explicit direction should be gradually withdrawn so that learners learn to self-regulate these processes. The benefits of investment in preparation and early guidance are eventually realized in increased ability by learners to tackle subsequent listening activities and make progress in listening comprehension ability.

Research on the Use of the Metacognitive Pedagogical Sequence

Is there any evidence for the success of a metacognitive pedagogical sequence, such as the one described in this chapter? Do learners who experience this kind of L2 listening instruction develop greater awareness of the metacognitive processes that underlie successful L2 listening? Even more importantly, does this instruction lead to better listening performance? The final section of this chapter will focus on research related to this pedagogical sequence. The first part will describe studies on the development of metacognitive knowledge about L2 listening and the second part on improvement of L2 listening ability.

Developing Metacognitive Knowledge About L2 Listening

The following qualitative studies investigated student response to the pedagogical sequence in the listening activities described earlier. The first study was based on a number of formative assessment instruments for core French learners in Canada (see Vandergrift & Bélanger, 1998). Three text-specific activities, similar to Activity 3, were piloted with 17 different primary school core French classes from different provinces in Canada (see Vandergrift, 2002). After learners completed the activities, the class reflected on the following: (1) what they learned; (2) what they discovered about their abilities in French; and (3) what they would do to improve future performance. The second study involved piloting preliminary versions of Activities 1 and 3 with university learners learning French (Vandergrift, 2003b). Learners kept a reflective journal in which they considered different dimensions of their learning and their progress. Learners were asked to consider the effectiveness of this approach to listening for facilitating listening comprehension. There was no course evaluation associated with these activities.

What effect did these listening activities have on student perceptions and awareness of the process of listening? Overall, learners responded positively, citing many similar responses: improved comprehension, greater motivation, awareness of the importance of prediction and other strategies, and greater ease in understanding. Student responses also demonstrated many instances of increased metacognitive knowledge about L2 listening.

Most evident in student responses was renewed motivation engendered by the success learners experienced with this approach to listening. Learners commented on the feelings of confidence they experienced when they understood all the important information by the third listen (". . . the last listen . . . I usually understand the whole thing so it makes me know that I can understand a whole conversation, which is a real confidence booster"). These beginner-level learners recognized the potential of this approach to help them access authentic-type texts and to transfer the strategies learned inside the classroom to situations outside of the classroom, in spite of their limited proficiency in the language (". . . when you are successful with the exercises in class, you feel more confident . . . I can be sure that I will understand at least part of what people might say to me"). Most important, they felt they were better able to cope with the demands of listening, enhancing their feelings of self-efficacy ("I have learnt to cope with listening comprehension. I have become more conscious of what I think when I listen to the text"). These comments support the argument that consciousness-raising of learning processes can motivate learners through success that makes them feel good about themselves and their abilities (Paris & Winograd, 1990).

Learners also commented positively on the role of collaboration. Listening is, by nature, an individual act, but collaboration with a partner proved to be beneficial for verifying and enlarging initial predictions (". . . it helps to talk about it [because] it helps you to think twice") or developing further predictions for the second or third listen (". . . the information you missed and your partner heard provides you with key phrases and ideas to actively listen for in the next session"). Work with a partner was also deemed useful for verifying comprehension since it encouraged more active monitoring (". . . when your partner has heard information that contradicts your listening conclusions . . . in that scenario you learn a lot from listening to the reasons why one of you has heard it wrong"). The importance of collaborative dialogue in the development of metacognition was also underscored by Cross (2009b), who found that dialogue between learners raised awareness of strategies, text features and comprehension processes. Learning is more than an individual cognitive enterprise: the development of self-regulated learners is facilitated through social and collaborative settings.

The questionnaire responses also revealed evidence of growth in metacognitive knowledge. Learners who experienced these process-based activities are more aware of what needs to be done to accomplish a listening activity and how to overcome difficulties in listening. With regard to person knowledge, learners often commented on their ability to understand more than they thought they could, and to manage affective factors related to listening. Most evident in the student comments were instances of strategic knowledge. In particular, learners highlighted the powerful role of prediction strategies, the importance of monitoring comprehension, and, for the younger learners, the importance of attending to the activity and concentrating. Taken together, the qualitative data from these studies reflect an emerging awareness of the processes underlying L2 listening. Learners are aware of the purpose and nature of the listening activity (activity knowledge), they have some understanding about themselves as L2 listeners (person knowledge) and they are aware of effective strategies they can use to approach listening activities (strategy knowledge). Figure 5.2 in the previous chapter provides more examples of metacognitive knowledge.

The process-based approach to teaching listening in this pedagogical sequence appears to have positive effects on the acquisition of metacognitive knowledge about listening, student perception of the listening process, and motivation to listen. However, we need experimental studies to verify the tacit assumption that a group of learners exposed to similar activities over a period of time would demonstrate superior achievement in listening (e.g., a unit of study, a semester, or an academic year). The next section will present empirical evidence for the success of this pedagogical sequence in improving L2 listening ability.

Impact of the Pedagogical Sequence on Listening Performance

A high degree of metacognitive knowledge is a mental characteristic shared by successful learners; in fact, metacognition accounts for a relatively high percentage of variance in learning performance (Veenmanet al., 2006). There is extensive evidence that learners' metacognition can directly affect the process and the outcome of their learning (Victori & Lockhart, 1995; Wenden, 1998; Zimmerman & Schunk, 2001). Research shows that it is positively linked to motivation and self-efficacy (Dörnyei, 2005; Paris & Winograd, 1990; Vandergrift, 2005) and that it can help learners regulate their comprehension (Pressley, 2002). There is, indeed, a strong theoretical basis for arguing that this pedagogical sequence can enhance listening success. Empirical support for metacognitive instruction as applied in this approach has been documented in recent studies with (1) federal public servants learning French; (2) Japanese-speaking learners of English; and (3) English-speaking learners of French.

Civil Servants in Language Training in Canada

The pedagogical sequence was investigated by Mareschal (2007) with two groups of civil servants in intensive language training (French) for purposes of meeting bilingualism requirements in Canada. One group, at the low-intermediate level, had been assessed as poorly motivated, low achievers; the other group, at the low-advanced level, had been assessed as motivated, high achievers. The study used questionnaires, stimulated recalls, think-aloud protocols, interviews, and listening logs to investigate the effects of the pedagogical sequence on development of metacognitive awareness of L2 listening processes, overall success in comprehension, and student perceptions of this approach to instruction.

Triangulation of the rich qualitative data from all sources suggested that both groups of learners responded positively to the pedagogical approach and that it had beneficial effects on metacognitive awareness, strategy use, and confidence and interest in L2 listening. The beneficial effects were most evident in the lower proficiency group, whose think-aloud protocols revealed a considerable improvement in listening comprehension success over the course of the 12-week instruction. This was not a controlled experiment, however, and evidence for increased listening performance was based on qualitative data only. From the beginning to the end of the study, substantial differences were observed in the difficulty level of aural texts and demonstrated comprehension of these texts, through analysis of the think-aloud protocols by the lower proficiency group. While similar increases in listening achievement were not observed in the higher proficiency group, these learners responded positively to the metacognitive instruction. In particular, they noted the opportunity to discuss their comprehension with a partner and to consult a transcript of the text as beneficial for improving their listening comprehension skills.

Adult Learners of English in Japan

The effect of strategy instruction was investigated by Cross (2009b) over a 10-week period with advanced-level Japanese learners of English. In this controlled experiment, both groups experienced the pedagogical sequence while listening to news videotext. The experimental group received explicit strategy training in addition to the implicit, activity-based, process-based instruction underlying the pedagogical sequence. Results showed that both groups made significant gains in comprehension scores on the listening post-test, but that there was no significant difference for the group receiving the additional explicit strategy instruction. Cross attributes this result to the salience of the pedagogical sequence. In other words, systematic practice using the pedagogical sequence prompted learners in both groups to activate metacognitive processes and other appropriate cognitive strategies embedded in the listening activity.

In addition to providing empirical support for the pedagogical sequence, the Cross study is important for our understanding of explicit strategy instruction in listening. There is some evidence that explicit strategy instruction can result in successful use of one or two strategies, but only immediately following the instruction period (Graham, 2003). The Cross study suggests that systematic practice with strategy-embedded activities using the pedagogical sequence, cued by activity performance, can better lead to overall listening improvement.

University Learners Learning French in Canada

Vandergrift and Tafaghodtari (2010) examined the effects of the pedagogical sequence with three intact classes of university learners. Over the period of one semester (13 weeks), learners in one high-beginner and two low-intermediate French classes were guided through a process approach to listening, using the pedagogical sequence as outlined in the opening scenario of this chapter and described in the discussion of Activity 1. Learners recorded their predictions in a listening log where each page had three columns: a prediction column and one column each for the first and second listening notes. The bottom of each page included a line for goal-setting for the next listening activity. Each week, the classes followed the same procedure with a new listening text, and the teacher took a less active guiding role as the semester progressed.

All variables were carefully controlled. The control group of three similar level classes was taught by the same teachers; one teacher taught both high-beginner groups and another teacher taught all four low-intermediate groups. The control group also listened to the same texts three times. Before beginning the activity, similar to the experimental group, learners in the control group were given the same contextual information. The listening log for the control group differed in that it had only three columns for notes, one column for each of the three listens to the text. Learners in the control group did not engage in any formal prediction activity, nor were they given an opportunity to discuss, predict, or monitor their comprehension with a classmate. After the third listen, the instructor engaged the class in a discussion in order to confirm comprehension of the text. No discussion of strategy use took place, nor did learners engage in any formal reflection on their approach to listening or goal-setting for their next listening activity.

The hypothesis that the experimental group would significantly outperform the control group was confirmed. There was a modest but significant difference between the two groups on the post-test, after initial differences in the listening ability between the two groups was taken into account. A closer examination of the final scores established that the difference in favour of the experimental group could be accounted for by the less skilled listeners: that is, the learners scoring below the median in the listening pre-test made greater gains than their more skilled peers. This finding demonstrates that, similar to findings by Goh and Taib (2006), less skilled listeners in particular can benefit from this kind of guided listening practice. The researchers attribute these results to the fact that the experimental group acquired implicit knowledge on an incremental basis over time.

Summary

Buck (1995) recommends that language learners experience lots of listening practice in order to become successful listeners. This can be facilitated, he suggests, if teachers understand the underlying cognitive processes, sensitize learners to the intricacies of listening, and provide "optimum" listening practice.

This chapter provides teachers with the tools to provide such optimum listening practice. We have shown how the metacognitive processes of planning, monitoring, problem-solving, and evaluation can be incorporated into a pedagogical sequence that encourages learners to activate the processes involved in real-life listening. Different listening activities were presented to illustrate concretely how this pedagogical sequence can work. Finally, we have discussed the extant research that verifies the positive impact of this kind of listening practice on growth in learner metacognitive knowledge and increased success in L2 listening.

Systematically leading language learners through the process of listening as part of regular listening activities encourages them to practice metacognitive processes and enables them to more readily participate in communicative experiences outside of class early in their language learning.

Discussion Questions and Tasks

1. Chapter 1 suggested that metacognitive instruction, applied as a pedagogical sequence in this chapter, is more holistic than other approaches to the teaching of L2 listening. Why is it more holistic and why is this important in listener development?
2. What does it mean that learners need to learn to regulate or control their listening processes? Why is this important?
3. Is there room for explicit strategy instruction in the classroom? Under what circumstances and how?
4. Take a listening text from your course materials and use an approach similar to Activity 1 in presentation to your class. What happened? How did learners respond to the activity? How did they respond to the process during the reflection stage?
5. Examine Figure 6.3 for Activity 2 and explain how it guides learners through the process of listening by (1) indicating where the stages delineated in Table 6.1 occur, and (2) how the different metacognitive processes at each stage are developed. Is it exactly the same as in Activity 1?

Suggestions for Further Reading

Chamot, A.U., Barnhardt, S., El-Dinary, P.B. & Robbins, J. (1999). *The learning strategies handbook*. White Plains, NJ: Longman.
   Chapter 2 (Metacognitive model of strategic learning) briefly presents the model in the context of all four language skills and provides concrete information for teachers on the four metacognitive processes and associated cognitive strategies, how these work in coordination to assist learning, and how instruction can help learners reflect on and self-regulate their learning.
Field, J. (2001). Finding one's way in the fog: Listening strategies and second-language learners. *Modern English Teacher, 9*, 29–34.
   This article presents an activity-based approach to listening instruction that leads learners through the stages of real-life listening, with the aim of helping L2 listeners access authentic texts and experience success.
Vandergrift, L., & Tafaghodtari, M. H. (2010). Teaching learners how to listen does make a difference: An empirical study. *Language Learning, 65*, 470–497.
   This article describes in detail the methodology, results, and implications of the study described in this chapter.

Chapter 7

Activities for Metacognitive Instruction

Scenario

Aida selects a DVD on global warming and prepares to watch it in a corner of the media center of her college library. She reads through a handout that her language instructor, Ms Fanaz, gave the class that morning. Each of several sections has a number of prompts that Aida will respond to before and after watching the video. The prompts ask Aida to note some of her existing knowledge about the topic and the strategies that she can apply during her viewing of the video. The prompts divide the listening practice into stages; for each stage, Aida will record thoughts on how to improve listening comprehension.

She recalls Ms Fanaz explaining to her class that the purpose for these prompts is to help them break down their extensive listening practice into several stages and reflect on how they can learn to improve their listening comprehension. The prompts elicit some of her existing knowledge about the topic and the strategies that she can apply during her viewing of the video.

Aida thinks this is an interesting way to learn listening and none of her previous language instructors has ever done anything like this before. They told her to "listen more" and "work harder" but never really taught her how to work at improving her listening on her own. She never had to think quite as much about how to listen. All she did then was to make notes when she was listening to a recording or watching a video recording. Her homework was usually a summary of what she had understood. What Ms Fanaz is asking her to do reminds her of the preparations she makes when she has to write a composition or give a short talk. She feels that the prompts in the handout guide her to better manage her learning. Aida goes through the first section of the handout again and writes down her responses to the prompts. Then she turns her attention to the screen, adjusts her headphone, and clicks the "play" button with the mouse.

Pre-reading Reflection

1. Aida's teacher wants to use prompts to help direct learner listening. In what ways do you think this activity will achieve that objective?
2. Aida sees how the prompts can help her in her learning, much like preparing to write a composition or preparing and rehearsing for a talk. What is your view?
3. Before beginning to read this chapter, try to recall what is meant by a metacognitive approach as explained in Chapter 5. Make a list or draw a concept map. In what way does Aida's task contribute to her metacognitive development?

Introduction

Listening and thinking processes are not easily observed by others or even by learners themselves. This often makes the teaching of listening difficult. Teachers can adopt a metacognitive approach to provide guidance on how to listen and facilitate learner listening development. They can teach students how to plan, monitor, and evaluate their listening development. This approach helps learners attend to implicit processes in their listening and make their knowledge of these processes more explicit.

Chapter 5 explained the theoretical basis for metacognitive instruction and highlighted principles for teaching. Metacognitive instruction focuses explicitly on learning how to listen. It heightens learners' awareness of their own abilities and limitations as L2 listeners, their understanding of the nature of listening and the challenges of listening tasks, and last, but not least, strategies they can use to improve and manage short-term comprehension and long-term development as L2 listeners. Learners also share their individual reflections with one another and engage in dialogue to jointly construct knowledge about listening and understanding of the listening text. Metacognitive instruction also provides opportunities for learners to practice listening skills and familiarize themselves with the sounds of the target language; this improves their understanding of the demands of fast connected speech.

The metacognitive pedagogical sequence demonstrated how processes of planning, monitoring, problem-solving, and evaluation can be integrated with existing listening instructional materials. This provides learners with listening practice that can lead to enhanced performance and heightened metacognitive awareness. In this chapter, we will present a number of other activities that can also help learners develop their listening ability and metacognition. In these activities, learners respond to comprehension- and strategy-focused prompts, and also focus on themselves as L2 listeners in areas such as self-concept, motivation, and anxiety. It is important for learners to understand and manage these affective variables because they have an impact on listening success.

Metacognitive Instructional Activities

In this section, we present two types of activities that can fulfill the goals and objectives of metacognitive instruction. See Figure 7.1.

Integrated experiential listening tasks weave metacognitive awareness-raising activities with listening comprehension activities. Through these tasks, learners can experience the cognitive and social-affective processes of listening comprehension and at the same time practice their listening comprehension skills. The integrated experiential listening tasks proposed in this chapter can be adapted for use with prescribed published materials and included at key stages of a listening lesson sequence: that is, pre-listening, post-listening, and during listening. By integrating everyday listening activities with metacognitive activities, we help learners become aware of the various processes that are involved in L2 listening. In turn, they can learn to apply this knowledge to their listening development beyond the classroom, be it to explore their own self-concept as listeners, use appropriate strategies during listening, or identify factors that influence their own performance in different listening tasks.

Metacognitive activities for listening can also include language-focused activities, in which learners examine the linguistic features of a listening text from an earlier listening task. Such activities can help learners develop better task knowledge—in particular, knowledge about spoken texts. Integrated experiential listening tasks can also take the form of learning extension tasks that are carried out after formal instruction time; these extensive listening tasks require learners to work together to co-construct metacognitive knowledge about listening.

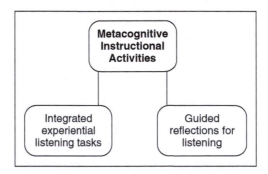

Figure 7.1. Two Types of Activities for Metacognitive Instruction in L2 Listening
Based on Goh, 2008

Guided reflections for listening, the second type of metacognitive instructional activities, aim to help learners plan and evaluate their learning. The purpose in using guided reflections is to elicit learners' implicit knowledge about L2 listening and to encourage them to construct new knowledge, as they make sense of their own listening experiences. These activities are used mainly as stand-alone activities after class, but they can also be adapted for use with other activities in a listening lesson, before or after listening tasks. These specially designed reflective activities, initiated by the teacher, require learners to set aside time to plan, monitor, and evaluate their listening and learning experiences. These activities, which direct attention to specific aspects of learning, enable learners to reflect on their listening performance and overall progress. In addition, they can be used with enrichment activities when learners practice listening on their own with recorded or downloaded materials.

By using a range of metacognitive tools, we engage learners in thinking back to events that have taken place and in looking ahead as a way of managing their own learning. While the activities focus a great deal on understanding the processes of listening and learning to listen, some also have a language focus. This focus is appropriate and necessary because learners benefit a great deal from reviewing what they have heard and rehearsing their perception of the sounds and prosody of the language. An important principle in learning is that learners review and rehearse what they encounter, in order to increase automaticity in processing the information that they hear. A summary of the various activities is found in Figure 7.2.

Integrated Experiential Listening Tasks

Metacognitive Pedagogical Sequence

The metacognitive pedagogical sequence is a sequence of learning activities that integrate metacognitive awareness raising with listening input and comprehension activities that offer a structure to help learners improve their understanding of the content of the text and at the same time become more familiar with the metacognitive processes involved. These include planning, predicting, monitoring, evaluation, directed attention, selective attention, and problem-solving. The metacognitive pedagogical sequence can be modified to address different learning objectives but still capitalize on the benefit of re-listening. This will increasingly lessen the cognitive load as more and more of the input becomes familiar and, as a result, processing becomes less controlled and more automatic.

Figure 7.3 shows how the last two stages can be modified to improve knowledge about text characteristics and to enhance learner confidence. In this sequence, learners are asked to listen to the text for a third time to

Integrated Experiential Listening Tasks	
Metacognitive Pedagogical Sequence	Learners are guided at specific stages in a lesson sequence to orchestrate listening strategies to facilitate successful comprehension.
Self-directed Listening	Learners work with a set of prompts to make pre-listening preparations, evaluate their performance after listening, and make further plans for future listening tasks.
Post-listening Perception Activities	Learners work through language-focused activities, conducted after a listening task, to develop better knowledge about the phonological features that may have affected their comprehension of the text.
Guided Reflections for Listening	
Listening Diaries	Using guiding questions to reflect on a specific listening experience, learners record their responses to issues related to the three dimensions of metacognitive knowledge.
Anxiety and Motivation Charts	Learners draw diagrams to show changes in their anxiety and motivation levels for various listening tasks they do in and outside class.
Process-Based Discussions	Learners discuss ways of addressing listening problems, improving listening proficiency, and strategy use.
Self-Report Checklist	Learners evaluate their own knowledge and performance by referring to a list of pre-selected items of metacognitive knowledge about L2 listening.

Figure 7.2. Activities for Metacognitive Instruction

catch the details they have missed. In the alternate version presented here, the teacher-led discussion continues into the second last stage but now it focuses on raising awareness about language features, such as selected sounds and prosody (at a micro level) or the structure of the discourse (at a macro level), or both. In the last stage, learners do not write goals and plan for the next listening activity or listening event. Instead, they listen to the text again. No overt responses are required. Learners now simply enjoy the text with less effort, having rehearsed it in earlier stages and added awareness of certain text characteristics. This enables learners to shift from strategies to skills in a way that is typically experienced by more competent and confident listeners.

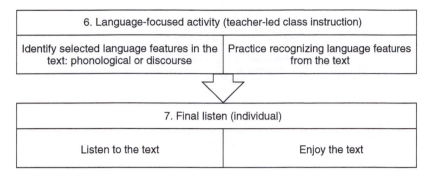

6. Language-focused activity (teacher-led class instruction)	
Identify selected language features in the text: phonological or discourse	Practice recognizing language features from the text

7. Final listen (individual)	
Listen to the text	Enjoy the text

Figure 7.3. The Metacognitive Pedagogical Sequence with Language-Focused Activities

Self-Directed Listening or Viewing

A great deal of informal learning takes place outside the classroom; this is certainly true for listening development. Learners can engage in extensive listening, selecting from a wide variety of materials available from mass media and the internet. Not all learners, however, are able to make the most of these opportunities because they lack the skills to direct their own extensive listening activities. Many still remain dependent on their language teachers to assign listening homework for further practice. Much of this homework requires learners to watch or listen to a program, and then write a summary of what they have understood or answer a set of questions prepared by the teacher. To help learners become more self-directed in learning to listen, teachers can assign listening homework that integrates both text-focused comprehension and metacognitive knowledge development.

To guide learners in their out-of-class listening efforts, using an approach similar to the metacognitive pedagogical sequence, we propose a self-directed listening guide that consists of a number of prompts that direct learners' attention to how they approach a listening task and accomplish it. These prompts should address three important metacognitive processes: planning, monitoring, and evaluation. In considering their responses to these prompts, learners will activate strategies for goal-setting, pre-listening preparation, reflecting on listening experience, and evaluating performance. Similar to the metacognitive listening sequence presented earlier, self-directed listening or viewing also capitalizes on the benefits of repeat listening and language-focused activities to develop better processing abilities and task knowledge. A self-directed listening or viewing guide should have several stages. The boxes in Figure 7.4 show the types of prompts that are used in four stages of self-direction. The

Figure 7.4. Four Types of Prompts for Self-Directed Listening/Viewing

circles show the stages in the extensive listening process and how they relate to the sequence of the prompts that guide learner reflection.

A sample of a self-directed listening or viewing guide is presented in Figure 7.5. The guide can take many forms. For example, specially designed handouts can be given individually to learners or compiled into a booklet like a journal or a notebook. Once the learners have completed a listening practice, they complete a handout and turn it in to their teacher. Alternatively, the guide can be distributed as soft copies, which learners can use to type in their responses. These completed guides can then be uploaded and shared with other learners on electronic platforms such as discussion boards, which are increasingly being used in many language programs.

Post-listening Perception Activities

The metacognitive approach can help learners recognize and understand how sounds and pronunciation are realized in connected speech. One of the most challenging parts of L2 listening is lexical segmentation, the ability to detect when one word ends and another begins (Field, 2003, 2008a).

Language learners often complain about the speed of L2 speech and that they are unable, as a result, to catch what is said. This sense of speed is often due to the learners' inability to perceive some spoken words or to make sound–script connections (Goh, 1999, 2000). They are also often baffled by phonological modifications that occur in connected speech. Understanding how sounds change and how written words are sounded in normal connected speech is therefore an important part of a language learner's metacognitive knowledge. Because it relates to the demands of different types of listening, it is part of a learner's task knowledge.

The benefits of the metacognitive approach for bottom-up processing skills can be illustrated by comparison with traditional approaches. In some traditional activities, learners are put through drills of pairs

Plan for Directing My Listening/Viewing Activity

Date: _____

Title of selected recording: _____Source: _____

I selected it because: _____

Before I Listen/View	

1. Setting my goal
   • What do I hope to achieve from listening to/viewing this recording?
   • How many times should I listen to/view it?	

2. Preparing to listen
   • What do I know about this topic?
   • What type of information can I expect to hear?
   • What words can I expect to hear? (Use a dictionary, if necessary.)
   • What difficulties can I expect?
   • What strategies should I use?	

After I Listen/View	

3. Evaluating my listening
   • What have I understood?
   • Was I able to make use of my prior knowledge about the topic?
   • What difficulties did I face? Were my strategies useful?
   • Write some words and phrases you heard.
   • What have I learned about learning to listen from this experience?	

Before I Listen/View Again	

4. Planning to listen/view again
   • What should I pay attention to this time?
   • What strategies can I use to improve my understanding?
   • What can I do to help myself enjoy the recording?	

Figure 7.5. Sample Guide for Self-Directed Listening/Viewing

of words (often referred to as minimal pairs)—for example, "lid" and "lead," "wrong" and "long"—to check if they can make out the differences in vowel lengths and consonants in the pairs. These exercises are rather meaningless for learners because the words are not presented in any communicative contexts, minimal or otherwise. Even if learners can recognize the phonological features in these exercises, it does not necessarily mean that they can do the same in connected speech at a normal speaking rate. The metacognitive approach provides both context and focused attention on perception skills.

Perception activities are best carried out after learners have completed a listening comprehension task, at the post-listening stage. At this stage learners no longer feel the pressure that often occurs during real-time listening, when they are mainly concerned with understanding meaning. After listeners understand the required information, they can revisit the spoken text to examine its language features and review difficult segments of sounds that they confronted during the listening stage.

Spending time on the language features they missed earlier can be immensely satisfying to learners. They can now pay attention to isolated features of speech and build up their metacognitive knowledge of authentic spoken texts. During these activities, learners often realize that the words they could not recognize are actually words they know. They are unable to make the sound–script connection because they are not able to segment the sounds of the word from other surrounding words or, in some cases, they do not recognize the word because of their own inaccurate or different pronunciation of it (Goh, 2000; Richards, 2005).

Time spent on post-listening perception activities can increase learner knowledge of sounds and phonological rules. This knowledge is particularly important for beginning learners to facilitate automatization of perceptual processing. Repeated exposure to unfamiliar sounds and knowing how some sounds change in connected speech will help learners understand different kinds of spoken input. Advanced learners may also find this activity useful for developing pragmatics if they focus more on intonation and rhythm that can directly influence meaning in context, particularly in interactive listening.

After post-listening perception activities, we recommend that learners listen to the text again, this time with new knowledge about the sounds in the text, as shown in Figure 7.3.

Guided Reflections for Listening

Listening Diaries

Typically, a diary is a record in which individuals write something that is personally significant on a regular basis, expressing their ideas and feelings, and reflecting on their experiences. Keeping a listening diary can help learners attend to what they implicitly know about their own listening abilities, behaviors, problems, and strengths (Goh, 1997; Kemp, 2010). To help learners get started, teachers can provide some structure or prompts on what or when to write. First, such instructions direct learners to focus attention on aspects of learning that the teacher is emphasizing at a particular time in a course of study. Second, prompts can help learners think more deeply about selected aspects of learning and analyze their practices from angles that they might not apply on their own.

In spite of its benefits, some learners might see keeping a diary as a monotonous activity when they have to do it over a long period of time. Diary entries may get shorter and shorter, as learners have fewer and fewer things to say and find that they are repeating themselves. To ensure that they continue to derive maximum learning benefits from the activity, teachers can vary the focus of diary entries, based on three kinds of prompts (see Figure 7.6):

- Reflections about a selected listening experience.
- Self-evaluation of listening skills learned from a unit or chapter of work.
- Thinking aloud immediately after a listening lesson.

These prompts direct learner attention to the three dimensions of metacognitive knowledge: person, task, and strategy. By varying the prompts, teachers can elicit fresh insights from learners, helping them to think

Prompts 1: Reflections on a Selected Listening Event	Prompts 2: Self-Evaluation of Skills Learned from Listening Lessons	Prompts 3: Think-Aloud Immediately After a Lesson
• What was the listening event? • Did you understand what you heard? • What did you do to help your understanding? • Are you pleased with the results? • Would you do things differently next time?	• List the listening skills you have been developing during the last week (e.g., listening for details in a description; inferring speaker attitude from tone). • How well do you think you have learned each of these skills?	• What strategies did you use during the listening tasks? • What made listening easy or difficult for you? • How do you feel about the class today? Why do you feel this way?

Figure 7.6. Examples of Prompts for Reflection in Listening Diaries

about their listening in different ways and from different angles. It can also help learners plan the development of their listening for various contexts. Many different kinds of prompts can be used: teachers can create prompts, based on the objectives of metacognitive instruction, or select from those presented in Figure 7.7.

Using Diaries to Develop Learner Metacognitive Knowledge About Listening

Duration: 5 weeks

Objectives (select according to contexts and purpose for individual diary entries):

Students will:

1. Examine personal beliefs about self-efficacy and self-concept with regard to listening in a second language.
2. Identify listening problems, causes, and possible solutions.
3. Differentiate different types of listening skill (e.g., listening for details, listening for gist, listening to infer information).
4. Analyze factors that influence listening performance (e.g., speaker, text, interlocutor, strategy).
5. Identify strategies that are appropriate for specific types of listening tasks and problems.
6. Demonstrate the use of strategies appropriate to the task and context.
7. Identify strategies that may not be appropriate for learning style or culture.
8. Set personal goals for listening development.
9. Seek appropriate opportunities for listening practice.
10. Make plans and preparations to address challenges in learning to listen.
11. Consider progress of listening development in light of what has been planned.
12. Assess chances of achieving learning goals.
13. Assess the effectiveness of overall plan to improve listening.
14. Assess the appropriateness of learning goals.
15. Assess the effectiveness of strategies for learning and practice.
16. Share learning experiences and knowledge about listening with other students.

	Types of prompts
Week 1 Prepare to use listening diaries as a reflective learning tool: three kinds of reflection.	Prompts 1: Reflections on a selected listening event Prompts 2: Self-evaluation of skills learned from listening lessons Prompts 3: Think-aloud immediately after a lesson

Week 2 Write diary entries daily for a week.	Prompts 1: Reflections on a selected listening event
Week 3 Share listening diaries of week 2 with other students; write diary entries for a week.	Prompts 2: Self-evaluation of skills learned from listening lessons
Week 4 Write short diary entries during class.	Prompts 3: Think-aloud immediately after a lesson
Week 5 Reflect on and summarize learning experiences from entries in the weeks 1–4; present in class or in a small group.	Prompts 1: Reflections on a selected listening event Prompts 2: Self-evaluation of skills learned from listening lessons Prompts 3: Think-aloud immediately after a lesson

Figure 7.7. Suggested Scheme for Using Listening Diaries

To create a sense of coherence over the weeks in which diaries are kept, a scheme can be created to integrate all the reflections during that period of time and culminate in something that consolidates the learner's metacognitive learning. The scheme suggested in Figure 7.7 spans five weeks. The sequence can be repeated immediately, with or without modifications, or following an appropriate interval of other tasks. One way to integrate the various reflection tasks is to combine individual diary writing with more collaborative activities, such as sharing diary entries in small group classroom discussions.

Emotional Temperature Charts

Language anxiety is a common phenomenon among language learners. Although it tends to be associated mainly with speaking, anxiety can also be caused by the pressure that learners experience when they listen to a new language. Not all listening experiences, however, trigger anxiety among learners. It is therefore useful for learners to identify and recognize which situations create anxiety and which do not. This is part of person knowledge development. With this knowledge, learners can use the right kind of strategies to deal with listening situations that they find problematic. It will also help them recognize that learning to listen as a whole does not necessarily have to cause anxiety. This will also help them improve their self-concept, because sometimes learners perceive themselves to be poor listeners as a result of their experiences in high-anxiety situations overshadowing other pleasant or low-stress experiences.

To help learners track their emotional temperature, they can make a note of how they feel in specific listening situations each day and depict their feelings in a diagram. Charts and graphs are a creative way for learners to reflect on and report their person knowledge. They are a change from diaries or journals because little writing is involved. Information is captured and presented in a concise and visually attractive manner; learners who may not enjoy writing will find it easy to do. Figure 7.8 gives

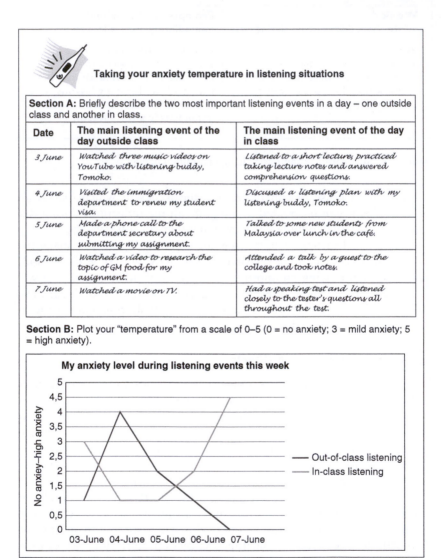

Figure 7.8. Sample Record of Listening Events and a Listening Anxiety Graph

an example of a listening anxiety graph, which offers a way by which learners can track their changes in anxiety levels according to the type of listening task they do in and out of class. In the case of children, teachers can ask them to draw smiley faces or affix stickers in a chart.

A diagram to help young learners track their emotional temperature is a confidence-level chart. This is presented as a collection of confidence bubbles in Figure 7.9. Language learners go through emotional highs and lows. There are times when they feel that they are making good progress but there are also times when they feel they have progressed very little or even feel stuck in a rut, not seeing any breakthroughs in spite of their best efforts. It is good for learners to make their feelings explicit and recognize what they are feeling. By doing this, they can objectivize their emotions and begin to take steps to overcome any negative feelings. Once they see themselves feeling confident on some occasions, they may be motivated

---

Confidence Bubbles

Reflect on your progress at the end of each week. Do you think you have made good progress in your listening development? Draw bubbles of different sizes to show how confident you are that you have made good progress and will continue to do so. You can trace the outline of your biggest coin to show you are very confident, a medium size coin to show you are a little confident and the smallest to show you are not confident at all. Write the date of your reflection inside the bubble.

My Confidence Bubbles in Learning to Listen in English

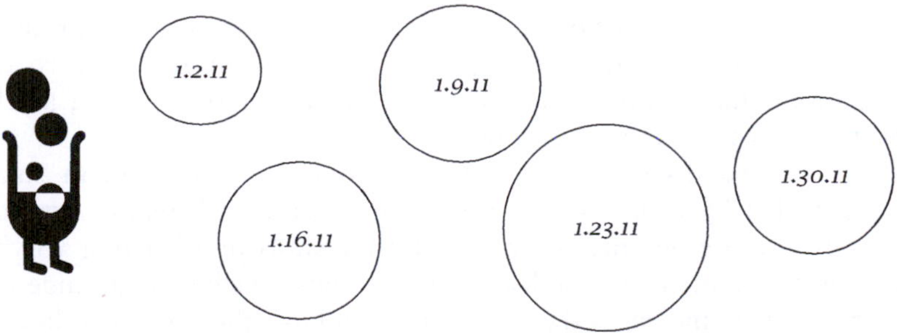

1.2.11   1.9.11   1.30.11   1.16.11   1.23.11

Look at all your confidence bubbles for the month of January and write your thoughts here:

_____

_____

_____

_____

Figure 7.9. Confidence Bubbles for Learning to Listen

to try harder to achieve greater success. This method works well with younger learners who may be drawn to the visual presentation.

Process-Based Discussions

Teachers often use small group discussions as a class activity; however, the focus is usually on content related to the topic of a particular unit of work. Group discussions can also focus on process by having learners talk about the way they learn. This can be a useful tool for raising learner metacognitive awareness (Goh, 1997). Process-based discussions can be integrated into the pedagogical sequence, replace content-focused pre-listening or post-listening activities, or be carried out as separate lessons. As with other metacognitive awareness activities, prompts are important for eliciting thoughts about listening and helping learners construct their knowledge about the process of learning to listen.

Prompts can be worded in different ways that are appropriate for the language and maturity level of the learners, but they should be based on a metacognitive framework that systematically elicits different kinds of person, task, and strategy knowledge. General prompts include "What I do to understand spoken English" and "How I practice my listening outside class." More specific ones can focus on strategies that learners use during a particular listening task, such as those used for listening diaries (see Figure 7.6). They can also share and comment on each other's beliefs and strategies as mentioned in their listening diaries, or feelings about learning to listen on emotional temperature charts. Some of the prompts presented for self-directed listening in Figure 7.5 can also be used for group discussion. Learners can also share their responses using a self-report checklist (see the next activity).

Process-based discussions can be carried out by learners in small groups or led by teachers as a pre-listening or post-listening activity. For example, after learners have completed a short pre-listening activity based on the contents of the listening materials, teachers can guide the class to predict challenges they might face and ask them what skills and strategies are needed to complete the task. As part of the discussion, teachers can also model a strategy and ask learners to comment on its usefulness.

Another way for teachers to raise awareness of listening processes is to explain the reasons for selecting the specific content-related pre-listening activities. By discussing what they are asked to do, learners notice that a planning strategy is included in a listening task. This provides a model for learners to plan their own listening tasks and develops learner metacognition. Figure 7.10 shows how a process-based discussion is integrated into a lesson to prepare for a national examination on listening.

Stage 1: Listen and Answer
This stage of the lesson is modelled after the listening examination format. To replicate examination conditions, no pre-listening activities are included.

Stage 2: Individual Reflection
After completing Stage 1, students reflect individually on how they have completed the listening exercises. Guiding questions are provided.

Stage 3: Self-Report and Process-Based Discussion
Students take turns reading aloud their notes on their reflections. The teacher facilitates a discussion by encouraging them to ask questions or give comments after each reflection.

Figure 7.10. A Three-Stage Listening Lesson Including Process-Based Discussion

Based on Goh & Taib, 2006

Self-Report Checklists

Self-report checklists describe beliefs and strategies that learners can use to assess their own learning. Open-ended reflection guides, such as listening diaries, are useful to focus on broad areas, but some learners may not know how to observe their learning beyond one or two familiar perspectives. They may not have the words in the target language to describe precisely what they think and feel. When metacognitive knowledge is limited, reflections may be narrow in scope and repetitive. We address this concern by suggesting the use of different kinds of prompts. Another way to overcome this limitation is to use self-report checklists. By using pre-selected items of metacognitive knowledge, we can direct learner thinking to specific areas of listening, such as what learners do to help themselves improve their listening (see Figure 7.11). To encourage learners to think more deeply, a simple scale can show how often they use a good practice, whether they enjoy doing it, and if they find it useful.

Self-report checklists are equally useful for adult and young learners. Learners can also use generic questionnaires to reflect on strategy use. The MALQ (Vandergrift et al., 2006) can be used as a teaching tool to help learners appraise their own listening, identify their level of metacognitive awareness and strategy use, and influence future strategy use in listening (see also Goh, 2002c).

Many teachers and learners find it useful to track learning and metacognitive development throughout a course of study. Self-report

---

What I Do To Improve my Listening

Below are 10 things that some language learners report doing to help them become better listeners in English. Do you do any of these things? Indicate how often, and whether you find it enjoyable or useful. Write your comments separately.
   To improve my listening ability, I do the following:

1. I seek to understand the specific problems I have with my listening.
2. I try to improve by listening to those things that interest me.
3. I have a plan for listening practice that I follow closely.
4. I practice specific skills, such as listening for details and listening for general meaning.
5. I familiarize myself with the organization of different types of spoken English (e.g., news, lectures, interviews, conversations).
6. I learn about the way sounds of words change when they are said in a sentence.
7. I encourage myself to practice listening even when I feel my progress is slow.
8. I try to be patient and build up my listening ability step by step.
9. I look for people who are fluent in English to talk with.
10. I look for other students to practice conversation in English.

Figure 7.11. Sample Self-Report Checklist on Strategies for Improving Listening

checklists such as the MALQ can be used at the start, mid-point, and end of a program.

Summary

Metacognitive activities can enable learners to uncover cognitive, affective, and social processes in listening. They provide scaffolded learning experiences where learners receive guidance and support from teachers. In this chapter, we have introduced a number of activities to develop better metacognitive knowledge about the process of learning to listen in another language. By making explicit what learners think they know and do, they can better monitor, evaluate, and plan their own listening development by setting tangible comprehension and learning goals. When learners see the benefits of engaging in these metacognitive processes, they will feel motivated and will want to persist in their efforts to improve listening, a language skill that many still see as the most challenging of the four language skills.

The integrated experiential listening tasks and guided reflection activities presented in this chapter can be used at various stages of a listening program, a lesson or a series of lessons. Teachers can use these activities within the metacognitive pedagogical sequence to plan lessons that guide learners in the orchestration of metacognitive processes. Learners who experience these activities regularly can gain greater control over their listening processes and become more autonomous learners.

Although a metacognitive approach is being used in many areas of learning, its role in L2 listening has only recently been explored and examined. Listening is to a large extent a hidden process; this makes metacognitive instruction all the more crucial for helping learners examine what they know and can do to enhance their listening development. Many traditional listening lessons overlook the important metacognitive dimension by involving learners only in listening to spoken texts and responding to questions about key points in them. A metacognitive approach to teaching listening, on the other hand, integrates these listening practice activities with learner-centered activities that directly raise learners' awareness about the listening process and themselves as learners of listening.

Discussion Questions and Tasks

1. Compare the two types of metacognitive instructional activities: integrated experiential listening tasks and guided reflections for listening. What are the relative strengths and limitations of each type of activity?
2. Read the scenario again and write a list of prompts that Aida's teacher might have used.
3. It is important for teachers to understand the processes that L2 listeners experience. Select an audio recording or a video that interests you. Use the self-directed listening or viewing guide presented in Figure 7.5 to accompany your listening or viewing. Share your thoughts and experiences with a colleague or classmate.
4. Draw up an alternative self-report checklist following the model given in Figure 7.11. Explain what the checklist is for and who could use it. Refer to Appendix A for more items on strategies.

Suggestions for Further Reading

Goh, C. (1997). Metacognitive awareness and second language listeners. *ELT Journal*, 51(4), 361–369.
   This is one of the earliest papers to report L2 listeners' metacognitive knowledge about learning to listen. It outlines activities that can be used to promote greater metacognitive awareness.
Kemp, J. (2010) The listening log: Motivating autonomous learning. *ELT Journal*, 64(4), 385–395.
   This article reports the benefits of using learner reflections on listening in two language programs in the UK. Kemp explains how the journals are

introduced and recommends their use as a tangible link between learner and teacher, as well as a means of formative assessment, feedback, and class input.

Richards, J. C. (2005). Second thoughts on teaching listening. *RELC Journal,* *36*(1), 85–92.

Richards discusses a two-part strategy where comprehension and acquisition are the goals of a listening course, highlighting the importance of noticing as a post-listening activity.

Chapter 8

Developing Perception and Word Segmentation Skills

Scenario

Today Mr. Park will work on developing sound and word recognition skills with his EFL learners. He announces that they will do a "Discovery Listening" activity today, using a text about the role of pets in people's lives. After clarifying the topic, he plays the text, delivered at normal speed, and the learners listen without taking any notes. The learners self-assess their level of comprehension (e.g., 40%, 60%, 80%), note it on their worksheets, and then listen to the text a second time. This time they write down all key words. The learners listen a third time to expand their notes by adding as many details as possible.

Mr. Park now asks the class to work together in small groups to reconstruct the text. The members of each group use the notes from their worksheets to reconstruct the text in writing as closely as possible to its original form. The learners share what they have heard, pool together the bits of information understood, and discuss problems they encountered and gaps in understanding. As they share information and resolve comprehension differences, the learners focus on specific words and important grammatical details to reconstruct a text that represents the combined effort of the group.

When the groups have completed the task, Mr. Park asks them to compare their reconstructed version with a transcript of the original. He asks them to closely examine their errors and determine the cause of those errors, according to the categories on the worksheet (e.g., couldn't hear the sound, couldn't separate sound into words, new word to me, etc.). He encourages the learners to assess the relative seriousness of their errors in relation to the overall meaning of the text, and to pay attention to differences between the text and their reconstruction of it. The activity ends with a final listen (without transcript) and the learners record another self-assessment of overall level of comprehension, comparing this assessment with the level recorded at the beginning of the activity.[1]

Pre-reading Reflection

1. How can this activity help listeners improve sound and word recognition skills?
2. Wilson (2003) claims that this activity helps learners discover their listening problems. How so?
3. To what degree does this activity develop listener metacognition? How is it similar to or different from the metacognitive sequence outlined in Chapter 6?
4. Why does Mr. Park have his learners do a pre- and post-self-assessment of their comprehension? What does that add to the development of their listening skills?

Introduction

For comprehension to happen, listeners need to parse the sound stream into meaningful units. This is challenging because the boundaries between words are often hard to determine. A common complaint of L2 listeners is that they have difficulty segmenting meaningful units from the sound stream. The acoustic signal comes so fast and then it is gone. In a study of listening difficulties reported by L2 listeners, eight of the ten problems were related to perception of the acoustic signal and segmenting words from the sound stream (Goh, 2000). This was particularly true for beginning- and intermediate-level listeners.

L2 learners also comment that reading is so much easier than listening comprehension. The most obvious difference between the two is the form in which the message is conveyed. Readers have the luxury of spaces that signal boundaries between words and the advantage of being able to return to the text. Listeners, on the other hand, need to do the hard work of segmenting the sound stream into meaningful units, without having the luxury of being able to re-examine the text. This adds to the cognitive burden of listening, compared with reading.

Indeed, the development of perception and word segmentation skills is an essential part of L2 listening development. Tsui & Fullilove (1998) observed that successful listeners need good perception and word segmentation skills because prior knowledge is not always adequate to compensate for unknown words in texts that do not always follow schemata precisely.

1 Based on Wilson (2003).

This chapter will deal with the important question of how L2 listeners segment speech in the new language they are learning and how teachers can use this information to teach listening. We will begin by examining some of the research literature to better understand the decoding problems faced by listeners and the cues that learners find helpful to segment speech in the target language. The second part of the chapter will examine the unique features of spoken language, the differences between planned and unplanned speech, and the importance of choosing texts that are "listenable" to facilitate listening development. Finally, the chapter will present a number of techniques and teaching activities that can be used to develop perception and word segmentation skills, to help language learners become better listeners.

Word Segmentation: Research Findings

Decoding Challenges

It is helpful for teachers to be aware of what research has uncovered with regard to the decoding problems that learners face when they try to parse input in a new language. Three types of problems are summarized by Cross (2009a) as intrusion, processing, and text problems.

First of all, L2 listeners experience intrusion problems from their native language. Research shows that they tend to segment speech involuntarily on the basis of their L1 segmentation procedures (Cutler, 2001; Goh, 2000; Graham, 2006). These language-specific habits are acquired early in life and become so solidly engrained in the listener's processing system that they are involuntarily transferred to listening in a new language, particularly at the beginning stages. This makes L2 listening particularly difficult when the new language is not rhythmically similar to the listener's L1.

Second, L2 listeners experience processing problems in that they are unable to rapidly locate word boundaries. In the case of learning English, a stressed syllable appears to be a fairly reliable cue for word onset. Content words, as opposed to function words, appear to be more salient, likely due to the fact that these words tend to be stressed.

Finally, L2 listeners experience text problems in that they possess inadequate L2 vocabulary knowledge to quickly recognize words. Furthermore, they are often unable to recognize words they do know when these occur in rapid connected speech, because the form of a word may be altered from its form when spoken in isolation.

Cross analyzed the notes written by learners after each of two listens to news videotexts in a classroom. Based on his analysis, he suggests that the learners in this study could be helped by a greater awareness of the phonetic variations that can occur in connected, spoken English, discrimination of certain sounds, and revision of poor word choices, drawn from other evidence in the text. Other research studies provide teachers with a better understanding of the cues that listeners use to help them deal with an unfamiliar sound stream.

Cues for Word Segmentation

Research shows that listeners use a number of different cues to help them segment a sound stream into meaningful units: semantic/lexical, prosodic, allophonic, and phonotactic cues. Semantic/lexical cues refer to L2 words that listeners may already know and recognize in connected speech, including words from their own L1 that are recognizable orally in the target language. Obviously, these cues play a greater role as proficiency in the target language grows. At the beginning stages of listening, however, listeners are confronted with unknown chunks of speech and will often resort to prosodic cues. Prosodic cues are the stressed syllables, the pauses in the speech stream, and the tone groups between those pauses (Brown, 1990). Allophonic cues refer to different sounds associated with a single phoneme that listeners use for segmentation. Phonotactic cues refer to the specific clusters of consonants and vowels that are characteristic of the target language.

Semantic/Lexical Cues

Sanders, Neville, and Woldorff (2002) conducted some interesting experiments to determine the respective roles of semantic, syntactic, and prosodic information in segmenting speech. They began by preparing and recording three parallel versions of a sentence: a semantic, syntactic, and acoustic version, each meticulously matched on as many physical characteristics as possible (see Table 8.1). The semantic version was a normal sentence. In the syntactic version, content words were replaced with non-words, retaining only recognizable function words and syntactic information, such as –ed endings for past tense verbs or –s endings for plural nouns. Finally, the acoustic version was changed to retain English prosody but with unrecognizable non-words. All three sets of sentences were recorded using identical intonation. Table 8.1 shows the three versions of a strong stress, initial position (*bot*tles).

Both L1 speakers of English and L2 learners of English listened to the sentences and performed a segmentation task. Not surprisingly, the L1 English speakers were best able to detect the targets in the semantic sentences, then the syntactic sentences and, finally, the acoustic sentences (see Table 8.1). These listeners used multiple cues, relying more and more on stress and rhythm (acoustic) cues when lexical and syntactic cues were absent.

Table 8.1 Performance on Segmentation Tasks by Cue Type (based on Sanders et al., 2002)

Cue type	Sample sentence	L1 speakers	Japanese speakers		Spanish speakers	
			L2 Eng	L1	L2 Eng	L1
Semantic	In order to recycle bottles you have to separate them.	1	1	3	1	3
Syntactic	In order to lefatal bokkers you have to thagamate them.	2	2*	1	2*	1*
Acoustic	Ah ilgen di lefatal bokkerth ha maz di thagamate fon.	3	2*	2	2*	1*

Legend: 1 = most accurate; 3 = least accurate; *no difference

L2 speakers were, understandably, less accurate. They included speakers of languages that are rhythmically different from English: Japanese (a mora rhythmic language) and Spanish (a syllable rhythmic language). Although the advanced proficiency groups for both languages were less accurate than the L1 English speakers, they performed the segmentation task most accurately in the semantic sentences, likely because they had access to multiple cues. On the other hand, there was no difference in performance on the syntactic and acoustic sentences, suggesting that these L2 speakers did not attend to syntactic cues to perform the segmentation task. When these listeners had to rely on syntactic and acoustic cues only, they were most successful in identifying words that followed normal English stress patterns. There was a slight difference between the performance of Japanese and Spanish L2 speakers, likely due to the influence of stress patterns in their first language.

L1 speakers of Japanese and Spanish also performed the tasks. Not surprisingly, given their minimal acquaintance with any English words, these participants performed least well on the semantic sentences. The Japanese L1 speakers performed slightly better on the syntactic sentences than the acoustic versions. There was not much difference in the performance of the Spanish L1 speakers on the syntactic and acoustic sentences.

A more recent study by Lee and Cai (2010) on unfamiliar word processing arrived at similar results for the salience of semantic cues. This was particularly true for higher proficiency learners. Prosody cues were used more by the lower proficiency learners.

In sum, not surprisingly, semantics appears to be the most salient cue in perception and word segmentation. Furthermore, based on other reviews of similar research (e.g., Field, 2008b), we can affirm that L2 learners make little use of syntactic cues. This corroborates research on the role of syntactic knowledge in listening performance (see Chapter 4).

The prominence of semantic cues points to the importance of instruction in both lexical knowledge and word recognition skills for the L2 listener.

Prosodic Cues

In the absence of semantic cues, prosodic features of spoken language, such as stress and tone groups, become increasingly salient for determining word boundaries. Some research shows that calling attention to these features is helpful to L2 listeners. Cutler (2001) proposed that, when listening to English, listeners use a metrical segmentation strategy: that is, a stressed syllable will most likely signal the beginning of a new word. Cutler concluded this from extensive research in oral language processing, based on earlier seminal work by Brown (1990). In fact, based on analysis of a corpus of spoken English, Cutler calculated that 85.6 percent of content words in speech contain only one syllable or are stressed on the first syllable (Cutler & Carter, 1987). This would make stress, listening for strong syllables, a fairly reliable cue for detecting word onset in listening to English. In similar research, Harley (2000) found that L2 learners of English with two quite different first languages (Polish and Chinese) paid attention to prosodic rather than syntactic cues in listening to English, regardless of the age and language background of the listeners. These results corroborate the findings of Sanders et al. (2002) with regard to the minimal role of syntactic cues and the importance of stress in the absence of semantic cues for L2 learners.

Allophonic Cues

A single phoneme may be produced in different ways, depending on its position within a word. For example, the phoneme *t* is aspirated in "keeps talking" but is unaspirated in "keep stalking." These are allophones, and allophonic cues, like prosody, are language-specific and may not be perceptible by all learners of English. For example, Ito and Strange (2009) found that Japanese learners of English had difficulty exploiting allophonic cues for word segmentation purposes; however, their ability to perceive and use aspiration and glottal stops (e.g., separating "ice cream" from "I scream" in English) improved with increased length of residence in an English-speaking environment. Altenberg (2005) found similar difficulties for Spanish learners of English. Knowing that L2 listeners can learn to override the segmentation cues of their first language and to use allophonic and prosodic cues of the target language to successfully segment continuous speech suggests that these processes are amenable to instruction (Cutler, 2001).

Phonotactic Cues

Each language has its own phonotactic constraints: that is, certain sound sequences cannot appear in a syllable or may only appear at either the beginning or end of that syllable. For example, in English the cluster *rt* can appear at the end of a syllable such as *shirt* but cannot be the onset of a word, whereas the opposite is true of *cr* as in *crust*. In order to test the degree to which L2 learners make use of this information in word segmentation, researchers use a word spotting task. Participants listen to a stream of sound that is nonsense and identify any target language words they hear. The same word is presented in different acoustic contexts, each representative of the language of interest. Responses are documented for both speed of reaction time and accuracy of recognition. Of particular interest to the researcher is the degree to which the phonotactic constraints of L1 facilitate or interfere with the constraints of L2.

As expected, research shows that listeners are more accurate in spotting words with boundaries that are prevalent in their L1. In their study of German learners of English and L1 English speakers, Weber and Cutler (2006) determined that, where word boundaries in English and German were similar, both listener groups performed equally well in identifying the English target word. When word boundaries were in the English condition only, both groups scored well; however, when words were in the German boundary condition, only the German group scored well. The English group had difficulty, even though the target word was English. Weber and Cutler conclude that this is good news for L2 learners: L2 listeners can approximate the word segmentation strategies of L1 listeners, although it is not clear how much experience with the target language is necessary in order for L2 listeners to suppress L1 probabilities when listening to L2. Building on this study, Al-jasser (2008) noted similar effects for L1 speakers of Arabic and conducted an eight-week study to teach them English phonotactics. After instruction, these L2 learners of English were able to more quickly detect target words in the English boundary condition.

Factors in Word Recognition

Word recognition involves an interwoven process of word segmentation and word activation (Rost, 2005). As listeners identify word boundaries, they attempt to activate a likely word candidate. How does the listener arrive at the best match? Based on his review of the literature, Cross (2009b) identified five interrelated factors that affect speed and accuracy in finding the best fit for a word: context and co-text of the utterance, density (number of potential competing words), frequency of occurrence of the word in the target language, recent activation of the word by the listener, and spreading activation of a network of associated words.

Probably the most important cue for the listener is the context of the utterance. Many segmentation challenges (e.g., "ice cream"/"I scream") are easily resolved by the larger context within the oral text, the co-text (what has been understood so far of the whole text) or the context in which the utterance is spoken. However, it is important to distinguish between lexical, syntactic or semantic contexts, and to consider how and when context has its effect.

Other factors are also important. Density is an important factor in that the onset of some words will activate many candidates. Some words take much longer to differentiate from other potential candidates; for example, a word beginning with a consonant cluster such as *scr* will be more quickly resolved than a word beginning with a consonant/vowel combination such as *li*. Words that occur more frequently in the target language are recognized more quickly and accurately. Not surprisingly, this includes mostly function words such as *the* and *it*, prepositions such as *to* and *with*, pronouns such as *you* and *his*, and content words such as *hot* and *make*. In the same vein, words that have most recently been activated by the listener, because there is still a trace in memory, will be more quickly activated.

Finally, activation of a network of topic-related words makes it easier to activate the correct word. This spreading activation of a network of words explains why contextualization before listening is so important. Discussion of the topic or reading something about the topic activates a network of words that can be more quickly accessed in a subsequent listening activity. It also explains why active prediction of words and/or content, as practiced in the metacognitive pedagogical sequence, is even more effective.

Word Segmentation: Synthesis

What can we learn from these studies on the problems and the cues listeners use to segment connected speech? Two types of research provide useful background for teachers. The research on specific cues and factors in word recognition, done in highly controlled conditions, provides technical insights and remediation suggestions. However, laboratory conditions in these studies rob the listeners of broader contextual support and therefore lack ecological validity for real-life listening. They also encourage word-for-word listening, which is a less productive strategy in real life. Research that focuses on identifying decoding errors, on the other hand, helps teachers understand the larger picture and choose both remediation of a technical nature and development of metacognition to improve specific components and general listening ability.

The studies with a more technical focus suggest that semantic and prosodic cues play a prominent role, and that syntactic cues are not significant. This contention is further corroborated by research on the predictor variables for L2 listening success, which highlight the powerful role of vocabulary and the negligible role of syntax. Phonotactic cues appear to be the next most important cues, followed by allophonic cues. The degree to which phonotactic or allophonic cues are used by L2 listeners may be a function of characteristics in their L1 and the target language.

The first important conclusion reached by many of the studies is that L2 listeners can be taught to overcome the word segmentation strategies of their L1. Second, the speed and accuracy of word activation appears to be influenced mostly by contextual factors. L2 listening can be facilitated by providing listeners with a context that allows activation of different knowledge sources and informed prediction, as part of actively planning for listening activities.

We will return to these questions later in the discussion on techniques to develop rapid and accurate segmentation skills. However, before doing so, we need to consider the types of texts used in L2 listening development. Some texts are more "listenable" than others, as we shall see in the next section.

Spoken Language: Planned Versus Unplanned Speech

Texts are created to be either read or spoken; far too often listeners are expected to be able to understand texts that are meant to be read. This adds to the burden of learning to listen. On the other hand, spoken texts enjoy a number of characteristics that can facilitate comprehension, if listeners are taught to capitalize on them. The degree to which a text is "listenable" will depend on the degree to which the speech is planned by the speaker. The differences between planned and unplanned speech are illustrated by comparing two transcripts of spoken language that refer to the same event: rescheduling a ski trip cancelled because of a snow storm. Read both transcripts and identify differences in linguistic features and presentation of information. The differences between the two texts are highlighted in Figure 8.1.

Text 1: Leader speaking to the assembled group
   I know some of you know already, but tomorrow . . . because we missed the ski trip today . . . tomorrow we're gonna leave around nine, nine-thirty . . . OK? . . . OK . . . so we're gonna try to be at the bus at nine-thirty and we're gonna go skiing there all day . . . but I'm gonna stay like in the cafeteria for individual meetings with people . . . like the two people who were supposed to have their meetings tomorrow . . . OK . . . like if it's in the morning, . . . they'll go skiing in the afternoon. I don't know for sure how long it's gonna take . . . like it's between . . . usually

Text Features	Text 1	Text 2
Sentence fragments	√	
Self-corrections	√	
High level of redundancy	√	
Complete sentences		√
Phonological contractions and assimilations	√	
Logical organization of information		√
Pauses for punctuation	√	
Hesitations and false starts	√	
Complex embedded clauses		√
Repairs with additional details	√	
Speakers are clear in what they wish to communicate		√
Short idea units	√	
Fillers (e.g., "uhm") as speaker finds next words	√	
Lexical density (number of content words in a clause)		√

Figure 8.1. Features of Planned and Unplanned Speech

it's between one hour and a half and two hours depending on the person . . . and . . . uhm . . . what he has to say, I guess. So this is for one thing tomorrow . . . and so I want to make sure that everybody agrees . . . do we want to go skiing and have the meetings over there instead? (Source: Tremblay, 1989, p. 12)

Text 2: Announcement over the public address system

Since our ski trip today had to be cancelled, I propose that the trip be rescheduled for tomorrow and that the two meetings planned for tomorrow take place in the cafeteria at the ski lodge. This means that the people involved will miss out on some ski time, depending on how long the meeting takes. If no one objects then, we will go skiing tomorrow instead. Buses will leave at nine-thirty. (Source: original)

Unplanned speech is more spontaneous in nature. It is often characterized by false starts in the form of incomplete sentences, hesitations and pauses of varying lengths, and fillers, as speakers search for the best word to express what they want to say. This results in shorter idea units, with frequent repetitions. Grammar errors may be present and the language is often colloquial, accompanied by reduced forms and assimilations. Overall, these features make unplanned speech easier to comprehend because the redundancy, fillers, pauses, and repairs give listeners more time to process the message. Speakers may also do self-repair: that is, change a word used or rephrase an idea in order to express the message more clearly and create the desired impression for the listener. As they rephrase, speakers may also add extra details, which often lead to strings of idea units that are not very cohesive and may make the message appear somewhat incoherent, if the listener is not familiar with the context.

Planned speech reflects more of the characteristics of written texts. These texts use complete sentences, placing greater emphasis on content and condensing information into fewer words. Since planned speech reflects a clear intention to communicate precise information, ideas are usually presented in a more logical fashion with more embedded clauses. This makes the text dense and, consequently, difficult for a listener to process in real time.

As noted earlier, many of the features of unplanned speech (pauses, redundancy, shorter idea units) can facilitate comprehension, particularly at earlier stages of language learning. Shohamy and Inbar (1991) suggest that these characteristics contribute to the "listenability" of a text because they better reflect the oral nature of language. They argue that the more a text reflects spoken language, the more "listenable" it will be and the easier it will be for L2 learners to understand. This is important information for the teaching of L2 listening.

Samples of spoken language can usually be classified on a continuum of planned and unplanned speech, not entirely one or the other; the more the speech is planned, the less likely one will find the characteristics of unplanned speech enumerated earlier. As a general principle, therefore, texts with the features of planned speech, or texts meant to be read, should not be used for L2 listening practice. Listeners, particularly low-proficiency listeners, do not have the time and attentional resources to process densely packed information. This is equally true for L1 listeners since, unlike a written text, information in a spoken text cannot be consulted again, unless one has the option of confirming understanding or asking the speaker to repeat. Therefore, if teachers wish to use texts with the features of planned speech, these texts should be adapted to include more of the features of unplanned speech.

Develop Perception and Word Segmentation

How can teachers help learners overcome intrusion, processing, and text problems and, at the same time, improve learner ability to decipher the variety of cues involved in word segmentation and recognition? Training in perception and word segmentation can take many forms. Indeed, motivated language learners can make significant progress on their own by listening to texts appropriate to their age, proficiency, and interest level, and consulting a transcript of the text only after using all strategies at their disposal. In addition, teachers can include activities that can make learners more aware of the bottom-up aspect of listening development and increase their comprehension skills. This section of the chapter will discuss a range of approaches teachers can consider, from text selection to specific techniques for skill development, to targeted activities with a metacognitive orientation that integrate development of bottom-up processing skills with broader listening development.

Text Selection

A first step in the design of teaching activities for the development of perception and word segmentation is text selection. As noted earlier, texts with the features of unplanned speech are more "listenable." Texts that include pauses, false starts, rephrasing, and fillers provide listeners with necessary redundancy and extra time to process what they hear. At beginning stages of language learning, this would mean choosing samples of oral language that are less dense and more literate in nature, such as dialogues and conversations, discussions, interviews, radio phone-in dialogues, telephone conversations, and answering machine messages. These texts should be short, free of too much colloquial language or a strong accent, and limited to two or three speakers (Goh, 2002a). The pedagogical benefits of selecting listenable texts were confirmed by anecdotal evidence in a study by Jensen and Vinther (2003). In response to a questionnaire, learners listening to texts at a natural speed (in contrast to slowed-down versions of a text) claimed that it was the pauses that provided them with the necessary processing time to understand.

Reducing Speech Rate

Some of the well-known methods for facilitating comprehension address the fact that learners find the speed of listening texts too fast. One of these techniques is slowing down the speed of the text. Teachers can draw on research to decide if reducing speech rate is useful in helping students develop real-life listening skills.

It is self-evident that speech rate affects comprehension. Even the comprehension of L1 listeners begins to decline for texts with a speech rate above 300 words per minute (wpm). Griffiths (1990) found that this number drops to about 200 wpm (or 3.8 syllables per second) for intermediate-level learners of English. In other words, for texts with a speech rate of more than 200 wpm, the scores of L2 listeners on comprehension questions related to the content of the text are appreciably compromised. After determining that many texts are delivered at rates higher than 200 wpm, Griffiths (1991) investigated the comprehension of stories spoken at three different speech rates. Stories delivered at 188 wpm resulted in better comprehension scores than texts delivered at 250 wpm. Similarly, stories delivered at 127 wpm resulted in better comprehension scores than those delivered at 188 wpm. The difference in comprehension scores for the two texts with faster speech rates did not differ significantly, suggesting that a speech rate of about 127 wpm can be beneficial in facilitating comprehension for intermediate-level listeners. For comparison purposes, audio books in L1 are usually delivered at the speed of about 150–160 wpm.

However, the results obtained by Griffiths are not corroborated by other research on speech rate (e.g., Blau, 1990; Rader, 1991). This prompted Zhao (1997) to examine speech rate from a different perspective. He gave learners the option of choosing the speed for listening to a text, using technology that could control speed without distortion to pitch. Zhao found that listeners performed better on the comprehension task when they had control over speech rate and repetition, although the chosen speech rate varied greatly by listener. While this result appears to support the results obtained by Griffiths, Zhao cautions that L2 listeners are unique individuals with different perceptions of what is fast or slow. Furthermore, he cautioned that learners who use this approach may not "push" themselves adequately, instead opting to slow down speech rate to a level of comfort below what they might actually still be able to understand.

The studies by Griffiths and Zhao provide empirical evidence for enhancing comprehension through reduced speech rate; they do not, however, answer the question as to whether speed reduction can help L2 listeners develop the skills and strategies necessary for real-life listening. In other words, does practice at reduced speech rates improve the comprehension of texts spoken naturally by competent speakers of English in authentic contexts?

The effects of reduced speech rate and exact repetition of the oral text were examined by Jensen and Vinther (2003), using a pre- and post-listening measure. Three experimental groups and a control group listened to videotaped dialogues in different modes, Fast (F) and Slow (S) in different patterns. All three experimental groups, F–S–S, F–S–F, and F–F–F, outperformed the control group in detailed comprehension of the text and in acquisition of phonological decoding strategies. Reduced speed, however, did not account for better performance since the F–F–F group outperformed the other two experimental groups on comprehension and decoding skills. In view of the fact that this difference was not statistically significant, the researchers conducted a similar experiment to tease out the separate contributions of reduced speed and text repetition. When the texts were presented three times at the same speech rate, the results did not change significantly, leading the researchers to conclude that repetition was the determining factor. Furthermore, questionnaire responses showed that most of the learners appreciated being able to do the final listening at normal speed, suggesting that comparing the slower, comprehended version with the authentic, faster version helped listeners learn to understand better and become more aware of the irregularities of spoken language. The researchers rightly argue that this approach, which also provided training in detailed decoding skills, helped listeners improve their ability to manage listening to high-speed input for immediate comprehension.

Is there a place for varied speech rate in the language classroom? A great deal of listening practice also takes place through teacher interaction with the class or individual learners in the target language. As teachers speak to their classes, they can vary their rate of speech as necessary. By slowing down the speech rate occasionally, articulating a word or an expression more clearly, supporting the oral with a visual representation of a word (a picture, or pointing to concrete referents), and further elaborations are some of the ways in which teachers speak at a natural pace and make the target language comprehensible to learners on a daily basis. Much of the consolidation of initial target language vocabulary in memory occurs during these interactions.

Repetition

Another technique to reduce barriers to comprehension is repeated listening to the same text. Teachers can draw on research findings to determine when and under what conditions repetition is a useful teaching technique.

The effects of repeated listening to a text, already noted in the discussion of the Jensen and Vinther (2003) study, was also examined by Chang and Read (2006), in addition to other kinds of listening support. They compared four different types of support: (1) preview the questions only; (2) repetition of the text; (3) providing background knowledge on the topic; and (4) vocabulary preparation. The last three conditions also involved preview of the questions before listening and, in the case of repetition, between the first and second listen. Results showed that repetition and provision of background knowledge had a significant effect on the final listening test performance. This was particularly the case for the higher proficiency learners in each group. The vocabulary preparation group performed the poorest of all the groups.

Repetition in and of itself is not sufficient for improvement, however. In the research with the metacognitive pedagogical sequence, experimental and control groups listened to the same text three times (Vandergrift

& Tafaghodtari, 2010). The experimental group that engaged in prediction and focused monitoring during each of the listens significantly outperformed the control group that listened three times with no explicit focus for each listen. In the same vein, an opportunity to examine the questions between listens allowed listeners in the Chang and Read study to verify what they understood and to focus their attention on information related to what they still needed to resolve. In a more recent study by Sakai (2009), using written recall protocols in the listeners' L1, the second listen did lead to more precise comprehension, particularly for the advanced proficiency group. This result was likely due to the opportunity afforded by the second listen to fill in details that memory overload did not allow the participants to retain during the first listen.

Clearly, repetition of an oral text at normal speech rate, as practice, is beneficial for improving listening comprehension. What appears to make repetition more powerful is the opportunity for listeners to apply a greater range of strategies to each subsequent listen. Listeners apply metacognitive knowledge by reflecting on what they have understood and where they need to pay greater attention, and then by planning for more focused attention to selected areas of the text during the next listen. These strategies, in combination with repetition, improve comprehension of rapid L2 speech.

In sum, the research base on techniques to increase perception suggests that repetition of the text can be beneficial for real-life listening skills, while reducing speech rate may not transfer benefits to real-life listening. In the case of repetition, it is the opportunity to strategically plan for and focus on different aspects of the text in subsequent listens that may explain the success of this technique.

Post-listening Activities to Develop Perception Skills

Perception and word segmentation skills can also be developed as part of a regular listening lesson within a metacognitive approach. Perception activities are best carried out at the post-listening stage: that is, after learners have completed a listening comprehension task. Figure 8.2 illustrates where these activities can be incorporated into a regular listening lesson. They help L2 listeners make sound-form connections and become more aware of phonological modifications, to improve their bottom-up

Pre-listening
(Planning, preparations, etc.)

Listening and viewing

Post-listening
(Language-focused, perception activity)

Figure 8.2. Place of Perception Development in a Regular Listening Lesson

processing ability.

These activities can be particularly helpful in making learners aware of the variations and irregularities of spoken language. In English, these include phenomena such as:

- assimilation: adjusting the sound of the end of a word to make it easier to move to the sound of the next word (e.g., *these sheep→thee sheep; spot light→spod light*);
- elision: omitting individual sounds within a word (e.g., *grandmother→granmother; internet→innernet*) or between words (*next time→negz time*) to make them easier to pronounce;
- resyllabification or liaison: relocation of sounds so that the consonant at the end of a word is attached to the beginning of the next word (e.g., *these apples→thee zapples; made out→may doubt*); and,
- reduction: reshaping less important words within a tone group to make them easier to pronounce (e.g., *I am going to eat→I'm gonna eat; it must have been me→it musta bin me*).

Figure 8.3 illustrates in greater detail how teachers can use this phase of a listening lesson to raise metacognitive awareness about phonological features of authentic spoken texts. The procedure can be adapted to help learners focus on a variety of key features of speech such as the phonological irregularities noted earlier: rhythm, word stress, prominence, tone, and pauses. Depending on the length of the excerpt to be examined, the second step (transcription by the learners) could be omitted so that learners work with the transcript immediately.

It is important that learners listen to the text one final time as a closing step, using their new knowledge about the sounds to confirm comprehension of the text as a whole. By increasing awareness of sound-form relationships, learners are developing metacognitive knowledge about lis-

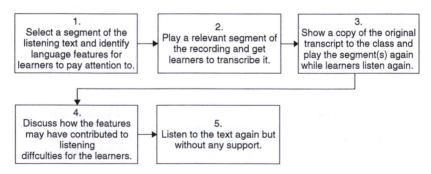

Figure 8.3 Suggested Procedure to Develop Sound Perception Ability

tening—in particular, task knowledge.

Within a metacognitive sequence, teachers can use common bottom-up activities to develop perception skills and modify them to contribute to metacognitive awareness as well. The traditional dictogloss, for example, can take on added value with feasible modifications. A closer look at some of these activities will focus on how they develop bottom-up processing skills and how to make them more metacognitive.

Cloze Exercises

A popular listening activity in language classes is the cloze exercise. Learners listen for missing words that have been deleted on a print version of an oral text (often a song) and write them in the blanks. The principle underlying the cloze procedure is that deleting every *nth* word (e.g., the seventh) forces listeners to activate their expectancy grammar: that is, their knowledge of the sequences of words in normal discourse. The cloze can be a useful tool for assessing general language proficiency through reading. As learners read the text, they activate various knowledge sources, such as linguistic, syntactic, or pragmatic knowledge, in order to determine the correct word. The deletions can also be more meaning-based by removing content words instead of every seventh word, for example.

Although the cloze procedure has value as a tool to force listeners to attend carefully to the sound stream and engage in exclusive bottom-up processing, it has some limitations as a meaningful listening activity. The primary limitation is that the cloze can, in fact, be successfully completed without understanding the full meaning of the text. It is possible to listen for the missing words only, insert them in the blanks and never actually pay attention to meaning. Not only does this make the task relatively meaningless: it does not encourage listeners to use contextual information to activate potential word candidates. Context, as we noted earlier, is the most important cue for rapid word recognition.

The cloze procedure can be made more meaningful and metacognitive if listeners are first required to read the text and predict the missing words. This has a number of advantages. When listeners first read the text, they can activate (1) prior knowledge that will help in predicting the missing content words, and (2) syntactic knowledge (or expectancy grammar) to predict the missing function words. Once learners have inserted their predictions (e.g., in pencil or below the line), they listen to the text for the first time, monitor the accuracy of their predictions, and insert the correct words, as required. An opportunity to compare either the predictions and/or the results of the first listen with a peer could add greater intensity to monitoring efforts. Adding a planning element to the cloze procedure makes it more than just development of bottom-up listening skills: it demonstrates to learners how bottom-up processing can be facilitated by top-down processing, as in real-life listening.

Dictation

The dictation, or *dictée*, has a long tradition in language learning. Originally conceived as a tool for testing written language proficiency, similar to the cloze procedure, it entails very strict rules for spelling and accents. Dictation can be a tool for remediation in listening if teachers target specific words and language features that have proven difficult in recent listening activities. Field (2003) recommends dictation as a particularly useful tool for calling attention to variations in spoken language that can create problems in word segmentation. Field suggests that teachers read, in a natural manner, short, unpaused sentences that target one of more of these phenomena, or read sentences from an authentic text. Strict rules for correction do not apply in this scenario; since teachers are looking for understanding of meaning, approximate spellings are acceptable. Dictation obliges listeners to pay careful attention to all the words in the sound stream; as such, it is a good tool for developing bottom-up listening skills, particularly if the sentences are unrelated. The more the dictation sentences are connected, the more listeners will be able to use metacognitive knowledge and other knowledge sources to help them anticipate words and resolve problems.

Although dictation appears to have potential as a method for improving perception and word segmentation in L2 listening, this has not been confirmed by research.

Reading While Listening

This activity allows listeners to read a transcript of a text while listening to the spoken version, without first listening to the text alone. Several studies by Chang have examined the use of this technique as a tool for developing perception and word segmentation skills. In a recent study, learners who read the text while listening outperformed a control group that listened only (Chang, 2009). However, the test used to establish improvement in comprehension was not independent of the text used in the study. The comprehension test involved reading elements of the same oral text: sequencing (ordering statements from the text in chronological order) and gap filling (filling in missing words from the transcript just read). Proof for the effectiveness of this technique would require pre- and post-test scores on an independent test that reflected the characteristics of real-life listening, without any written support. Although this activity may have value for making sound-form connections, it is unlikely to help learners develop skills for real-life listening, since learners construct meaning through reading (not listening) and it encourages them to listen for every word, not a productive strategy for comprehending speech in real time.

Dictogloss

The opening scenario of this chapter presented the dictogloss as a method for raising awareness of the process of listening. It focuses on both bottom-up and top-down dimensions of listening. Called "Discovery Listening" (Wilson, 2003), this activity involves three phases. In the listening phase, learners listen to a short oral text three times: first, without taking notes; second, making notes of key words; and, third, expanding on the notes taken during the second listen. During the reconstruction phase (dictogloss), learners work in small groups and use their notes to reconstruct the original text as closely as possible in writing. Finally, in the discovery phase, learners compare their reconstructed text with a transcript of the original and classify the causes of their mistakes. During the last phase, learners make sound-form comparisons and develop greater metacognitive knowledge about the target language.

Figure 8.4 presents the worksheet that accompanies this activity. As argued by Wilson, the dictogloss can help L2 listeners notice differences between their reconstructed text and a written transcription of the original, and gain greater insight into their comprehension errors. The activity is also metacognitive in that learners plan, monitor, and evaluate their listening, learning to problem-solve with peers when they confront difficulties in their reconstruction of the text.

"I Minus I" Listening

In order to develop skill in automatic word access, Hulstijn (2001) recommends listening to "*i minus 1* level" texts. In contrast to Krashen's principle of *i plus 1* (Krashen, 1985), this activity requires learners to listen to oral texts that they are able to understand almost completely the first time with relatively little effort. As suggested by Hulstijn, this can be very motivating for L2 listeners, especially when the texts are new to learners, relate to their interests and life experience, and are humorous. A variation of this activity requires listeners to follow along with a transcript of the text (fully grammatical, with no unfamiliar words) that has been slightly altered by the addition, deletion, and/or modification of some words. Listeners are forced to pay close attention to every word in order to identify slight discrepancies between the aural and written forms of the text. In that sense, the variation of the activity is more useful for making the sound-form connections since listeners must consciously use bottom-up processing in order to detect any discrepancies.

1. **First Listen: How much of the <u>meaning</u> do you think you understood?**

   ☐ Almost   ☐ Less than   ☐ About   ☐ More than   ☐ Almost all
      nothing   40%   50%   60%

2. **Second Listen: Make notes of key words.**

3. **Third Listen: Add more notes.**
   a.
   b.
   c.
   d.
   e.
   f.

4. **In your group, try to write the sentences completely. They don't have to be perfect, but try to make the meaning as similar to the original as possible:**
   a.
   b.
   c.
   etc. (continue on back of page)

5. **What problems did you have?**
   (Circle the problem words above [exercise 4], and write a, b, c, d, e or f beside them)
   a) I couldn't hear which sound it was.
   b) I couldn't separate the sounds into words.
   c) I heard the words but couldn't remember their meaning quickly enough.
   d) This word was new to me.
   e) I heard and understood the words but not the meaning of that part of the sentence.
   f) Other problems (write on the back of the page).

6. **Which of these words (or phrases) caused you most difficulty in understanding the general or overall <u>meaning</u>?**

7. **When you read the transcript of the listening, did you have any trouble understanding it?**

   ☐ No   ☐ Yes   (If yes, write the problem on the back of the page)

8. **Final Listen: Can you hear and understand clearly now?**

   ☐ Almost   ☐ Less than   ☐ About   ☐ More than   ☐ Almost all
      nothing   40%   50%   60%

Figure 8.4. Worksheet for Discovery Listening

Source: Wilson, 2003

Development of Perception and Segmentation Skills: Synthesis

L2 problems related to perception and word segmentation have received some research attention. Research studies have also identified important factors for teachers to consider in lesson planning, such as text selection, and teaching practice has developed techniques and specific activities that can be included within a metacognitive approach to listening development.

At the same time, however, there is very little research on the impact of activities designed to help L2 learners become aware of the phonetic and phonological properties of the target language. As we have noted, many of the activities presented in this section, although compelling for their potential to help L2 learners improve the bottom-up dimension of listening, are not yet supported with empirical evidence.

Finally, although these activities are important for teaching and remediating L2 listening, one other caveat is in order. When we encourage learners to attend to each word in the sound stream, we may be fostering a word-for-word translation approach to L2. Unless listeners are doing remedial work with certain sounds, they should work with the transcript of the text only after they have attempted to understand the text as a whole, using a metacognitive approach and strategies that help to compensate for gaps in understanding. This encourages L2 listeners to use prediction and monitoring strategies to greater advantage for deeper cognitive processing of the target language.

Summary

This chapter has discussed the bottom-up component of listening comprehension in greater detail and the related problems faced by L2 listeners. We examined some of the research on cues in the sound stream that listeners exploit to segment speech and select the word that best fits the context. We analyzed the features of spoken language that listeners can use to their advantage, and then discussed the importance of choosing "listenable" texts, particularly in the early stages of language learning. Finally, we presented and discussed a number of activities teachers can use to help listeners pay closer attention to the sound stream and increase awareness of how sounds combine to create words in connected speech.

To conclude, teachers should be aware that the pedagogy associated with the bottom-up component of listening development can easily fall into a simple focus on form with little attention to meaning. Listeners must learn to sort out these sounds in the context of connected speech where the larger context, as in real-life listening, can often help listeners sort out and identify sounds that may initially seem unintelligible.

It is imperative that remediation take place within the context of meaning-based practice that allows L2 listeners to actively plan, monitor, and evaluate their listening efforts in order to regulate their comprehension and improve their listening ability.

Discussion Questions and Tasks

1. Select a listening textbook to examine the types of texts used for listening practice. To what degree does this book use texts that contain features of unplanned speech? What kinds of activities are used to improve learner bottom-up processing skills?
2. Many of the activities used to help learners listen are often critiqued for being inauthentic since the support provided within the activity would not be available in real-life listening contexts. In that light, is repetition of an oral text authentic practice? Explain.
3. How should teachers deal with different accents in the target language? Should teachers introduce different accents? If so, when is the best time to introduce listeners to other accents?
4. Compare the dictogloss with the cloze exercise. List some advantages and disadvantages of each technique. Would you use these techniques for developing bottom-up listening? Explain.
5. What is the role of bottom-up listening practice where the focus is on the identification of sounds only, with no reference to the meaning of those sounds in the context in which they occur? What are the advantages and disadvantages of this kind of listening practice?

Suggestions for Further Reading

Cross, J. D. (2009). Diagnosing the process, text and intrusion problems responsible for L2 listeners' decoding errors. *Asian EFL Journal, 11*, 31–53.
  This paper includes a comprehensive review of the current literature on word activation in L2 listening and a classroom study on decoding problems experienced by Japanese learners of English while listening to authentic videotext. Common decoding errors are noted and remedial action proposed.
Cutler, A. (2001). Listening to a second language through the ears of a first. *Interpreting, 5*, 1–23.
  An excellent review of the large body of literature on speech segmentation in a language other than the first, which concludes that segmentation is language-specific and that listeners need to learn to inhibit the application of L1 language-specific habits when learning another language that is rhythmically different.
Field, J. (2003). Promoting perception: Lexical segmentation in second language listening. *ELT Journal, 57*, 325–334.
  A practical article analyzing in greater detail the types of difficulties listeners experience in trying to understand English—in particular, reduced forms,

resyllabification, assimilation, and elision. Further examples and remediation suggestions are provided.

Wilson, M. (2003). Discovery listening—improving perceptual processing. *ELT Journal, 57,* 335–343.

This paper presents and discusses in detail the classroom activity presented in the opening scenario of this chapter.

Chapter 9

Task-Based Listening Lessons

Scenario

Elaine is training to be a Teacher of English to Speakers of Other Languages (TESOL). She is excited because her TESOL lecturer will be observing her listening lesson next week. She is careful to choose materials that cover a wide range of topics and interests for her class of 18 year olds. Two weeks ago, she chose a TV interview with a female singer from the UK because she had overheard some of her students talking enthusiastically about the singer. For her lesson next week, Elaine has identified two possible sets of materials. One is a DVD on global warming hosted by a well-known American personality. Another is a BBC podcast on the same topic. She knows her students have some prior knowledge because it was the topic of a reading comprehension passage, and she is confident that they will find the topic of global warming interesting. She is, however, still unable to decide which set of materials to use for the lesson.

To begin planning her lesson, Elaine goes through her notes from her TESOL course on teaching listening. She runs her highlighter pen over the heading "Teach not test" and reads what she has written under it: "Don't make learners listen and produce answers to show their comprehension. Help them. Let them help one another. Scaffolding is the key! Support their listening." She runs her highlighter pen over another heading, "Teach listening as communication." Her notes read:

> Listening is a communication skill. People listen for a purpose. Make listening lessons communicative. Why should learners listen? Give learners a reason to listen. Make them want to listen or they'll be bored!! What do they do after they have listened? People use the information from listening in real life. They store it for a reason. Listening to a recording and answering multiple-choice questions is not communicative. Plan tasks, not exercises!

Elaine then reviews her notes on selecting materials: "Use authentic materials. Be mindful of student interest but provide a wide range of materials and themes. Consider visual support— not all visuals are helpful."

Pre-reading Reflection

1. What criteria does Elaine use to select listening texts for her students? Do you think they are useful and adequate?
2. How can Elaine create a reason for her students to listen purposefully?
3. What kind of support do you think teachers can give learners before they listen or when they are listening?
4. Do you agree with Elaine's notes on "Teach not test"? Think of the last listening lesson you experienced either as a student or a teacher. In what way did it test listening? In what way did it teach listening?
5. If you were Elaine, would you use the DVD recording or the podcast for your next lesson? Why?

Introduction

Listening, unlike writing, speaking, and even reading, is typically done in real time where the input is transient and there is little record of what happens during listening. Teachers therefore find it difficult to teach listening in the way they teach the other language skills. Chapter 6 described a pedagogical sequence that encourages students to activate the processes of real-life listening through planning, monitoring, problem-solving, and evaluation. This is an important way for teachers to make the processes of listening explicit and show learners how they can develop greater facility in the execution of these processes. The different stages of discussion and repeated listening offer learners the opportunity to revisit the input, giving some degree of permanence to what would have been ephemeral and transient. Re-listening helps learners comprehend more of the content, which can motivate them to continue their practice. The pedagogical sequence is a direct metacognitive approach to teaching that deconstructs the listening process and the listening text. It is one of two ways to plan listening lessons discussed in this book.

The second way that we present here will help teachers plan lessons that teach listening for communication, focusing on the development of both one-way and interactive listening competence. These listening lessons are based on principles of task-based learning in which purpose, meaning, and outcomes are paramount (Skehan, 1998; Willis, 1996, 2005). Metacognitive instruction is embedded within the task-based lesson to help learners develop their metacognitive knowledge about listening. The task-based lesson structure and the pedagogical sequence are complementary and form twin organizing principles for a listening curriculum and for the listening component of an integrated language skills program.

Listening Comprehension Tasks

We begin by focusing on a smaller unit of the lesson—the task. According to Willis (1996, 2005), a task is an activity in which learners use language for a communicative purpose in order to achieve an outcome. By focusing on learning activities and communication goals, task-based listening lessons foreground the importance of comprehending meaning during listening. Teachers need to have a principled and systematic way of designing tasks that supports learners in their comprehension. They need to engage learners cognitively and affectively by motivating them to pay attention to meaning and to use strategies and skills to achieve comprehension. Listening tasks should also offer opportunities to develop core skills such as listen for details, listen for global understanding, listen for main ideas, listen and draw inferences, listen and make predictions, and listen selectively (see Figure 9.1).

Skills are what we use to carry out a task without much conscious attention. Strategies, on the other hand, are controlled and require effort; they are activated according to the purpose of the task. Learners employ strategies when they encounter difficulty in comprehending input or when they have to manipulate their cognitive processes or manage their affect. Language learners use both skills and strategies according to the degree of challenge they encounter and the purpose for listening. Typically, if the input is something they can easily manage, learners will demonstrate better proficiency in comprehension by using a variety of listening skills that are similar to those used by competent listeners.

In everyday listening events, listeners often combine the six core skills in different ways to understand the meaning in the input. The skills used to achieve comprehension are mainly influenced by the purpose for listening. For example, someone listening to instructions will pay attention to the main details that a speaker gives. Someone listening to an argument will pay attention to the key points in the speaker's argument and assess critically if the argument is a convincing one. In real-life communication we usually do not listen in one particular way for a long time. For example, we do not normally pay attention to details for an extended period of time because this can be tiring. In many listening events listeners tend to listen for global understanding, using inferences and predictions to

Listen for Details
Understand and identify specific information in a text: for example, key words, numbers, and names.

Listen for Global Understanding
Understand the general idea in a text: for example, the theme, the topic, and the overall view of the speaker.

Listen for Main Ideas
Understand the key points or propositions in a text: for example, points in support of an argument, or parts of an explanation.

Listen and Infer
Demonstrate understanding by filling in information that is omitted, unclear, or ambiguous, and make connections with prior knowledge by "listening between the lines": for example, using visual clues to gauge the speaker's feelings.

Listen and Predict
Anticipate what the speaker is going to say before and during listening: for example, use knowledge of the context of an interaction to draw a conclusion about the speaker's intention before he/she expresses it.

Listen Selectively
Pay attention to particular parts of a message and skim over or ignore other parts in order to achieve a specific listening goal or, for example, when experiencing informational overload, listen for a part of the text to get the specific information that is needed.

Figure 9.1. Core Skills for Listening Comprehension

complete their understanding whenever possible. The way we listen will depend on a number of other factors too, such as interest or the speaker. How we listen in interactive listening is also heavily influenced by the context: that is, where and when the interaction takes place, the relationship between the participants, and what is being discussed.

Figure 9.2 presents examples of listening texts and the type of communication associated with each one. The term "text" is used broadly to refer to any piece of discourse associated with an event, including dialogues. A lecture is a text for listening and so is interactive speech. Designing listening tasks based on these communicative events can help learners develop listening competence for real-life communication. We use the term "authentic listening" to refer to listening experiences in the classroom that reflect the purpose, skills, and outcomes of listening in real-life

Texts for Listening Practice	Communicative Events and What Speakers Do
Conversations, talks, interviews	Recount: Retell events or incidents from the past, describing them in chronological order and reflecting on their significance for their listeners.
Narratives, anecdotes, tales	Story-telling: Tell a story formally or informally by explaining the setting, the characters' actions and motives, a problem or crisis they are involved in, and how it is eventually resolved.
Commentaries, explanations, instructions, demonstrations	Language-in-action: Talk about an action as it takes place to provide greater clarity for listeners or add a dramatic effect to an event.
Conversations, interviews, group discussions, forums, talks	Views and perspectives: Give comments and opinions from various perspectives, based on questions asked by listeners or motivated by other communicative purposes.
Expositions and persuasive texts	Debate and argument: Express views, theories, plans, or recommendations from defined positions, typically in a formal or semi-formal situation in order to convince listeners.
Conversations, short exchanges, announcements	Service encounters: Offer and receive goods and services in formal or informal transactions involving one or more people.
Lectures, seminar presentations, talks, group discussions, show-and-tell, class-room instruction	Language, learning, and interaction: Talk about a range of subjects and topics in formal or semi-formal situations within the contexts of academic institutions such as universities and schools, often inviting responses from the listeners.
News reports, documentaries, presentations	Information giving: Present reports, explanations, and descriptions of important events and happenings in order to inform or educate listeners.
Songs, movies, TV, and radio programs	Entertainment and appreciation: Interest, amuse, or inform an audience or individual listeners for their pleasure, appreciation, and relaxation.
Conversations, TV talk shows, counselling, interviews	Problem sharing: Talk about a personal problem or issue so as to get help and understanding from the listeners.

Figure 9.2. Texts for Listening Practice Based on Authentic Communicative Events

Based on Carter & McCarthy, 1997; Burns, Joyce, & Gollin, 1996; Wolvin & Coakley, 1996

communication. For example, teachers can use recordings of texts in a specific genre and identify communicative goals that are typically associated with these one-way listening events to plan listening tasks that work towards these goals. To develop skills for interactive listening in the real world, tasks that include discussions, simulation, and role-play should also be used. Learners will practice their listening through activities that have a degree of communicative authenticity.

To enhance this learning process further, metacognitive instruction can be incorporated into the lesson to develop knowledge about the features of different types of texts in the respective communicative events. When learners become familiar with these features, they can use appropriate strategies for planning, monitoring, and evaluating their listening. In the case of interactive listening, they can respond by predicting what they will hear in the discourse routine. It is advisable to plan listening lessons with a range of texts to ensure that learners have wide exposure to real-life communicative events. Figure 9.2 offers examples of texts that should be considered for such a purpose. The texts are relevant to the contexts of both one-way and interactional listening.

One-way Listening

Selecting Tasks

One-way listening tasks do not require learners to interact with a speaker. The goal is to understand a text they hear according to specified communicative purposes. Two types of listening texts can be used for one-way listening: direct and indirect authentic listening texts. Examples of direct authentic listening texts include lectures, talks, radio broadcasts, podcasts, TV programs, and movies that are aimed at a general audience. In such situations, learners engage directly with the speaker(s): that is to say, they respond to the speaker(s) and the message overtly or covertly because they are the ones being addressed. With indirect authentic listening texts, however, learners play the role of "overhearers" of the conversations and other exchanges in an interaction where they are not a participant.

Regardless of the type of text, there are a number of tasks that learners can do during or immediately after listening in order to achieve specific communicative outcomes. Figure 9.3 presents a selection of one-way listening tasks and the response that learners could make in each task, the listening skills that are practiced, and the expected outcome(s). The tasks are arranged in order of increasing cognitive demands and relative complexity of the tasks. The listening skills highlighted are the main ones that learners are expected to use and which teachers can foster. They do not, however, preclude other skills and strategies that learners can use

Task Type	Listener Behavior and Response	Listening Skills in Focus	Listening Outcomes
Restoration	Listen to a text to compare it with a written version and to correct details in the written text by adding, changing, or deleting words.	Listen for details	An amended written text.
Sorting	Use information in a text to sequence, categorise, or rank items such as jumbled up texts and pictures.	Listen for details	A rearranged sequence of a text or pictures.
Comparison	Identify similarities and differences in the contents of a number of short texts that have a common theme or topic.	Listen for details	A list of similarities or differences.
Matching	Listen to a number of short texts and match each one with with the most appropriate theme given (e.g., friendship, stress, conservation).	Listen for global understanding	Matched themes or topics.
Jigsaw Task	Listen to one part of an original text, memorize the main points and share the information with learners who listen to other parts of the same text in order to understand the entire text.	Listen for main ideas or listen selectively (if learners all listen to the same text but focus on different parts)	A summary of the information heard.
Narrative Completion	Listen to a story with one missing part (e.g., the beginning, the transition, or the	Listen and predict Listen to infer	The beginning, the transition, or the

	ending) and speculate on the contents of the missing part using clues from the text and background knowledge.		conclusion of a text.
Embellishment	Listen to a "bare" text and at each appropriate juncture elaborate on a point or a description by adding interesting and relevant details such as names, words, phrases, and numbers. Use the words to embellish the original text.	Listen for details Listen to infer	Notes on what was added to the text. An embelished oral or written version of the original "bare" text.
Evaluation	Assess the information or message contained in what is heard by checking for accuracies, merits, inconsistencies, and contradictions.	Listen for main ideas Listen and infer	Ranked information; a list based on relative merits.
Reconstruction	Listen and take notes of key content words or key points in a text (e.g., problems, solutions, and recommendations), which are then used to produce a text as close in meaning as possible to the original.	Listen for main ideas Listen for details	An oral or a written text based on the contents of the original. (The structure of the text may vary according to the purpose for which the information is used.)

Figure 9.3. One-Way Listening Tasks, Listener Responses, Skills Practiced, and Task Outcomes

to complete the task. For example, the teacher may begin each task by asking learners to listen to the text once for global understanding before concentrating on the requirements of the task.

Most one-way listening tasks require little teacher intervention once the tasks are planned and the accompanying listening materials, such as worksheets, checklists, and templates for note-taking, are prepared. It is important to ensure that appropriate listening texts are selected so that learners find the task manageable and interesting. Selecting texts that are easy for students may have the short-term benefit of building up their confidence, but in the long term texts with some degree of challenge should be included so that learners also get opportunities to learn to apply listening strategies. A combination of natural and effortless use of listening skills and some effortful processing, facilitated by comprehension strategies, will help learners develop their overall listening competence in the long run. Well-chosen listening texts can also be an important source of language input that can be further exploited after the listening task to enhance overall language acquisition.

Authenticity of response should be a consideration when planning the kind of response elicited from learners. In other words, we ask the question "Is this one of the ways in which people normally respond when listening?" For example, people normally compare the information they hear with something else they have heard, predict the way stories or recounts unfold, improve something that they are working on, look to others to get advice on how to handle a problem, or critically evaluate the merit of something they hear. If we decide to elicit listener responses that are low on authenticity, it is important to articulate why they might be useful for language learners. For example, a popular listener response in many classroom listening activities is asking learners to listen to a song or a news report and fill in the blanks in a copy of the lyrics. The purpose is to get the learners to listen for details as a way to demonstrate understanding. It can be argued that such activities are useful for training learners to focus on details but there should be ways of compensating for this lack of authenticity in a listening task in the overall lesson. One way in which we can create greater authenticity in the overall listening experience of learners is the use of post-listening activities that put the listening outcomes to authentic use.

Listening outcomes should, as far as possible, reflect the ways people use information obtained through listening. Examples include: using the information to draw up a list, incorporating it into a piece of writing or a draft for a presentation, writing a short message, revising a report, editing texts, etc. Once the outcomes have been produced, teachers can encourage learners to evaluate the outcome of their listening by comparing it with those of other students or checking it against a model outcome by a competent user of the language: for example, the teacher's own outcome.

This will also develop the important habit of self-evaluating what they have understood. It is important, however, to avoid situations where learners feel that they are being constantly tested by focusing too much on what they can or cannot do with the listening texts. Teachers should in fact scaffold learner listening during the task. These points apply also to interactional listening tasks; we will return to them later in the chapter when we discuss pre-listening and post-listening activities.

Selecting Texts

One-way listening tasks rely heavily on texts to develop listening competence. It is therefore important that texts are carefully selected for this purpose. As a general principle, it is beneficial to use authentic materials as frequently as possible. Authentic materials for listening are texts that have not been produced or scripted for the purpose of language teaching but are recordings of natural speech taken from everyday sources where speech is produced (Underwood, 1989). Authentic materials for one-way listening can be found in a number of sources, such as videos, radio and television broadcasts, songs, audio recordings, CD ROMs, the internet, and situations in which speech is performed, such as drama and poetry recitals.

Authentic materials are intrinsically interesting because they contain information on current topics and well-known personalities of interest to learners of all ages and backgrounds. This can motivate learners to want to listen (or watch in the case of videotext). Moreover, authentic materials are found in a large variety of language use domains and include a range of speakers whom language learners are likely to encounter in real-life communication. However, natural speech in this context has features that can be both helpful and problematic to language learners. These include hesitations, pauses, fillers, redundancies, a range of accents, and rapid speech rate. For beginning listeners, some of these features may pose too much of a challenge and, therefore, there may still be a need for scripted or "semi-authentic" materials to be used (Rogers & Medley, 1988). These materials contain some degree of authenticity since many of the qualities of natural speech are incorporated, such as normal speech rate, fillers, and repetitions. Scripted speech produced at a normal rate allows students to activate strategies and learn to cope with gaps in comprehension that they may encounter in real life. Speaker pronunciation in these texts is usually clearer, the utterances are better structured, and the text is generally less "messy" than in authentic materials.

Besides authenticity, other points also need to be considered when selecting texts for listening. These are reflected in the seven questions below. The first four questions pertain to the communicative context for the material while the remaining three focus on features in the text:

1. What is the original communicative purpose for the material?

The quickest way to decide whether a text should be considered further is to establish its original purpose. This does not mean, however, that you must have a total match of the original purpose with the listening purpose for the classroom. Knowing what a text is for will give you an idea of whether it will be suitable for your particular group. Should you want to adapt the material for teaching listening, it will also alert you to the things you need to do and the extent of what needs to be done.

2. Who is the intended audience?

It is useful to match the intended audience of the listening text with the profile of your learners because the content and even the style of delivery may be more attractive to one group of listeners than to another. Finding a good fit between the intended audience for a text and a group of language learners will ensure that the learners find their listening task relevant and appropriate. Another point to consider is the presence of any unfamiliar cultural elements. While there is common ground between different groups of people in the world, something that is produced for a group of teenagers in one country, for example, may not necessarily be accepted by their peers in another culture.

3. Who is speaking?

The characteristics of speakers can have a huge influence on L2 listening comprehension. These include speech rate, accent and pronunciation, fluency, clarity, and even gender. It is best to avoid speech that is too fast by the standards of competent speakers while at the same time speakers who speak too slowly, haltingly, or in a monotonous manner should also be avoided. When a task requires learners to play the role of "overhearers," the number of speakers in an interaction should also be a consideration. An audio recording with several speakers may sometimes create a problem for learners who are not able to follow the change in turns, particularly when the voices are quite similar, or when the speakers are speaking fast.

4. What kind of visual support is available?

Visual support can provide useful contextual clues to enhance comprehension through drawing inferences and monitoring understanding. Illustrations, maps, pictures, etc. can also help learners focus their attention on the listening input and predict what they will hear. Not all forms of visual support, however, are useful for learners. TV news reports may provide an example here. It is quite common for TV viewers to watch video footage while listening to a voice-over reporting on details of an incident. Sometimes, what is showing on the screen bears little relation to what is actually said by the reporter. In such situations, the visuals do not provide support for listening and may even be a source of confusion for non-proficient listeners.

5. Is the level of language appropriate?

Ideally, the text you choose should be at a level that your students will be able to understand minimally at a global level. It should also present some challenges that will push them to use listening strategies in order to achieve the listening outcomes. The level of acceptable difficulty relates to the task. A difficult text can be manageable for learners if all they have to do is listen for global understanding. A text that is normally considered easy could be used for a more complex task, which requires not merely listening for details or main points, but also eliciting judgments or evaluations from the listener. In other words, learners have to listen critically, using high-level skills such as inferencing to listen between the lines. This can be made more challenging by including other factors that influence listening and its outcomes, such as listening to something from the perspectives of people in different roles. Avoid texts for which learners have very little background knowledge, which contain a number of unfamiliar lexical items, or which are spoken in an unfamiliar accent. Texts that contain such linguistic challenges, but on a familiar topic, can be used to practice skills such as listen for main points, listen for global understanding, or listen and predict. Of course, listener processing of input can also be supported by relevant preparatory activities before the listening task. As a rule of thumb, there should not be more than one aspect of a text that learners will find challenging.

6. Is the length (duration) of the text appropriate and realistic for the learners?

One way to assess whether the length of a text is suitable is to consider the listening purpose and the intended listening outcomes. For example, if learners have to obtain detailed information, then a long text will not be appropriate because it will require prolonged attention to details and this can be tiring. On the other hand, if the purpose is to produce a short summary, learners will be listening for main points and global understanding, and they can use different strategies to enhance their understanding. If a long text is particularly relevant to the lesson objectives, you may consider segmenting it for use with a sequence of listening tasks in a lesson. Very short texts (less than a minute) present a different set of challenges. Some learners need time to "tune in" to a topic and part of this "tuning in" involves getting the ears used to the way the speaker sounds. Thus, if the text is not long enough for this "tuning in" to take place, learners may end up feeling frustrated.

7. Is the text really meant for listening?

This may seem like an odd question to ask, but in reality many written texts meant for reading find their way into listening classes; this does a great disservice to L2 listeners. Texts meant to be read silently tend to be high on content or lexically dense. Clauses in spoken language, on the other hand, tend to have fewer content words (e.g., nouns and adjectives) and more function words (e.g., prepositions, auxiliary verbs, articles), thus allowing meaning to build up over more words and utterances. Speech is organized differently: spoken grammar differs from the grammar of written language (Carter & McCarthy, 1997). Instead of multiple clausal embeddings, the coordinator "and" is used frequently to link ideas together. These features of spoken language are mainly due to limited cognitive capacities to process and produce speech, but they are in fact helpful to listeners who are also limited by similar constraints while processing spoken input. As a general principle, therefore, written texts that are meant to be read silently should not be read aloud or recorded for learners to practice their listening. Unlike the printed word, listening input is transient and not reiterative under normal circumstances. If written texts are used, select those with features of the spoken language or adapt them so that more features of speech are included to facilitate listening.

Interactive Listening Tasks

Interactive listening, as noted in Chapter 2, requires learners to engage in face-to-face interactions where they often alternate between the roles of listener and speaker. As listeners, learners will have opportunities to seek clarifications and improve their comprehension in other ways. Interactive listening tasks normally involve talk with a broad range of purposes of an interactional or transactional nature (Brown & Yule, 1983). The purpose of interactional talk is to create and maintain relationships between participants. The turns are generally short and more equally distributed among the participants. Transactional talk, on the other hand, focuses on giving and receiving information; the speaker who is giving the information does most of the talking while the listener may ask questions or give comments during or after listening. In some situations, both types of talk occur in the same interaction, but in all situations the learner alternates between the role of listener and speaker.

Figure 9.4 presents a selection of interactive listening tasks that require learners to work in pairs or small groups. The tasks are based on information- and opinion-gap activities that are commonly used in speaking classes. Speaking is integrated with listening in these tasks, but the emphasis is on listening, a dimension that is usually overlooked in speaking classes. These activities can be used to practice both skills as long as the teacher and the learner recognize that the listening skills need to be made explicit. The types of listener behavior and response as well as expected outcomes are highlighted. In addition to core comprehension skills, reception skills are important because the listening event involves face-to-face communication. Consideration must be given to how the tasks can be delivered in such a way that learners understand the importance of using constructive strategies to enhance their comprehension and interaction. For example, in the first two tasks, which are essentially information-gap activities, teachers must insist that the learners not show anything in writing or diagrammatic forms to their partners or group members. They should say everything only once to encourage other learners to use strategies to ask them to explain, repeat, or rephrase what they say. These ground rules create the need for learners to interact with one another and practice the use of important reception skills.

Interactive listening tasks reflect the contextual conditions under which people normally communicate: there is a clear purpose and the participants' goal is to ensure that meaning is understood and necessary information is shared successfully. In social interactions, participants may also work towards greater solidarity and mutual understanding among themselves. In interactive listening tasks, listening and speaking skills are practiced in an integrated manner: learners need to cooperate with one another to accomplish the task. Typical tasks include activities with a gap in knowledge between participants. For example, learners working in pairs need to obtain information from each other to complete their own understanding of a topic or they need to find out the opinion of other participants concerning an issue. The key to purposeful listening is a gap in information or opinion that can sufficiently interest and motivate learners to want to fill it through meaningful cooperation. Many existing speaking tasks in communicative teaching classrooms can be used for this purpose if they are carefully selected to meet the profile of learners in a class. To avoid situations where listening is overshadowed by speaking, it is important that listening skills and strategies necessary for these tasks are highlighted or pre-taught to remind learners that listening well is just as important as speaking fluently.

Developing Process-Based Lessons from Listening Tasks

We have concentrated so far on how to design listening tasks that encourage learners to process meaning in one-way and interactive listening. While an interesting task is an important component of a good listening lesson, it has to be complemented by other process-based learning activities that support learners in processing input for meaning. In addition, activities that apply, synthesize, and extend the knowledge they have

Task	Listener Behavior and Response in Focus	Listening Skills and Reception Strategies	Listening Outcomes
Creative Dictation*	Each student has an incomplete version of the same text. To complete it, they listen to each other's dictation of the text and complete the gaps in their incomplete version by writing down the missing words. Listeners ask each other for clarification and repetition where necessary.	Listen selectively Listen for details	Clarified understandings of all involved, leading to the production of a restored and complete text.
Description	Each student has a drawing or written information that his/her partner or group members do not have. They listen to each other's descriptions to complete their goal for listening. Listeners must ask each other for clarification and repetition when necessary.	Ask for clarifications Ask for repetition Paraphrase to check understanding	Clarified understandings of all involved, leading to production of the pictures, maps, sketches, ranked objects, and information.
Simulation	Students form small groups and take on an assigned role in a simulated situation to discuss a problem or issue. They listen to each member's views closely, make notes, and respond to views. A moderator is assigned to ask questions, elicit views, challenge assumptions, and clarify understanding.	Listen for main points Listen and predict Listen and infer	A list of views and suggestions or a set of notes following a problem-solution pattern. A presentation of recommendations made by the fictitious group.
Discussion	Students form small discussion groups to plan something or suggest solutions to a problem.	Ask for clarifications	A list of views or a set of notes

* Adapted from Davis & Rinvolucri (1988).

	Description	Skills Practiced	Listening Outcomes
	They listen to each member's views closely, make notes, and respond to views. A moderator is assigned to ask questions, elicit views, challenge assumptions, and clarify understanding.	Ask for repetition Paraphrase to check understanding Send back-channelling cues	following a problem-solution pattern. A mind map that shows the interconnected views of members in a group. A summary.
Role-play Interview	Students work in pairs to role-play an interviewer and an interviewee on a selected topic. The interviewer asks questions and listens to the responses of the interviewee. The roles are reversed. This can also be conducted over a "live audience" in class. At the end of the interview, members in the audience ask the interviewee more questions.		Notes on views on a selected topic. A written or an oral summary.
Presentation or Debate	Students listen to a presentation by the teacher or classmates, or a class debate, and make notes. They prepare some questions to ask the presenter at the end of the presentation and seek further clarifications if necessary.	Listen for main points Listen and predict Listen and infer Ask for clarifications	A set of notes. A list of questions. A mind map of information. A summary.

Figure 9.4. Interactive Listening Tasks, Listener Responses, Skills Practiced, and Listening Outcomes

gained are needed to make listening more purposeful and directed. Last but not least, process-based lessons should include metacognitive activities through which learners deepen their understanding of how to facilitate and improve listening comprehension. What kinds of activities are useful to achieve these aims? We now recommend a number of activities for different purposes that can be carried out before and after listening.

Pre-listening Activities

Pre-listening activities are carried out before an actual listening task to prepare learners for listening. The rationale is based on our understanding of how prior knowledge or schema about facts and language can assist individuals in processing any kind of information encountered. Pre-listening activities retrieve existing knowledge and create new knowledge to help learners process listening input more efficiently when they eventually encounter it during the listening task. These activities have three main functions:

1. Language Orientation

Pre-listening activities with a linguistic function can prepare learners to process the language in the text by anticipating the occurrence of these words. This can help to reduce learner anxiety. One of the problems that many learners report is the presence of unfamiliar words and phrases; another is the challenge of recognizing words they know in print but not in spoken form. Pre-listening activities can prepare learners for these linguistic challenges to make word recognition and lexical segmentation easier. This will make perception and parsing more efficient during listening.

2. Knowledge Generation

Because listening is an active and constructive process, having the necessary background knowledge will greatly enhance interpretation of the text. Pre-listening activities with a knowledge orientation serve to activate relevant schema or create opportunities for learners to acquire more knowledge needed for the task; this facilitates top-down processing. Such activities enhance the efficiency of the utilization phase during listening, enabling learners to achieve the communicative outcomes planned for the listening tasks.

3. Strategy Activation

For many learners, listening is a conscious and strategic process, especially if the texts are not within their linguistic or schematic grasp. Process-oriented activities help learners plan and prepare for the skills and strategies they will need for the task and the type of text. The prediction activities in the metacognitive pedagogical sequence are examples of strategy activation activities.

Figure 9.5 presents a number of generic activities that can be carried out by learners before they engage in the listening task. These activities focus

Activity	What Learners Do	Interaction
Brainstorming	Think of words and phrases associated with the topic; teacher writes them on the board or screen.	C
Mind-mapping	Create a map of all ideas interconnected with the topic by using words and, if necessary, pictures.	I, P
Discussion	Based on prompt questions from the teacher, discuss possible responses or discuss an idea or issue that is related to the topic of the listening text.	P, G
Games	Play word games or language games where the responses can be linked to the meaning or language in the listening text.	C
Questions	Draw up a list of questions to ask about the topic.	I, P
Reading	Read a short text provided by the teacher that is based on the topic of the listening text, and note down ideas and vocabulary that can help with the listening task.	I, P
Pictures	Study photos, maps, diagrams, etc. that are linked to the content of, or theme in, the listening text.	G, C
Research	Conduct simple research on the internet about the topic of the listening text or the situation in which the topic may be discussed.	I, P

Figure 9.5. Language-Oriented and Knowledge-Oriented Activities for Pre-listening Learning

P = pair work; G = group work; C = teacher-led class work; I = independent work

Adapted from Goh, 2002a

focus mainly on language and knowledge aspects of the task. The types of interaction that support the aims of each activity are also included: pair work (P), group work (G), teacher-led class work (C), or independent work (I).

Post-listening Activities

Post-listening activities, as the name suggests, are carried out after a listening task to extend the communicative listening outcomes. These activities are useful for increasing the authenticity of the overall listening task, particularly when the listener response is not something that people would normally do when listening, such as filling in blanks. Post-listening activities can also provide an opportunity for learners to notice specific language in the input they heard, thus helping to facilitate their overall acquisition of the target language. Opportunities for reflection and evaluation can also be included as post-listening activities. These uses of post-listening activities are elaborated below.

Meaning Elaboration

Listening is meaningful when there is a purpose for doing it. This purpose is usually related to end goals that we hope to achieve with the knowledge and information that we acquire through listening. Based on this principle meaning elaboration activities enable learners to apply, synthesize, or evaluate what they have learned by organizing and presenting their thoughts through other modes of language use, such as writing or speaking. From a language development perspective, this gives learners opportunities to develop their writing and speaking skills at the same time. Listening texts can also be an important source of information and knowledge for learners, particularly those who are learning a language through the academic content of a course. Through post-listening activities, learners can be asked to do further research on the content of the listening text by reading other online or print materials. This helps learners develop their reading skills in a focused and meaningful way, and it allows teachers to recycle language and concepts in the development of another language skill.

Language Analysis

Listening gives learners access to an important source of language input that can contribute to their overall L2 acquisition. Although listening to carefully selected texts during a listening task is useful, it is insufficient for deeper language learning to occur. This is because learners tend to have limited processing capacities and they will mainly focus on meaning and not on language forms (Skehan, 1998). Focusing on language is best done after the listening task to allow learners to shift their attention and other cognitive resources from meaning to various aspects of language, such as grammar, vocabulary, and pronunciation. Learners can be asked to focus on words that they are unable to recognize, new or unfamiliar vocabulary items, or phonological modifications of words as they occur in connected speech, as well as grammatical features, structure, and organization of different types of spoken text. In other words, after learners have listened to the text for the required number of times, teachers can "mine" the text for language forms and features that will be helpful for language development. They can do this by asking learners to study the transcript of the text, for example.

Evaluation and Planning

This type of post-listening activity has a clear metacognitive emphasis. It is important for learners to reflect on their listening experience to understand what they have done well and what they might need to improve. Similar to process-based pre-listening activities, evaluation and planning activities at the post-listening stage are meant to enhance understanding of the listening process. Reflecting on their listening experience helps learners find ways to understand their problems, direct future learning, and manage any negative emotions that may arise from the experience.

The timing of post-listening activity depends on at least two factors. The first is the length of lesson which varies. A post-listening activity may be carried out immediately after the listening task, continued as homework, or carried out at the start of another lesson. The second factor is the nature and demands of the activity. Some of the activities presented in Figure 9.6 can be readily completed within a short time while others of a fairly substantial nature will require a great deal more work. If necessary, the more demanding activities can be carried out as a separate lesson of a larger unit of work. This should fit in particularly well with language programs that emphasize the integration of all four language skills. Figure 9.6 presents a number of post-listening activities for elaborating meaning and focusing on language.

Lessons that Promote Authentic Listening and Metacognitive Awareness

Now that all the components needed for a lesson are in place, what does a teacher need to do to design a lesson? For teachers who have to teach from prescribed materials, how can they adapt their materials to ensure that the lesson or the unit of work addresses the various aspects of listening that

Activity	What Learners Do	Interaction
Personalization	Relate contents from a listening text (e.g., stories, poems, discussion of an issue) to their own experience through writing or an informal group sharing.	I, P
Writing	Write short texts such as letters, emails, messages, or diary entries, or longer ones such as summaries, reviews, reports, or expository essays.	I, P
Oral Presentation/ Forum	Use the information from a listening text or the outcomes of a listening task to prepare an oral presentation or a discussion forum.	G, C
Dramatization/ Role-Play	Enact parts of a narrative, recount for an audience, or role-play the parts with a partner.	G, C
Joint Construction	Share information from the listening text with another person who does not have it (e.g., in jigsaw listening) in order to complete a joint task.	P, G
Café Talk	Move from group to group to share listening outcomes (e.g., outcomes of simulation or discussion tasks of their group).	G
Publication	Publish the written outcomes of selected listening tasks for dissemination to other students in the institution or a wider online group.	I, P
Perception	Examine the spoken text for phonological features that influence the bottom-up processing of a text.	G, C
Transcription	Listen to the text again and transcribe a section of it for further analysis or for problem identification.	I, P
Vocabulary Building	Review selected vocabulary items from the transcript of a listening text and use selected words in a related writing or speaking task.	I, P

Figure 9.6. Meaning Elaboration and Language-Analysis Activities for Post-listening Learning

P = pair work; G = group work; C = teacher-led class work; I = independent work

Adapted from Goh, 2002a

have just been discussed? Normally teachers would start by determining the skills and strategies that they want learners to practice and then plan a lesson to practice those skills. Another common approach is to select a text, decide what to do with it, and plan activities that can be used to achieve that purpose. While these two approaches are useful in their own ways, we would like to propose an alternative way of planning that starts with the communication goal for listening in mind. The goal can be aligned to the theme of a unit of work or a higher instructional objective for the unit. We start by asking the following questions: Why do learners have to listen to a text or participate in a planned interaction in this lesson? How will they be using the information and knowledge obtained through listening? How does this knowledge and information contribute to a larger communication goal?

By beginning with the listening outcome and the communication goal, we focus on creating an authentic listening experience for learners. Examples of listening outcomes are found in Figures 9.3 and 9.4, while examples of communication goals are found in meaning elaboration activities used after listening (see Figure 9.6). Next, we consider how this experience can be realized through appropriate listening tasks and supported by pre-listening activities. It is important that teachers share with learners what the expected outcomes and communication goals are. Listening lessons should not be a mystery that unravels with each activity because we may lose learners along the way. Those who encounter problems initially may become disheartened and stop engaging with the task. Others may lose interest because they do not see the point of the activities. On the other hand, when learners know why they are listening and how the information and understanding derived from listening can be helpful for achieving a larger goal, they become more engaged in the task and may even seek help with their comprehension. In addition, learners develop better task knowledge as they become more aware of the nature and demands of each activity and more strategic in the way they achieve the final goal for listening.

The term "lesson" is used here to refer to any coherent unit of learning activities that engages learners in a systematic and principled manner, carried out over an appointed duration in a day. The duration may vary, however, according to different learning contexts and requirements. Figure 9.7 shows the process of designing a listening lesson, comprising eight stages, starting from the listening outcome and the communication goal for the lesson.

Teachers who do not have the opportunity or the need to design their own lessons because they teach from prescribed materials can refer to Figure 9.8. It contains a list of questions to ask in order to evaluate the degree of authenticity in the listening experience that the lesson or unit of work offers learners. These questions follow the normal sequence of activities expected in a language course book, starting with the pre-

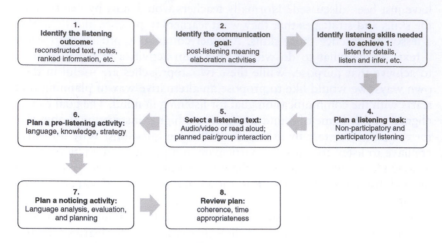

Figure 9.7. Designing an Authentic Listening Lesson

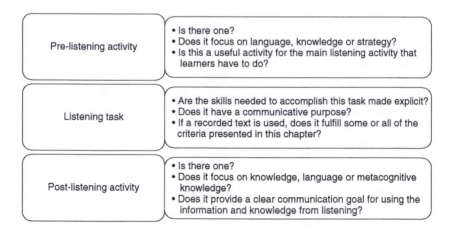

Figure 9.8 Evaluating the Authenticity of Listening Experiences in Prescribed Materials

listening activity. If the answer is "No" to two or more of the questions in Figure 9.8, chances are you will need to adapt the materials if you wish to apply some of the principles outlined in this chapter. To adapt materials and include task-based and process-based elements in the lesson or unit of work in the course book, you will find the sequence presented in Figure 9.7 useful. For example, if a unit in the book does not have a pre-listening activity, you can include a strategy activation activity so that learners do some predicting and planning beforehand. You may also need to include a communicative outcome for the listening task to make the experience more authentic and purposeful for your students.

To conclude our discussion of planning a task- and process-based lesson, we present three lesson outlines to demonstrate how the different components can be organized into coherent wholes. These outlines can be adapted for learners of various age groups by varying the listening text, task complexity, and support given to learners. Figure 9.9 shows a one-way listening lesson. Since it requires some dramatization, the lesson may be more suited for a group of adolescent learners than for adult learners. The outline can also be used with young learners if the story is suited to their level and the teacher offers plenty of help and support in planning for the dramatization. For adult learners who may be more inhibited, the post-listening activity can be a personalization task such as writing a response to the short story or short movie, which can then be compiled and published with other responses from the class.

Figure 9.10 shows an outline for an interactive listening lesson. It is aimed at lower proficiency learners and includes many stages where learners are prepared and supported for listening and interaction. The interaction is structured and predictable, allowing learners to prepare for what they can expect to hear from the other participant in the interaction. The teacher can also help them with language that accompanies strategy use. For example, learners are expected to ask the speaker for clarification or repetition, so the teacher can teach some useful language for expressing such requests before the task begins.

Finally, Figure 9.11 demonstrates how one-way listening and interactive listening tasks can be integrated in a single lesson. This plan will work with a group of fairly proficient learners. For groups of learners who need more time to complete the activities, the post-listening activity may be postponed to the following class.

In all three lesson outlines, the focus is on the use of tasks and pre- and post-listening activities to create authentic listening experiences for learners. The metacognitive dimension of the lesson, however, must not be overlooked. Pre- and post-listening phases of a lesson can also offer opportunities for metacognitive development by including activities that help to activate strategy use for comprehension and encourage reflections on learning. These types of metacognitive activities do not have to be included in every lesson but they should be done regularly.

Summary

Teaching is the process by which novices learn a skill or acquire knowledge with the help of expert input, scaffolding, and guidance. Task-based lessons with a process orientation teach listening through a sequence of activities that prepare learners to listen, construct, and monitor their

---

Lesson Outline

Listening outcome(s): Write a short ending of a story heard
Communication goal: To dramatize a story with an original ending for the class
Listening purpose: To listen to a story, understand its theme and plot development in order to provide an original ending
Listening skills: Listen for global understanding, listen for main points, listen and predict
Task knowledge: Structure of a narrative
Listening text: Recorded short story of about 5–6 minutes in duration
Lesson duration: 120 minutes
Proficiency level: Intermediate

Lesson Phases and Learning Activities

Introduction	Explanation of the listening outcome, communication goals, and learning goals of the listening lesson.
Pre-listening	Questions: Make a list of questions to ask about the story that the students will hear, based on title or other clues provided, such as pictures.
Listening Task	Narrative completion: Speculate about the ending of the story based on all other parts that are heard.

    a. Students listen to a short story or watch a short film.
    b. Students work in pairs and discuss what they think would happen (i.e., how a problem is resolved and what the characters think and do after that).
    c. Students write the ending and read it aloud to the rest of the class.
    d. The class compares all the endings and votes for the one they think is the most plausible or the most creative.
    e. The class listens to or watches the ending of the story and, in groups, compares the ending with their own version and identifies the one that is closest to the original.

Post-listening Task	Dramatization: Selected students enact part of the story that they have listened to or the alternate ending they have created. The class compares the performance of the various groups and selects the group(s) with the best ending and the best performance.
Closure or Extension Activity	Listening diary: Students write an entry in their listening diary to describe their experiences and lessons learned about listening, predicting, and working with others.

Figure 9.9. Outline for a One-Way Listening Lesson

Lesson Outline

Listening outcome(s): Clarified understandings leading to the production of a restored text
Communication goal: To share information with another student in order to obtain all the missing details in a text
Listening purpose: To listen to specific parts that are missing in the copy of song lyrics
Listening skills: Listen for global understanding, listen for details, ask for repetition
Task knowledge: The role of reception strategies in interactive listening
Listening text: A copy of lyrics for a song; a recording of the song
Lesson duration: 60 minutes
Proficiency level: Lower-intermediate

Lesson Phases and Learning Activities

Introduction Explanation of the listening outcome, communication goals, and learning goals of the listening lesson.

Pre-listening Mind-map: Create a map of all ideas interconnected with the topic by using words and, if necessary, pictures.
a. Students are given the title of the song.
b. They draw a mind-map to show all the ideas (in words and pictures) that they associate with the title.
c. They pass their mind-maps around to show other students.

Listening Task Creative dictation: Each student has an incomplete version of the same text in a handout. To complete it, they listen to each other's dictation of the text and complete the gaps in their incomplete version of the text by writing down the missing words.
a. Students listen to the song being played once.
b. They tell a partner what they understand the song to be about.
c. The teacher checks their global understanding and discusses with them how they arrived at that understanding.
d. Next students work in pairs as A and B.
e. A is given a version of the lyrics with a number of missing words and phrases.
f. B is given another version that contains the missing items from A's version but has other missing words and phrases.
g. Students first practice reading aloud the text they have. They check with the teacher the

	pronunciation of unfamiliar words. They can also use the dictionary to look up meanings of words. h. When they are ready, the students take turns to dictate their text to each other. Whenever they reach a blank space, they stop and let the other person dictate what is in their text. They may ask their partners to repeat as many times as they want. i. When they have finished, the teacher reads the entire set of lyrics aloud for the students to check what they have noted down. j. Students can ask the teacher to clarify or repeat or even to spell unfamiliar words for them. k. They listen to the song again and follow along by reading their completed lyrics.
Post-listening Task	Personalization and reflection: Students listen to the song without looking at the lyrics. After that, they write, in their listening diary, their personal response to the song and what they think of the listening task. They also write down three to five new words that they learned from the song.
Closure or Extension Activity	Each student selects a song to share with the class in the next lesson. They prepare copies of the lyrics, bring a recording of the song to class and play it for everyone's enjoyment.

Figure 9.10. Outline for an Interactive Listening Lesson

comprehension with the help of peers and teachers. Use of a variety of one-way and interactive listening tasks presented in this chapter can help learners focus on listening as a communication and learning tool. The overall aim of using the set of listening tasks, pre- and post-listening activities, and metacognitive activities is to facilitate the *teaching* of listening and avoid a singular focus on a demonstration of comprehension by the learners. These activities raise learners' awareness, activate their prior knowledge, enhance their language knowledge, and integrate their understanding with other meaningful language tasks. By doing that, teachers are in fact showing learners how to use internal and external resources to improve their comprehension and overall listening development. Like the metacognitive pedagogical sequence, a process-based lesson developed from communicative tasks can demystify the process of learner listening. When learners become aware of it, they will become more

Lesson Outline

Listening outcome(s): Prepare two sets of notes
Communication goal: To share information gleaned from a talk and original ideas in order to collate information for a class forum
Listening purpose(s):
- To listen to a talk on a topic and then share the information with other students who have not had had a chance to hear it
- To listen to original ideas from each group member in order to augment the information obtained earlier

Listening skills: Listen for main points, listen for details, listen to infer
Task knowledge: The structure of an expository text
Listening text: A five-minute video recording of a talk on the same topic (four different talks for four different groups).
Lesson duration: 180 minutes
Proficiency level: Upper-Intermediate

Lesson Phases and Learning Activities

Introduction	Explanation of the listening outcome, communication goals, and learning goals of the listening lesson.
Pre-listening	Reading: Read a short text on the issue that will be discussed by speakers in the recorded talks. Planning: Use a self-directed listening guide to write down possible challenges that may arise during listening, and consider the strategies that can be used to cope with these challenges and facilitate comprehension.
	a. Learners are given a short passage to read so as to create or activate the necessary background knowledge for listening.
	b. They identify unfamiliar or key vocabulary items associated with the topic.
	c. They also prepare for their listening by activating their knowledge of some useful strategies to cope with potential challenges.
Listening Task 1	Jigsaw: Learners are divided into groups. Each member listens individually to one part of a text, memorizes or makes notes of the main points, and shares the information with others in the group. Together they have the complete pieces of the "puzzle" to construct their understanding of what the text is about. This task is slightly modified below:
	a. Students are divided into four groups to watch the video recording of a talk meant for their respective group.

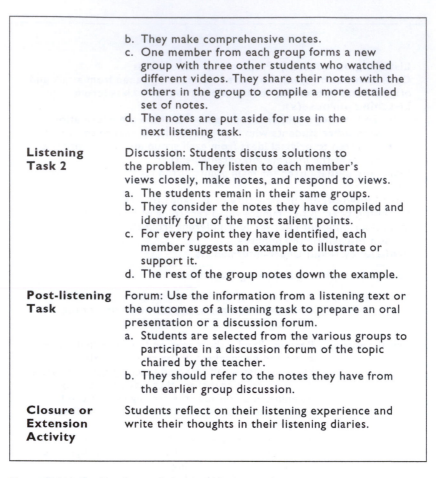

	b. They make comprehensive notes. c. One member from each group forms a new group with three other students who watched different videos. They share their notes with the others in the group to compile a more detailed set of notes. d. The notes are put aside for use in the next listening task.
Listening Task 2	Discussion: Students discuss solutions to the problem. They listen to each member's views closely, make notes, and respond to views. a. The students remain in their same groups. b. They consider the notes they have compiled and identify four of the most salient points. c. For every point they have identified, each member suggests an example to illustrate or support it. d. The rest of the group notes down the example.
Post-listening Task	Forum: Use the information from a listening text or the outcomes of a listening task to prepare an oral presentation or a discussion forum. a. Students are selected from the various groups to participate in a discussion forum of the topic chaired by the teacher. b. They should refer to the notes they have from the earlier group discussion.
Closure or Extension Activity	Students reflect on their listening experience and write their thoughts in their listening diaries.

Figure 9.11. Outline for an Integrated Listening Lesson

confident, motivated, and skillful L2 learners, as research has shown. Teachers working with prescribed materials can apply the discussions in this chapter to adapt their materials in order to make listening a more authentic experience and promote the development of metacognitive knowledge and strategy use.

Discussion Questions and Tasks

1. Do you think learners' listening and metacognitive knowledge is affected by whether they are listening to direct authentic listening texts or indirect authentic listening texts? Explain.
2. Here is a list of possible listener responses for the two sets of listening tasks presented in the chapter.

(a) Select a few of the responses and categorize them according to their degree of authenticity and cognitive demand in the appropriate sections of Figure 9.12.

(b) Do you think there is a place for listener responses that do not reflect authentic communication? Discuss your views with another course participant.

1. Mark/check items in pictures/diagrams
2. Match pictures/diagrams with text
3. Rearrange pictures
4. Complete pictures/diagrams
5. Draw pictures/diagrams
6. Label pictures/diagrams
7. Carry out actions/instructions
8. Take dictation
9. Separate main ideas from less relevant
10. Express opinion
11. Offer recommendations and solutions
12. Frame appropriate questions
13. Summarize information
14. Reconstruct original message/text
15. Paraphrase original message/text
16. Edit text
17. Restore text
18. Trace a route
19. Complete texts with long gaps
20. Elaborate by quantifying or qualifying
21. Predict the next part
22. Take notes
23. Complete grids/tables
24. Complete texts with one-word gaps
25. Identify true/false
26. Identify factual and opinion statements
27. Spot mistakes/differences/inconsistencies
28. Confirm pre-listening speculations
29. Identify specific items of information, e.g., content, grammar items, discourse markers
30. Identify attitudes/relationships/mood

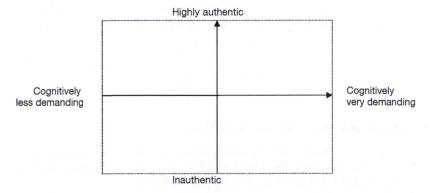

Figure 9.12. Degree of Authenticity and Cognitive Demand of Listener Responses

3. Select an interactive listening task and identify the type of reception strategies (see Chapter 2, Table 2.2) that learners might need to help them participate effectively in the interaction. Prepare a list of useful expressions (in order of formality) that you can teach learners before they begin the listening task.

4. Read the following paragraph that has been abstracted from a newspaper report. The text contains many features that are typical of written texts. It is lexically dense, contains complex grammar structures and each sentence is long. If a teacher were to read this text aloud in a listening task, the linguistic features just mentioned would affect processing of the information. In other words, it is not a "listenable" text for the language classroom. How would you edit this text to make it more like a spoken text so that the listening experience for the students can be a more authentic one?

Heavy snowfalls forced some of Europe's busiest airports to close and wreaked havoc on roads and railways on Wednesday as an unreasonable cold snap swept the continent, claiming at least 15 lives. Transport chaos hit the whole of the continent as the snow spread, and Britain—shivering in the earliest widespread snowfalls of winter since 1993—was one of the countries worst affected. Part of the motorway orbiting London, one of the busiest cities in Europe, was shut and there were severe delays on north–south routes, while serious accidents were reported on the main road between Prague and the eastern Czech city of Brno.

---

5. Select a unit of work with a listening component from a course book. Evaluate the material based on the questions suggested in Figure 9.8. Suggest how you might adapt the materials, if necessary, so that the listening lesson will promote metacognitive development as well as provide an authentic listening experience for the students.

6. Based on the structure of a lesson outline presented in this chapter, prepare a lesson for a group of learners of your choice. Where possible, include more details about the text and the task used for this lesson.

Suggestions for Further Reading

Morley, J. (2001). Aural comprehension instruction: Principles and practices. In M. Celce-Murcia (Ed.), *Teaching English as a Second or Foreign Language* (3rd ed.) (pp. 81–106). Boston, MA: Heinle & Heinle.

In this chapter, Morley gives a summary of learner listening. Of particular interest is her discussion of the "Listen-and-Do" format for listening activities and the outcomes or objectives for real-world listening.

Skehan, P. (2003). Task-based instruction. *Language Teaching*, 36, 1–14.

This article gives the theoretical basis for task-based instruction, outlines research perspectives, discusses approaches to sequencing activities in task-based lessons, and offers insights into practical implementations of tasks within language teaching.

Underwood, M. (1989). *Teaching listening*. Harlow: Longman.

In Chapter 8, Underwood compares and considers the use of both recorded material and "live" presentations by teachers and students as a basis for listening comprehension work. Chapter 9 makes a case for the use of authentic and "near authentic" materials, and discusses the usefulness of such materials, even for beginning learners.

Chapter 10

Projects for Extensive Listening

Scenario

Mr. Williams believes in the role of listening in language acquisition and is convinced that his class of Korean freshman university students needs regular engagement with comprehensible input in order to develop their English further. He also thinks that learners should listen to authentic texts so they are better prepared for the natural speech they will encounter outside of the classroom. Because these learners do not have many opportunities to listen to English, Mr. Williams decides to set up some resources for them to practice listening on their own. He sets about designing a small project that will encourage these learners to listen to a wide variety of texts regularly on their own. The project is a listening resource package that contains links to a variety of internet audio and video texts that learners can listen to free of charge. To develop their metacognitive awareness of the listening process, he has included the use of a listening journal that encourages learners to assess different stages of their listening process.

Based on past experience, Mr. Williams knows that providing learners with resources alone is not enough and he wants to improve the quality of their independent listening experiences as well. He wants his learners to take an active role in regulating their efforts at learning to listen outside class and to be motivated to do so without any pressure from him. Last but not least, he wants them to enjoy their listening experiences. To help these learners, Mr. Williams teaches them listening strategies in class and encourages them to try these strategies when listening on their own. He also includes perception exercises as post-listening activities whenever possible.

Mr. Williams decides to try out this extensive listening project for two months. He prepares a schedule for the learners to listen on their own every day. In addition to writing journal entries twice per week, he sets up an online discussion forum where the learners can share their reviews of different listening texts with one another.

Pre-reading Reflection

1. Are Mr. Williams' concerns about his students' lack of exposure to listening in English justified? Explain your views. How will the projects facilitate the language acquisition of his students?
2. Do you think language learners will listen to a wide variety of texts on their own? What would motivate them? What would hinder their participation?
3. How long do you think projects such as this should take? What would contribute to their success?

Introduction

Language learners who want to improve their listening proficiency often want to engage in L2 listening experiences beyond the classroom. They exploit listening resources available outside the classroom, such as self-access materials and the media, to increase their exposure to the spoken language. This practice is called "extensive listening." Although extensive listening is recognized as important by teachers and learners alike, not every learner derives the same amount of benefit and satisfaction from it. While some learners enjoy listening to the target language on their own, others find the routine monotonous and become discouraged when they do not see improvement. Some may also find the listening resources difficult as they struggle with problems such as speaker accent or insufficient background knowledge.

This problem stems from a lack of structure and guidance in extensive listening activities. Students are left to their own devices, quite literally speaking, to practice listening after class, and many continue to struggle with pre-existing listening problems. Findings from a survey of 118 ESL learners illustrated this (Goh, 2002c). While nearly 100 percent of the learners said they had a plan for listening practice, only 18 percent said they followed their plan closely. Although many of them said they practiced listening by talking with fluent English speakers, only 16 percent said they did this frequently, even though they lived in an environment where English was widely spoken. The learners did not focus on developing specific skills, and less than half paid any attention to the linguistic features of the text, thus missing opportunities to use listening strategies.Interestingly, most of the learners said they would persevere in order to improve their listening and were content to build up their listening proficiency gradually. The learners, however, reported that they some-times felt discouraged because of a lack of tangible progress. There is great value in learners practicing their listening on their own with differ-ent types of materials, but this may be inadequate for success. There is much that teachers can do to facilitate extensive listening practice.

In this chapter, we discuss how regular extensive listening practice can become more relevant and outcome-directed by embedding more structure and teacher scaffolding into a number of project tasks. Like the project in the opening scenario, the suggested listening projects will encourage learners to listen more frequently and also develop their metacogni-tive knowledge and strategy use individually and collectively. Carefully designed projects will benefit weaker learners who need to increase their exposure to listening texts and improve their processing skills at their own pace; and they increase metacognitive awareness about L2 listening. More advanced learners also benefit from engaging in authentic listen-ing tasks beyond the classroom to further develop their listening ability. The suggested listening projects can help learners deepen their under-standing of listening, use listening and learning strategies, and at the same time practice their perception and interpretation skills. Each project is a set of systematically planned, process-based activities in which learners work individually and with their peers to listen to the target language for communicative purposes and to achieve specific outcomes. The projects provide learners with the direction and focus that are often lacking in extensive listening that learners do on their own.

Principles for Planning Extensive Listening Projects

There are two kinds of extensive listening practice. In typical individual practice, learners access different kinds of listening resources to supple-ment their input of spoken text. Specially designed projects, the second kind, integrate listening practice with elements of metacognitive instruc-tion. A listening project is composed of a task that requires learners to plan and work towards definite listening outcomes and to work collab-oratively with others over a period of time. The projects proposed in this chapter are based on a metacognitive approach. They are also based on three principles that are important for extensive listening: variety, frequency, and repetition.

Variety

Learners should listen to as many different types of authentic listen-ing texts as possible, on a wide variety of themes and topics. Types of texts include narratives, recounts, information, reports, instructional or procedural texts, expository or argumentative texts, and conversations. This will enable learners to become familiar with the way each type of text is structured. This knowledge can greatly facilitate processing and understanding of similar types of speech in real-life listening. A variety of themes and topics is equally important because learners acquire vocabulary through different content. It is natural that learners prefer to stay within their comfort zone by selecting materials that they find interesting and easy to comprehend, but this does not help for long-term listening and language development.

Frequency

Listening, like many other skills, needs to be practiced frequently, in manageable and realistic chunks of time. Learners should be advised to follow a planned daily or weekly routine of sustained listening for a defined amount of time, between five minutes to an hour, depending on age, background, motivation, and capacity. As far as possible, learners should set their own goals for what they intend to do and achieve. A common challenge is uneven practice, due to flagging interest, loss of motivation, or competing demands for time. To help learners deal with this, teachers can show them how to monitor their progress and to adjust their planned schedules without compromising too much on the original goals they have set for themselves.

Repetition

A major problem in independent listening is that many learners listen to something only once. This is usually the case with listening to broadcasts, an important source of listening input for many L2 learners. EFL learners, for example, have found the BBC World Service to be invaluable listening practice for decades. In the past, most learners could only listen to radio programs once, unless they managed to catch a repeat of the program in a different time zone. Today, many radio programs are freely downloadable podcasts which learners can store on their mobile devices and listen to as many times as they wish.

Repetition provides an unbeatable cognitive advantage for learners because listening to the same text again allows learners to become familiar with the content, vocabulary, and structure of the spoken text. This can greatly reduce the learners' cognitive load for each listen, freeing their attention and limited working memory resources to focus on other points or features of the text. With repetition, listening processes become automatic in the long run, a key to effective listening. At the same time, repetition reduces anxiety, a factor that can greatly hinder comprehension.

Projects for Extensive Listening

Figure 10.1 presents four projects in which learners engage in one-way and interactive listening, and learn to apply strategies in authentic language use contexts.

Each project takes at least two weeks to complete. We recommend that a project be carried out in its entirety as far as possible. However, if the scope of a language program does not support the demands and length of a project, teachers can adapt it by scaling down the requirements. The projects are designed mainly with adult and older adolescent learners in mind, but the last three can be adapted for younger learners by reducing the demands and complexity of the tasks and increasing teacher scaffolding and monitoring. Regardless of whether an entire project is implemented or only some tasks are selected, it is useful to apply the principles discussed earlier. The principles are also useful for advising learners on how they should carry out listening practice on their own.

Project	Description
Peer Listening Task	Learners work in pairs to design a listening lesson for the rest of the class. They select relevant listening materials from a variety of texts and prepare some relevant listening tasks.
Facilitated Independent Listening	Learners select listening materials from a teacher-prepared resource package to practice listening individually. They meet after each phase of the project to share what they have learned about their listening, the contents and ideas in the materials, and new vocabulary.
Listening Buddies	Learners work in pairs to plan their extensive listening program by selecting materials from a wide range of text types. They also co-monitor their listening development.
Authentic Interview	Learners plan structured interviews with competent speakers in their community so that they can practice interactive listening skills and use appropriate strategies to support their learning and understanding.

Figure 10.1. Projects for Extensive Listening

Learner awareness of the listening process will be raised through participating in each project and learners will also have a chance to work cooperatively and creatively with their fellow students. As with any collaborative project, problems may arise because of different personalities and a lack of shared understanding of the purpose. It is useful to lay down some ground rules to help everyone work together smoothly to achieve their goals. Learners should also be told where to find help if they have problems. It is crucial that teachers not only encourage learners to practice listening through extensive listening, but that they also guide and regulate learners' practice by giving instructions and stating expectations.

Peer Listening Tasks

Learners develop metacognitive knowledge about listening by thinking about the skills that are required for a specific task and the ways in which those skills can be developed. In this project, learners work in pairs to identify appropriate audio or video materials, and to devise suitable activities for helping their peers practice their listening. They use a simple project planning template to guide their work (see Figure 10.2). The products are shared with other classmates during lesson time, if the class is small, or collected by the teachers and compiled for all to use during their own listening practice.

The goal is that learners will understand the listening process better by the end of the project while, at the same time, collectively creating additional class resources for listening. To plan the task, learners have to think about the kind of listening materials that their classmates would find interesting and relevant, and the activities that can enhance their listening ability. In making these decisions, learners will draw on metacognitive knowledge they developed through earlier lessons. When they use activities that enable their peers to tap into prior knowledge, for example, learners demonstrate their understanding that listening is more than receiving information and completing exercises in the book. This can reinforce their own listening strategies and skills. Learners also engage with listening practice more purposefully because they listen to a number of texts before deciding which one to use.

This project is based on Liu's (2005) original idea for a group project in which learners assume the role of the language teacher to prepare a listening lesson. She observed that, when we ask learners to assume the role of a teacher, they will draw on what they have learned about the nature of listening in previous lessons. By discussing these ideas and applying them in their project, learners develop greater collective metacognitive knowledge. She also argues that teachers can gain valuable insights into what learners understand about listening comprehension by observing the activities that they prepare, and then the teachers can better identify

Stages in the Task	What You Need to Do
Understand the objective of the task: to plan a listening task for your classmates	Discuss with your partner or group what you need to do, and why this project is helpful to your own listening development.
Decide on the purpose of your task	Discuss the purpose of your listening task. Should your classmates listen simply to understand what they hear? Or should they listen for other purposes such as listening critically or empathetically? Identify the skills that you want your classmates to practice. For example, would you like them to listen for details, to understand globally, or to predict what they will hear?
Identify your listening material and explain the reason(s) for your choice	Before you decide on the material to use, listen (and view) at least <u>five</u> recordings. Make a list of these, stating the titles and the sources. Pick the one that is the most suitable and explain why.
Prepare a task of about 10 minutes for classmates	Decide what your classmates need to do to prepare themselves for listening or viewing. State what they need to do when they listen, and suggest how they can use that information after they have finished listening or viewing. Identify some words or phrases that they may not be familiar with.
Experience the task yourself first	Try out the task yourselves. Does it work? Is it interesting and useful? Why? Do you need to modify it?
Ask your teacher to review the task	Show your plan to your teacher and, if necessary, he/she will give you some feedback on how you can improve it. (Optional: revise the task and try it out again)
Share your task with classmates	Share this task with your classmates. Your teacher may ask you to exchange it with another pair, or it may be collated into a package for all in the class.
Reflect on your task	Meet as a group to talk about what you have learned from selecting the texts, planning, and delivering the lesson. Obtain mutual feedback on how each pair did on the task.

Figure 10.2. Instructions to Learners for Peer Listening Tasks

areas of knowledge that may be lacking or inaccurate. In our adaptation, we have added the stages "Experience the task yourself first" and "Ask your teacher to review the task." By trying out their task first, learners will know whether it will work. Review by the teacher gives learners feedback on the assumptions they made for their task. In this way, any misunderstandings about the listening process can be identified and the task modified before it is delivered. Requiring a preliminary selection of five sets of listening materials helps to ensure that learners increase their own time in listening to a wider range of listening texts before settling on one. Delivering the task to the class may take up more time than one language course can afford. Our suggestion is to have two pairs of learners exchange their planned activities. After this, all activities can be collated into a package to be used for further practice. In the next section, we will explain how such a listening package can assist learners in their listening comprehension development.

Facilitated Independent Listening

Language learners usually do not have the luxury of time for listening widely during class time. Facilitated independent listening is one way teachers can support learner listening efforts beyond the classroom. A listening package can make details of important sources of listening texts available to learners and help them improve the quality of their independent listening experience. In doing this, teachers also increase the amount of linguistic input that learners receive, which can have an impact on their rate of language acquisition as a whole. The package contains a variety of useful listening resources, including titles of CD recordings and links to a variety of internet audio and video texts. This listening project will provide additional opportunities for learners to experiment with and apply the strategies they learned during formal instruction time. As part of the project, learners also keep a journal to record what they listen to, how they practice their listening, and how they assess different stages of their listening process. The idea of this project, shared with us by David Holmes (Korea University), has been adapted to include specific stages and learner milestones. Figure 10.3 shows the stages of the project and highlights the groundwork that teachers need to do.

The stages help learners develop greater confidence to listen independently. In the preparatory phase, learner needs, interests, and resources are identified. The teacher reviews strategies learned in class and, if necessary, carries out further strategy instruction and selects appropriate listening materials from different media. The teacher also needs to prepare materials to support independent learning, such as self-directed listening guides or listening journal prompts. At the same time, the teacher draws up a schedule and identifies stages in the schedule when learners can come

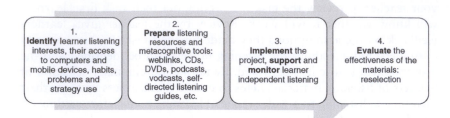

Figure 10.3. Teacher Planning in Facilitated Independent Listening

together to talk about their learning; this provides additional support for independent listening. It may also be necessary to have learners report to the teacher on progress made, at different points in the project. Finally, when the project is completed, the teacher can get comments and feedback from the learners on the relevance and appeal of the materials that have been selected. This helps assess the suitability of the listening resources selected. Appendix C provides a number of listening sources that can serve as a starting point for the selection of suitable materials for this project.

To motivate learners to persevere in their listening practice, the project can also include different "milestones" when learners come together to discuss what they have learned and to share interesting learning points about the target language, listening strategies, and the content of what they have been listening to. Figure 10.4 demonstrates the ways learners are engaged during this process.

The duration of the entire project and each phase can vary, depending on different contexts. In each phase, learners begin by selecting a number

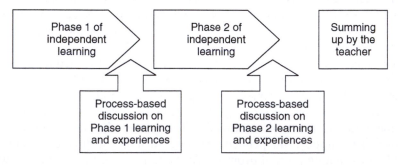

Figure 10.4. Learner Involvement in Facilitated Independent Listening

of listening materials. They make a schedule on when and how they will listen to the materials. The schedule also includes when they will review the materials before the end of the phase. At the same time, learners keep a listening diary to record their experiences with each listening. At the end of each phase, there is a process-based discussion: learners gather in small groups to share their experiences, learning points, etc. (Refer to Chapter 7 on the materials and procedures that can accompany each phase.) The listening package can be a physical package of purchased materials or take the form of a webpage with links that learners can access on their computers or mobile devices. It is important that teachers check copyright and conditions for use before including the links in a personal page. It is also useful to include practice activities that allow learners to select their own listening materials. The next project idea will demonstrate how this can be done.

Listening Buddies

The "Listening Buddies" project asks learners to work in pairs to plan a personalized extensive listening program. This project motivates learners to persevere in their listening practice with each other's support. It also creates opportunities for them to learn from each other. This activity is somewhat similar to the self-directed listening or viewing activity described in Chapter 7; however, learners now select texts together and jointly construct their metacognitive knowledge about the listening process. They plan their own listening practice by selecting from a range of resources: radio or TV broadcasts, videos and movies, podcasts, web videos, "live" talks, etc. The teacher can specify how long each practice session (excluding selection of texts) should be; we recommend something between 30 and 45 minutes. Figure 10.5 gives a sample structure for a personalized listening program. It should include details of the pair's schedules, information about the listening texts they select and the playback resources that they will need (e.g., MP3 player, computer, iPod, mobile phone).

When learners are first introduced to this activity, the program can be short: for example, a week or at most a fortnight. Although it is possible to set a longer duration, keeping the partnerships short has advantages. First, learners get a chance to work with different people in the class and learn from them. Second, it ensures that each individual gets a chance to work with different types of listening texts, because pairs can become set in their choices and seek out the same type of materials each time. To ensure that learners get adequate exposure to different types of listening, teachers could identify types of listening texts that learners must use at least once in the program: for example, each program must have one each of the following types of texts: radio or TV news broadcasts and programs, videos and movies, and internet programs. The self-directed

LISTENING BUDDIES
Our Listening Enrichment Program

Buddy 1: _____
My favourite type of listening materials:

Buddy 2: _____
My favourite type of listening materials:

Our agreed goals for our listening program:
1.

2.

Start date: End date:

Frequency: Daily/Every two days/Twice weekly

Types of listening materials we will choose (e.g., video clips from
YouTube, BBC news broadcasts, podcasts, songs, MTV):

Resources that we will be using:

Materials we have selected for the program
Session 1
Title: _____
Source: _____

Session 2
Title: _____
Source: _____

Session 3
Title: _____
Source: _____

Session 4
Title: _____
Source: _____

Figure 10.5. Sample of a Personalized Listening Program Outline for Listening
Buddies

listening guide presented in Figure 7.5 of Chapter 7 can also be modified for listening buddies to reflect on the collaborative nature of the task.

Authentic Interview

This project is a collection of activities in which learners practice listening by communicating with competent speakers of English. Teachers can leave the choice of activities relatively open and encourage learners to seek whatever opportunities they can find to practice listening in authentic communication. Learners keep a journal of their experiences. A better way, however, is to provide learners with some scaffolding for the types of activities they can choose and the tools they can use to reflect on and evaluate their learning. Here we suggest an authentic listening project that involves learners interviewing other people. The structure of an interview is useful because it reduces uncertainty and helps learners predict what they might hear. This helps learners become more confident in their listening. The learners have some degree of control over the interaction because they formulate the questions, unlike a conversation where the topics can be diverse, the words may be unfamiliar, and the ideas may be beyond the knowledge and experience of the learners. Figure 10.6 illustrates the three stages of the project and how each stage can support learner listening and language development in a holistic manner: (1) planning the interview; (2) rehearsing the interview; and (3) conducting the interview and reporting results.

Planning the Interview

Learners work in groups of four to prepare and conduct a structured interview, using a questionnaire that they design themselves. They start

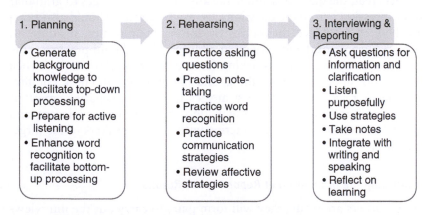

Figure 10.6. Stages in an Authentic Interview Project

by identifying a topic or an issue that interests them. They draw up a list of questions to elicit the views of other people: for example, the learners and teachers in their school, their neighbours, or other people in their community. After they have drawn up a preliminary list of questions, they research the topic by reading about it in the library or on related websites. This helps to activate and increase their background knowledge, which will assist them in top-down processing during the actual interview. They identify different perspectives on the issues and make notes on a range of possible responses to their questions, based on what they have researched and what they expect to hear. This helps learners to predict, and prepares them for active listening. Learners will pay particular attention to new and unfamiliar words that they come across in their preparations, and they will find out how these words are pronounced so that they will recognize them when they hear them. Next, they review their questions by editing, adding, or removing questions.

Rehearsing the Interview

Once the list of questions is complete, learners rehearse the interview through role play. This helps them build greater confidence in the task and anticipate what might happen in the actual interview. Two members will be the interviewers while the other two will take the role of interviewees, one at a time. One of the interviewers asks the questions while the second person takes notes on the responses. The "interviewees" are encouraged to refer to the set of notes prepared by the group, based on their research. This creates further opportunities to learn to recognize unfamiliar words associated with the topic of their interview. To ensure that questions are properly structured and easily understood, teachers read the questions and make any necessary changes to grammar and expression before the questions are used. Learners should also practice how to introduce themselves by stating their names, institutions, and the purpose of the interview. In addition, they should practice using reception strategies, such as asking for repetition or clarification when they do not understand something, and paraphrasing to check comprehension. A review of affective strategies to manage negative emotions is also recommended. Learners will find these strategies relevant and timely because they will be interacting with "real" speakers of the target language.

Conducting the Interview and Reporting the Results

Once learners are ready, they will form pairs to carry out the interviews with the people they have planned to approach. During the real interviews, one student asks the questions while the other writes down the answers, just as they did during the rehearsal. The one asking the questions should also pay attention to what is said. Learners will get a chance to use the communication strategies they have learned to manage their interviews and affective strategies to cope with anxiety, which some learners would doubtless feel. At the end of each interview, the pair will discuss the answers they have understood. They will also individually chart their anxiety temperature daily. When both pairs in the group have completed their interviews, the learners will collate all their findings and write a report. If there is time, teachers can also organize sessions where learners present the results of their interviews to the rest of the class. The presentations can also include learner reflections on metacognitive components of their learning throughout the project. The pair and group discussions, as well as the class presentations, create further opportunities for learners to listen to one another purposefully.

In some situations this project may take up too much time and coordination, but the idea of authentic interviews can still be implemented on a smaller scale. One way to do this is to have learners work in pairs throughout the project. Instead of going to interview people, they can arrange for some of the interviews to be done online through Skype or other forms of oral computer-mediated communication platforms (see Chapter 11). Instead of class presentations, learners can present within smaller groups that meet in class at the same time.

Projects for Extensive Listening: Closing Remarks

Some commentators on L2 listening suggest that teachers should spend most of classroom time getting learners to listen to "a lot of meaningful, enjoyable, and comprehensible spoken text" and not spend time on teaching strategies (Renandya & Farrell, 2011, p. 52). While it is clearly useful to have learners practice listening frequently, much of this practice would be better done outside class time so that more time in class can be spent on learning to listen. Strategy instruction and listening practice need not be mutually exclusive. Metacognitive instruction during class time can support task-based listening practice and further support learners when they practice their listening at their own pace outside class. A recent study by Kemp (2010) showed that learners do take on board the importance of skills taught in a language course and use them to manage their listening in real-world communication. Equally important, metacognitive instruction gives learners the confidence to move beyond comprehensible listening texts to select input that is slightly more challenging and that can stimulate greater learning. These sources of listening input can be equally meaningful and enjoyable, if not more, when learners have the metacognitive knowledge and skills to approach them confidently. At the same time, when learners have the opportunity to report back to the class or the teacher what they do when listening extensively, they also have the benefit of teacher and peer input. This creates a cycle of learning that provides crucial continuity between formal and informal ways of learning to listen. In the long run, a meta-cognitive approach to extensive listening will greatly benefit learners and help them develop real-world listening skills that can "ensure that the acquisition of L2 continues in the world beyond courses and classrooms" (Field, 2007, p. 31).

Summary

Listening beyond the language classroom is clearly useful for language learners, but it often leaves the learning too much to chance for some learners and does not make use of the expertise of teachers to add value to their efforts. This chapter proposed four projects that can offer structure and teacher scaffolding for extensive listening. Some of these projects, such as facilitated independent listening and listening buddies, can be used to help learners get into the habit of extensive listening practice. A project on peer listening tasks can be introduced after learners have had adequate experience with task-based listening lessons. Authentic interviews can be carried out at most stages of language learning and are particularly suited to language programs where the curriculum integrates the four language skills. Although the projects focus mainly on listening, the different activities in the projects also help learners develop their overall language knowledge and language use.

Normal listening practice may work well with some learners, but many learners need to be motivated to persevere after an initial period of enthusiastic response, as other activities take over their heavy learning schedule. Extensive listening projects can help to develop a listening routine and instil commitment to listening practice beyond the classroom. Learners who do not have a habit of practicing their listening beyond the classroom may begin to do more of it on their own. For learners who are already attempting to improve their listening proficiency through extensive listening, the skills and thinking processes they develop through these projects will help them become more effective.

Discussion Questions and Tasks

1. Read the following listening diary entry of Susi, a 20-year-old college student. Which project could she be referring to? Comment on Susi's attitude to learning to listen and how the project could be helpful to her.

I met Min in our college cafeteria to plan our next assignment for the listening class. Ms Lee has asked us to plan a listening activity for the class in a fortnight's time. We tried to select two short video clips from YouTube but we kept getting distracted by what we came across. It wasn't so bad because we also practised our listening when we watched all the different videos. Ha! Ha! Maybe this is just an excuse! Anyway, after 2 hours of watching and laughing at some silly ones, we finally found two videos. We think our friends in class will like them. Each recording is about 5 minutes long. In one of them, a woman is talking about why it is important to eat lots of fruit and vegetables. Good reminder! ☺ In the other recording, a man is talking about how he changed his diet after he suffered from a heart attack. We think we can use this to get our friends to do a jig-saw listening, like what Ms Lee did with us last week. But I think ours are better!!! Tomorrow I will meet Min again and we will have to plan a listening lesson. I think it's going to be quite fun. We will have to think of how to teach listening like what Ms Lee does. Min says Ms Lee is lazy because she asked us to prepare the lessons. That way she doesn't have to prepare them. I don't think so. I believe Ms Lee when she said this task will help us understand listening better. I hope that after this activity, I will be able to understand how my friends listen, especially Vincente. He's so good. Maybe I can learn from him, too. I think we should make the task really hard for the class!!

2. How much do you think learners should decide for themselves what they do for extensive listening. How often do you think listening projects should be used? Why?

3. The listening projects in this chapter may need to be scaled down for learners in some language programs because of a lack of time or other circumstances. Select one of the projects and modify it so that it can be used for a specific group of learners you have in mind. As a start, consider how the task demands can be simplified and the duration of the entire project shortened. Share your modified project plan with some colleagues and explain the rationale for your modifications. Include other considerations that may have guided your plan.

Suggestions for Further Reading

Field, J. (2007). Looking outwards, not inwards. *ELT Journal, 61*, 3–38.
   This article makes a case for extensive listening and reading as a way of empowering learners to be truly autonomous, and it offers suggestions on how learners can extract linguistic information from the rich resources in the real world.

Krashen, S. (1996). The case for narrow listening. *System, 24,* 97–100.

Krashen extends the idea of narrow reading to narrow listening in which learners become familiar with a limited range of topics in the speech of a small number of selected speakers. Guidelines on how to select input and use it for repeated listening are offered.

Liu, X. L (2005). Teaching academic listening. In P. F. Kwah, & M. Vallance (Eds.), *Teaching ESL to Chinese learners* (pp. 70–79). Singapore: Pearson Longman.

Liu describes proven successful ways of engaging English language learners in an academic listening course to listen beyond the classroom through practical teacher-prepared activities.

Renandya, W. A., & Farrell, T.S.C. (2011). "Teacher the tape is too fast!" Extensive listening in ELT. *ELT Journal, 65,* 53–59.

Applying perspectives from extensive reading, the authors suggest using an extensive listening approach to teach listening to lower proficiency EFL learners. The article offers suggestions on where to find materials for listening.

Part III

Listening in Other Contexts

Chapter 11

Listening in Multimedia Environments

Scenario

It's Wednesday, the day when Ms Nguyen's class works in the school's multimedia learning center. Today, as part of their unit on sports, her classroom learners will listen to a videotext on the history of the World Cup, the coveted international football/ soccer prize. With the help of specialized software,[1] the digitized videotext has been divided into short fragments of several seconds each. The transcript of the text matching each fragment has been programmed on a separate track.

Learners begin by consulting a worksheet provided by the teacher. The first part asks them to predict some of the information they think they will hear, including some of the specialized vocabulary. The learners then listen using Mode 1 of the text, which is a non-stop playing of the videotext without the text display (similar to watching television). After the first listen, they note what they predicted correctly, adding related ideas and any new information they had not predicted. The learners then listen to the text a second time, noting parts of the text where they had difficulty distinguishing words in the sound stream. They also add to their notes any additional information they have understood.

For their third listen, the learners listen using Mode 2 of the videotext. This mode allows them to play the videotext by fragments and, when desired, listen again to difficult fragments by clicking the *replay* button as often as necessary to comprehend the fragment. Once they feel confident that they have understood, they click the *text* button and read the transcript of the fragment to verify their understanding. The learners can return to the video/audio by clicking the *replay* button and listening to

---

1 123LISTEN (Hulstijn, 2003)

the fragment as often as required. They complete the activity by listening to the entire text once again, using Mode 1.

Finally, the learners complete the worksheet. In the second part they write down new words, L2 expressions, or cultural knowledge they learned from the text. In the third part, they note what was easy and/or difficult about the text and, based on their reflection, write down any goals for future listening activities.

Pre-reading Reflection

1. What are the teacher's goals for (a) the listening activity and (b) the worksheet?
2. What are the roles of the different parts of the worksheet?
3. What does the technology allow the teacher to do in the multimedia learning center that she could not do in the regular classroom?
4. What is the purpose of repeated listening to fragments in Mode 2, besides comprehension?
5. Another mode would allow the learners to listen to the entire text with simultaneous text display, similar to watching a movie with subtitles. How useful might this mode be for listening practice? What might be the disadvantages of using this mode?

Introduction

Listening instruction has been associated with technology ever since the acoustic signal could be captured in a form that permitted repeated listening. This was a huge advancement. The face of teaching L2 listening changed, not with the advent of computers, but the invention of the phonograph, as pointed out by Hulstijn (2003). The acoustic signal could now be recorded and repeated as often as desired for purposes of comprehension.

Technology has evolved greatly since the phonograph, with major advances in the last few decades. Starting with the phonograph, film, television and audiotape, we now have DVD, digital video and audio, computer-mediated audio and video, hand-held MP3 players and more. In fact, the ability to repeat delivery of audio or videotext and add captions or subtitles begins to turn the listening skill into a semi-recursive activity. As suggested by Robin (2007), listening is "inching its way closer to reading which is fully recursive" (p. 2). Indeed, the acoustic signal is not as elusive as it once was, opening up new avenues for teaching and learning L2 listening.

In his investigation of the pedagogical effectiveness of different technologies, Salaberry (2001) posed a number of relevant questions; two can be rephrased for listening:

1. Is increased technological sophistication correlated to increased effectiveness of L2 listening pedagogy?
2. Which technical attributes specific to new technologies can be profitably maximized for L2 listening pedagogy?

This chapter will attempt to answer these questions by exploring the ways multimedia can be used to facilitate the development of listening skills. Today language learners can access a huge range of input options through the internet and other innovative technological tools. How can L2 listeners best utilize these resources? Which of the tools are genuinely helpful for listening development? We will examine research on the effectiveness of individual tools and various combinations of media such as audio, visual, and written supports. Research on the modes of presentation, such as captions, annotations, and other help options, as well as functions such as repeated delivery and slowed audio delivery, will be examined and evaluated. The potential of media such as podcasts and oral computer-mediated communication will also be explored with regard to their usefulness for teaching L2 listening.

An assumption that use of multimedia always enhances learning to listen is tested and challenged in existing research studies. The findings are more complex, showing significant differences in impact by types of technology, modes of delivery, and function within the learning context. Teachers will do well to give detailed consideration to the various options available to them in multimedia teaching environments. In that light, we will conclude this chapter with (1) some considerations for teaching and learning listening in multimedia environments, based on the research findings, and (2) a discussion of the importance of metacognitive guidance for language learners to use multimedia efficiently.

Impact of Visual Media for Listening Instruction

Technology available for the purpose of listening development made leaps forward from audio recordings with the advent of visual media, such as film, television, and, eventually, digital video. Adding a visual component to listening instruction increased the authenticity of classroom listening practice. This is particularly true for situations where the visual component is a fundamental part of the listening context and fully supports comprehension as it would in real-life listening contexts.

The potential for a visual component to enhance language learning finds theoretical support in educational theories such as Mayer's generative theory of multimedia learning and Paivio's dual coding theory (Jones, 2006). The generative theory of multimedia learning (Mayer, 2001, 2002) assumes that mixed modes of delivery (text, audio, and video) affect cognitive processing for learning. According to Mayer, when L2 listeners comprehend a videotext, they select relevant pictorial and/or linguistic information from it, convert this information into coherent visual and verbal mental representations, and then integrate these into a new mental model of text comprehension (Jones, 2004). Similarly, in dual coding theory (Paivio, 1986), learning is facilitated when both verbal and non-verbal processing reinforce each other. Believing that human cognition can deal simultaneously with language and with non-verbal objects and events, Paivio argues that learners make referential connections between information gleaned from the two sources and then organize this information into knowledge that can be acted upon, or stored and retrieved for later use.

Both theories maintain that L2 listeners will comprehend more when visual and aural information support each other, because any recognized visual information is processed automatically in working memory and made available for processing further linguistic input. As a result, listeners have more attentional resources available in working memory to process the aural information which, in addition, will be segmented more efficiently because of the supporting visual information. In sum, information presented in both aural and visual modes together, when congruent, can lead to better comprehension for L2 listening. In fact, the importance of learning to process the visual with the audio prompted Ockey (2007) to argue for enlarging the construct of listening to include processing visual and audio inputs.

Impact of Visual in Listening Instruction: Research Evidence

A visual component adds an element of authenticity that more closely approximates real-life listening situations. Given the additional visual cues, the incorporation of visual media in listening instruction should make comprehension for L2 listeners easier than in audio alone. In a carefully controlled, longitudinal experiment with young children learning English, Verdugo and Belmonte (2007) demonstrated that weekly interaction with "an internet-based technology" using songs, games, and stories resulted in greater comprehension gains than regular textbook-based listening activities only. Although these results appear promising, it is not really clear what it was about the technology and activities that could explain the difference in results.

Listening to a speaker is facilitated by visual support; this more closely approximates authentic listening experiences such as lectures. Watching the speaker, in addition to listening, offers the option to attend to potentially helpful cues known as kinesics: that is, body language, facial expressions, hand gestures, and other non-verbal cues that can facilitate interpretation of a message. In a qualitative analysis of think-aloud protocols (Wagner,

2008), listeners indicated that they did use non-verbal information in a number of ways, although they varied in their ability to use this information for comprehension purposes. The degree to which kinesics are used appears to vary as a function of listening proficiency, which may explain the variability among Wagner's listeners. Sueyoshi and Hardison (2005) found that seeing the speaker's face and gestures produced the best results for lower proficiency learners, presumably because the gestures gave cues to meaning that compensated for what was not understood. On the other hand, the advanced group obtained the highest scores when they saw only the speaker's face, likely because their advanced proficiency allowed them to focus on lip movements and other facial gestures for additional cues to meaning. Only auditory input resulted in the lowest scores for all groups. Questionnaire responses revealed positive attitudes toward both gestures and facial features as cues of meaning, possibly because listeners perceived these cues to facilitate engagement with the speaker.

Visual media, such as video clips, can be used successfully to prepare learners for listening (Wilberschied & Berman, 2004). Seeing the setting of a listening event provides listeners with an immediate context to activate potential scenarios and related vocabulary. Guided by metacognitive knowledge, L2 listeners use the information elicited by the visual to activate strategies that compensate for inadequate linguistic knowledge. Clearly, listeners supported by a visual are better able to activate top-down processing strategies than those who only listen (Seo, 2002).

Visual media can provide helpful context to prepare for listening and to activate appropriate strategies. However, does the visual continue to support comprehension during the listening activity as the videotext unfolds? Ginther (2002) investigated the relative effect of context or content visuals for listening performance on the computerized Test of English as a Foreign Language (TOEFL). Content visuals, in contrast to context visuals, are pictures congruent with the actual sound track. Results indicated that content visuals slightly enhanced comprehension but that context visuals had a slightly debilitating effect on comprehension. Ginther concluded that listening comprehension is facilitated when the visual information is directly related to the content of the information presented in the audio.

The Ginther study has important implications for which kind of visuals are useful and when they are useful for facilitating listening comprehension. Context visuals, as suggested earlier, are helpful before listening for activating top-down processing strategies to compensate for inadequate linguistic knowledge. However, they are less helpful during listening because these visuals require processing in addition to the audio, thereby consuming additional attentional resources and limiting the amount of working memory capacity available to the listener to attend to the audio. On the other hand, when content visuals complement the audio, both sets of information can be processed together, with the visual informing the audio, as argued (see earlier) by Paivio and Mayer.

In a similar vein, the possibility that visual content might actually detract from comprehension, rather than enhance it, was investigated by Coniam (2001). A group listening to an audio version of a test obtained similar comprehension scores to another group listening to a video version. Of particular interest was the finding that over 80 percent of the video group felt that the video had not facilitated comprehension, and they expressed preference for audio. Coniam suggests that the nature of the text (a talk show discussion) may not have been as conducive for visual support as an action-oriented input, for which a visual might provide useful clues. The nature of the task, working from a test booklet, may also have affected performance since the video group felt they might have done better if they were not distracted by the visual images and did not have to look up and down from question paper to screen. Coniam concluded that, for high-stakes tests, the listening comprehension component should be implemented via audio only, and not video.

Ockey (2007) pursued the same question using think-aloud interviews with a small sample of listeners. All listeners agreed that still images were helpful for providing context (similar to Ginther's conclusions); with regard to video, however, there was a wide range of opinion about its usefulness. In the same vein, Suvorov (2009) compared the effects of visual support in (1) video-mediated texts, and (2) pictures and audio, with (3) audio alone. Results showed that scores on the video-mediated section of the test were significantly lower than for the audio plus pictures and audio alone sections. Interestingly, listeners who indicated a preference for audio outperformed the others on the audio part of listening test, suggesting that listening ability might be related to learning style. The potential of such a relationship finds further support in a study by Hernández (2004) who determined that listeners with high spatial ability performed better with visual support whereas those with low spatial ability performed equally well in both audio only and multimedia environments.

The mixed results of these comparative studies turn attention to questions about how learners actually process visual and audio inputs. A first question is how much attention listeners pay to the visual component of videotexts. In order to investigate this question, Wagner (2007) videotaped learners while listening to videotext (dialogues and lecturettes). He computed the amount of time each listener made eye contact with the video monitor and determined that listeners paid attention to the video monitor 69 percent of the time on average, with a greater percentage of time during the dialogues. In a later study, using the same texts, Wagner (2010) found much less attention to the screen, at only 48 percent of the time. In this case, viewing time negatively but significantly correlated with overall listening comprehension and with comprehension of the lecturettes. Wagner attributes this result to the inclination of weaker listeners to seek comprehension cues in the visual that might compensate for their inadequate linguistic competence. Stronger listeners, on the other hand, may have chosen to work more with the test booklets, focusing on the audio alone to selectively listen to the information required to answer the questions.

Mixed results in the research on the supporting role of visual input for listening comprehension led Gruba (2004) to examine how listeners process this kind of dynamic information. Until we know how learners attend to dynamic visual elements in listening activities, argued Gruba, the development of computer-based listening skills cannot move forwards. After interviewing learners who had watched Japanese video news clips and written a summary of each clip, he concluded that visual information has a differential impact on the audio information as the listener develops a fuller understanding of the videotext. The visual component can be as much of a hindrance as a help, depending on the degree of relevance to the aural input. In the case of weaker listeners, visual inputs that are not congruent with the content can lead them to a flawed interpretation of the text. A later study (Gruba, 2007) listed a number of ways in which the visual elements of the digitized newscasts influenced comprehension in beneficial and detrimental ways. Gruba concludes that teachers need to help learners understand different types of videotext. He argues for the development of media literacy where listeners learn to understand that the nature of the supporting visual may vary by text: for example, news clips.

Impact of Visual Input in Listening Instruction: Summary

In sum, the assumption that presenting a visual component with the acoustic signal will facilitate listening comprehension is contested; the research evidence on this question is not conclusive. Even though learners may initially appear to be positively disposed to visual media and make extensive use of it in their daily lives, they do not always appear to benefit from the dual mode of delivery for comprehending a language they are learning. Although a positive affective response to visual media is evident in the qualitative findings, the results are mixed with regard to how much the visual contributes to their comprehension of the videotext. It appears that attention to the listening task, the visual, and the aural may be too demanding or distracting. When they disregard the video monitor, learners are making choices about what will help them to best complete the listening comprehension task.

The results on this question may also be related to the listening task. Most of the studies report on the use of a visual component for a listening test. Questions about the value of adding visual are particularly acute for listening assessment. Given the potential for distraction as well as the need to move eye contact between the monitor and the test materials, great care is needed in choosing to add visual material. Assessors need to ask: are we assessing the ability to understand a target language speaker or the ability to interpret the accompanying visual?

Teachers will want to use multimedia because of its affective attractiveness for learners. What they can learn from the ongoing research is to make careful choices among the types of visual supports available and the nature of the images in the visual material. A key consideration is a close match between the content of the images and the aural input, especially for learners at lower levels of language proficiency. Using visual materials to prepare for listening by setting the context is less problematic; and it is particularly useful for activating metacognitive knowledge to predict potential scenarios and strategies to compensate for inadequate linguistic knowledge.

Teacher use of multimedia for classroom listening instruction is only one aspect of learning in multimedia environments. Multimedia technology has also opened up the availability of help options, the ability of learners to make choices about the tools they use, and the expansion of learning beyond the classroom. Furthermore, as suggested earlier, the benefit of using different media for purposes of comprehension may be related to learning style. In that light, the next section will explore what listeners do in multimedia environments where they can exercise choice and control to accomplish a listening comprehension task.

Listener Choices in Multimedia Environments

A distinct advantage of multimedia environments is the choice and control available to L2 learners (Hoven, 1999). Choice and control already became available to learners at a very basic level when sound was first recorded. With the help of three simple tools—a recording, a player, and a printed copy of text—listeners could implement a relatively unsophisticated six-step procedure to practice listening and word segmentation skills: (1) listen to the recording; (2) ask themselves whether they have understood what they heard; (3) replay the recording as often as necessary; (4) consult the written text to read what they have just heard; (5) recognize what they should have understood; and (6) replay the recording as often as necessary to understand all of the oral text without written support (Hulstijn, 2003). Technology has become much more sophisticated, however. Today, listeners have at their disposal a wide range of technological aids from which to choose.

This section will examine the pertinent research dealing with options available to listeners working in multimedia environments. Computer technology can track the pattern of choices made, providing some insights into how listeners process a listening task. To what degree do the choices made contribute to improved listening comprehension? Some research studies in this area explore how learners choose and use different help options; other studies compare the impact of particular types of help functions.

Support Options in Multimedia Listening: Research Evidence

The types of help functions learners used and the relationship between functions used and course performance were examined by Hegelheimer and Tower (2004). Although there was a high degree of variability in option choices, the "repeat previous sentence and transcription" function was used more by weaker learners and was negatively related to performance. Stronger learners relied more on the audio by making greater use of the "aural repeat only" function. The preference by weaker learners to consult written supports (to read) likely hindered the development of productive listening strategies. Weaker development of those strategies could explain their weaker performance in the course.

A wide range of help options, and the use of play/rewind/pause functions, were investigated by Pujolà (2002) for insights into strategy use in multimedia listening environments. The help options included: dictionary, cultural notes, transcripts, subtitles, feedback (on comprehension question responses), and an expert's module (to develop metacognitive knowledge about comprehension). Although options chosen varied greatly (reiterating the findings of other studies), two major patterns of listening behavior were identified. Listeners using a global approach tended to use help options less, relying more on prior knowledge and strategies. Learners who manifested a compulsive consulter approach repeatedly accessed the different help options as well as the pause and rewind buttons. The stronger listeners tended to use the written help options to confirm comprehension whereas the weaker listeners tended to rely on these options (to read) for comprehension.

These findings are amplified in research by Roussel (2008) and Roussel, Rieussec, Tricot, and Nespoulous (2006). They examined how learners approached listening to MP3 tracks in German, while online movements of the mouse were recorded on a computer screen. The researchers observed that listening behaviors could be summarized into four distinct approaches:

1. An initial global listen followed by a detailed listen with frequent pauses and short rewinds.
2. A detailed listen with frequent pauses followed by one or more global listens.

3. One or more global listens with no detailed listen.
4. One detailed, erratic listen with many rewinds but no global listen.

The first approach was characteristic of high-proficiency listeners who, apparently, first listened for gist and then verified details, problem-solving as they went along during the second listen. The fourth approach was generally used by the weaker, low-proficiency listeners who, ostensibly, got caught up in bottom-up processing without first determining an overall conceptual framework into which they could slot details of the text during a second listen. The researchers contend that the recorded movements of the mouse during the listening task visually represent learner self-regulation of a listening task and, as such, are good indicators of metacognitive activity. Computer tracking can often offer real-time immediacy and insight into the listener's work strategies.

One specific technical option listeners can choose is changing the speed of listening to a text, using technology that controls speed without distortion of pitch. Zhao (1997) found that listeners performed better on a comprehension task when they had control over speech rate and repetition, although the speech rate chosen varied greatly by listener. While slowing down speed of delivery has beneficial effects on comprehension, Zhao cautions that L2 listeners are unique individuals with different perceptions and internal references of what is fast or slow. Furthermore, learners may slow down the speech rate too much, opting for a rate of delivery that is comfortable rather than a faster rate of delivery approximating natural speech rate, where they would not be able to understand every word but could attain a reasonable level of comprehension, with the help of appropriate strategies.

Other research studies compare results by the type of support chosen by learners. The effect of student choices among pictorial support and written annotations for comprehension of oral texts in multimedia environments has been investigated extensively by Jones and Plass. Learners in beginning-level French classes were given the options of consulting either picture and/or written annotations during a listening task. Their final listening scores showed that learners acquired more vocabulary and recalled the text better with the help of both pictorial and written annotations than with pictures only or written annotations only (Jones & Plass, 2002). Delayed post-tests revealed that pictorial annotations had a stronger and longer lasting effect than written annotations, both for vocabulary retention and for listening comprehension. A later study confirmed these results; in addition, however, it was determined that learners using written annotations remembered vocabulary better on a written test than learners who used pictures, contrary to the hypothesis that pictures would be easier to process and would increase efficiency of learning (Jones, 2004).

Vocabulary learning and L2 listening comprehension were further elucidated by a study based on web-delivered ESL lectures. Smidt and Hegelheimer (2004) were able to ascertain that the incidental vocabulary learning that occurred was based on consultation of the slides and transparencies rather than the lecture. This finding helps to explain why listening comprehension did not improve significantly, leading the researchers to conclude that the incidental acquisition of vocabulary was likely due to reading, not listening.

Brett (1997) presents evidence for the greater success rate of multimedia (digital video, digital audio and text/comprehension questions) for comprehension and language recall, compared to audio or video alone. Brett attributes these results to the monitoring support from immediate feedback in multimedia. The feedback ensured that any errors in interpretation were corrected periodically and that listeners could continually move forward from a position of correct understanding. Brett rightfully questions whether learners will be able to transfer the monitoring support provided by technology to self-monitoring in real-life listening.

A comparison between the optional use of captions and transcripts by learners listening to short lectures was explored by Grgurovic and Hegelheimer (2007). When comprehension broke down, learners opted to consult the captions more frequently and for a longer time than the transcripts. Surprisingly, learners did not use these help options as often as anticipated (they were opened only 45 percent of the time), particularly lower proficiency listeners. Because of the wide variability in how and when these help options were accessed, the researchers recommend that both captions and transcripts be provided for comprehension support. In view of their prevalence, the use of captions and subtitles is explored in more detail in the next section.

Support Options in Multimedia Listening: Summary

Studies on the use of help functions in multimedia settings are useful to determine what listeners find useful for comprehension. Research findings suggest that use of options is quite idiosyncratic and that learners do not always make use of the options available to them. Learners may not be aware of how the various options can be used and they may not be aware of how to combine them synergistically to enhance their comprehension efforts, particularly lower proficiency listeners. In terms of outcomes, the options used appear to have beneficial effects for vocabulary learning. Although certain types of navigational patterns appear to be associated with better comprehension, there is little evidence to demonstrate that the options selected led the learners to improve their L2 listening ability. In fact, the choices made by some of the lower proficiency listeners led them to written support options and reading that likely precluded the development of productive listening strategies.

Providing listeners with more help options in themselves will not necessarily lead to better learning outcomes. As concluded by Vanderplank (2010), effective use of these tools by language learners cannot be taken for granted. Teachers will need to provide more initial guidance on the use of help options if these tools are going to improve listening ability.

Captions and Subtitles

Widespread availability of television programming and DVD video with multilingual soundtracks and captions provides increased opportunities for written support to enhance listening comprehension. These include subtitles and captions. Subtitles are translations of the sound track of a film or television program that appear simultaneously on the bottom of the screen, for the benefit of non-native viewers. Captions are translations that appear on the screen a second or two after they are spoken. These are commonly used to aid deaf and hearing-impaired audiences. The following overview examines relevant research on the potential benefits of these tools for L2 listening comprehension and vocabulary learning.

Captions and Subtitles: Research Evidence

To determine the most effective type of textual support for listening comprehension, Markham, Peter, and McCarthy (2001) compared the effect of different types of captions on the comprehension of a Spanish DVD. Results showed that the order of listening performance from high to low was: (a) English captions only; (b) Spanish captions only; and (c) no captions. A follow-up study (Markham & Peter, 2003), using a different type of comprehension measure, found similar results. The researchers argue that learners would benefit from a cycle of repeated viewing, progressing from L1 captions to L2 captions and finally to no captions, particularly with challenging video material.

Continuing the same line of research, Guichon and McLornan (2008) examined the effects of different modalities of presentation, using free written protocols as a comprehension measure. Participants were divided into four groups of similar L2 proficiency: (1) audio only; (2) video with audio; (3) video with audio and L2 subtitles; and (4) video with audio and L1 subtitles. An analysis of the number of semantic units understood showed that the subtitle groups obtained the highest scores, with the L2 subtitles group scoring slightly higher, and that viewing with L2 subtitles yielded more accurate vocabulary use. On the semantic units where the visual did not match the audio, listeners in the video/audio mode were less successful, presumably due to cognitive overload.

A more recent study by Winke, Gass, and Sydorenko (2010) extended this line of research with a much larger group of participants. Results revealed, first of all, that listeners who saw the videos twice with captions performed better on written and oral vocabulary tests of new words and a comprehension test, compared with those who saw the captions only once. Second, with regard to ordering effects, listeners who saw captions during a first listen scored higher on the oral vocabulary test than those who only saw the captions on the second listen. Comprehension test results were comparable for both groups. Third, with regard to any effects for language, captions appeared to be more beneficial for learners of Russian and Spanish, compared with Chinese and Arabic. Finally, with regard to proficiency, there were no differences, dispelling the conjecture that captions might be less beneficial for beginner-level listeners. Interviews with a random sample of participants uncovered five themes: (1) learners need multiple input modalities; (2) captions reinforce and confirm what is understood; (3) captions have an impact on where listeners pay attention; (4) captions help in word segmentation; and (5) captions may be a crutch. The last two themes were unanticipated by the researchers.

Captions and Subtitles: Summary

Taken together, the studies discussed appear to suggest unequivocal support for the usefulness of captions and subtitles in listening comprehension. Comprehensive reviews by Danan (2004) and Vanderplank (2010) make the same observation. There is no doubt that the use of L2 captions and subtitles can lead to better word identification and, ultimately, vocabulary learning, based on existing research. This conclusion is confirmed in a set of carefully designed experiments by Bird and Williams (2002) who observed that prior bimodal presentation (audio and captions in L2) improved recognition memory for spoken words and nonwords, compared with single modality presentation.

With regard to content, however, it is not clear whether improved comprehension is a result of listening or reading. The potential of L2 captions and subtitles for improving oral text comprehension needs to be verified with a comprehension measure that replicates listening in real-life contexts: that is, without the help of these tools. No claims can be made about the positive impacts of captions and subtitles on L2 listening comprehension until their effects are investigated using a measure that requires L2 listeners to fully rely on their L2 listening ability, compensatory strategies, and metacognitive knowledge about listening processes. In fact, Gruba (2007) suggests that incorrect decoding of captions can frustrate or cause overall misunderstanding.

Given that written support is usually not available in authentic, real-time listening, learners need to learn to rely only on the acoustic signal and relevant contextual factors, mediated by their metacognitive knowledge about listening, to construct the meaning of what they hear. The same observation is evoked in the Winke et al. (2010) study when participants suggested that captions might be a crutch. Furthermore, Danan (2004) concludes her review by confirming the use of subtitles and captions for improving listening "as long as viewers learn to take advantage of relevant strategies" (p. 76), although it is not clear what these strategies are. To conclude, before we can affirm the capacity of subtitles and captions to improve listening comprehension skills, we need longitudinal research comparing the performance of an experimental group using these tools with a control group, on a measure that assesses comprehension without the benefit of these tools.

Does this mean that subtitles and captions can play no role in the development of L2 skills? Certainly not. These tools can be beneficial to L2 listeners, as confirmed by the listeners interviewed in the Winke et al. study. Captions and subtitles help listeners note differences between what they hear and the written form of the message, improve word segmentation skills, and, thereby, gain greater insight into their comprehension errors. Similar to the caveats expressed earlier about the use of transcripts in listening development, captions and subtitles should only be used after learners have attempted to understand the text as a whole, by means of a metacognitive approach, using prediction, inferencing, and monitoring strategies that help to compensate for gaps in understanding.

Other Multimedia Tools for Listening Development

The rapid spread of technology has opened up new avenues for listening development. We will briefly discuss two such prominent tools for access to more authentic texts and listening practice outside the classroom: podcasts for extended listening and oral computer-mediated communication for interactive listening.

Podcasts

Podcasts are audio or video files published via the internet, designed to be downloaded to a MP3 player or laptop for future listening (McMinn, 2010). Given their widespread availability and mobility, podcasts offer new, creative, out-of-class possibilities for L2 listening practice and instruction. The findings of research related to videos can be helpful for podcasts as well, but there is also some research into podcast use specifically.

Integration of podcasts into a listening course was examined by O'Bryan and Hegelheimer (2007). These podcasts reinforced the listening strategies taught in class by offering learners opportunities to practice the strategies through listening to mini-lectures and/or completing related tasks. Benefits reported by teachers were extension of class time, and learners reported acquiring new note-taking tips and useful lecture cues.

With the goal of improving student academic listening skills, Vandergrift, Weinberg, and Knoerr (2010) scripted and recorded a series of podcasts to help French immersion learners better comprehend and prepare for lectures in French courses taken with francophone peers. Grounded in metacognitive (Wenden, 1998) and L2 listening theory (Goh, 2008), these podcasts targeted the development of listening strategies and processes to enhance lecture comprehension and note-taking skills. A controlled study of the impact of the pilot version of the seven podcasts revealed that learners who listened to the podcasts appreciated the content but not the presentation of the content. The experimental group showed a small increase on the Planning and Evaluation factor of the MALQ, which was administered before and after use of the podcasts to assess their impact on metacognitive awareness of academic listening.

Research into the usefulness of podcasts for L2 learning is just beginning. The potential for podcasts to improve L2 listening skills is unlimited; however, research into the actual use and benefits of this tool is needed, particularly how the relationships between listener proficiency, listening task, and text difficulty can work together to maximize comprehension and learning.

Oral Computer-Mediated Communication

Oral computer-mediated communication (CMC), which began with the advent of audio and video conferencing, is expanding rapidly with advances in broadband technologies and wider availability of laptops with cameras and microphones. Internet voice and video applications such as Skype,[2] with high picture and sound quality, present new opportunities for interactive listening, not available only a few years ago. These new, high-quality media offer boundless opportunities for speaking and listening development and L2 listening research.

Yanguas (2010) recently investigated three modes of interaction: video CMC, audio CMC, and face-to-face communication (FTFC) on a task seeded with unknown vocabulary. In terms of comprehension, the audio group attained a lower percentage of complete understanding (45 percent) of the targeted lexical items, compared with the video CMC (64 percent)

2 http://www.skype.com

and FTFC (70 percent) groups. A closer examination of the responses to communication problems indicated greater use of elaborations for the audio group, while the video and FTFC groups made equal use of elaborations and gestures. These results reinforce the earlier reported findings on the benefits of kinesics in facilitating comprehension. These results are also good news for the development of interactive L2 listening instruction in that video CMC and FTFC appear to be comparable contexts for learning. The reception strategies used for clarification were mostly of a global nature and, for purposes of confirmation, back-channelling cues such as *mhmm* were used (see Table 2.2 on p. 30).

Oral computer-mediated communication holds a great deal of promise, particularly for language learners in contexts with very little or no access at all to target language speakers.

Meta-technical Skills for Listening in Multimedia Environments

The benefits of using multimedia for listening development are both confirmed and questioned in this overview of existing research. Are all the "bells and whistles" worth the time and money? As suggested by Rost (2007), technology must be "intuitively helpful and elegantly efficient" (p. 102) in order to help us teach better than we do without it. If not, he concludes, we simply should not use it. Others (e.g., Robin, 2007; Vanderplank, 2010) suggest that the problem may not lie in the technology itself but in learner ability to appropriately apply the technology for efficient learning. When faced with an overabundance of information, some learners may attend to the wrong elements and have more difficulty extracting relevant meaning from the material (Smidt & Hegelheimer, 2004). Multimedia tools may be appealing, but that does not mean that their use will automatically lead to better learning.

Language learners may need guidance in navigating the options available to them. An interesting study by Mills, Herron, and Cole (2004) shows how language learners can feel lost and ineffective in a multimedia environment, without support by the teacher. Teacher-assisted viewing (TAV) in a classroom environment and computer-based individual viewing (IV) of videos were compared. There was no difference between the two groups in the final comprehension scores; in terms of self-efficacy, however, the TAV group felt significantly more confident in their ability to comprehend video. Level of engagement significantly predicted comprehension performance in the IV group, although there were considerable individual differences. This study underscores the value of training beginning-level language learners how to use videos in order to improve self-efficacy in self-access, independent learning environments.

Listening success in multimedia environments may also be related to learning styles and strategies, as suggested earlier. Initial evidence from research by Hernández (2004) suggests that spatial ability may be a factor. Robin (2007) insists that learners who are metacognitively aware can apply the available help options most efficiently: that is, they can choose when and which options and functions to apply in planning for a listening task and in problem-solving when difficulties arise.

In his overview of the potential for harnessing the panoply of "raw" electronic resources available today, Robin (2007) repeatedly underscores the need for teaching meta-technical skills so that learners can "use off-the-shelf technology to best facilitate their own learning in their own learning style" (p. 109). This likely needs to begin with teachers, leading Robin to conclude that the "daunting" future of technology and language teaching lies in the ability of teachers to advise and enable their learners to use the available raw electronic resources effectively to improve their L2 listening ability.

Listening in Multimedia Environments: Synthesis

We will now return to the questions about the pedagogical benefits of new technologies posed by Salaberry (2001), posited at the beginning of this chapter. What does the research literature on L2 listening reveal with regard to these questions?

Is increased technological sophistication correlated to increased effectiveness of L2 listening pedagogy? The answer to the first question is not yet clear. The promise that increased technological sophistication will lead to increased effectiveness of listening pedagogy has not yet been demonstrated, presumably because learners may not possess the meta-technical skills and strategic knowledge to use the support options efficiently. Furthermore, it is not yet clear how the interaction of the various media leads to comprehension. When is multimedia an overload? Can listeners pay attention to three different modes and still develop listening ability? Limitations of working memory dictate that supports provided to listeners should relate directly to the text and the listening task.

Which technical attributes specific to new technologies can be profitably used for L2 listening pedagogy? The answer to the second question lies mostly in evidence presented in Chapter 8 on the development of perception skills for L2 listening. The capacity provided by technology for repeated audio delivery, slowed audio delivery, and matching sound with text can be helpful to listeners in developing word segmentation skills. There is also evidence that use of this technology can lead to vocabulary learning.

More specifically, what does the research literature tell us about the use of multimedia for L2 listening development?

Considerations for Teaching and Learning L2 Listening in Multimedia Environments

Based on this overview of the research literature, we can tentatively deduce the following points for consideration by teachers and learners who want to use multimedia for L2 listening development.

Visual Media

- Use multimedia to engage learners in learning since it does trigger a positive affective response; however, the measurable impact of adding a visual component for text comprehension is less certain. Attention to both visual and aural inputs may be too demanding for working memory or too distracting.
- Use visual materials to prepare learners for listening. Appropriate visuals provide context quickly and activate metacognitive knowledge to predict potential scenarios and to use strategies to compensate for inadequate linguistic knowledge.
- Choose materials where content of the visual input closely matches the aural input, especially for learners at lower levels of proficiency.
- For assessment, careful attention is needed before including visual inputs. The potential for distraction and the need to move eye contact between a monitor and test materials may have a greater negative impact than the positive impact of the visual aids.
- Include instruction in media literacy somewhere in the student curriculum. Understanding the nature of different types of visuals and texts (e.g., the difference between news clips, interviews, comedy, and stories), is important for the effective use of visual media to enhance listening comprehension.

Help Options

- Provide learners with initial guidance on the use of help options, including how and when these tools can enhance comprehension and listening development. Without guidance, the use of help options is quite idiosyncratic and learners do not always make use of the options available to them.
- For lower proficiency listeners, provide more guidance in choice of help options to prevent a tendency to quickly resort to written support options (and reading) instead of developing productive listening strategies that are essential to become good listeners.
- If vocabulary learning is a goal, help options have beneficial effects on the outcomes.

- If L2 listening development is the primary goal, consider that there is little evidence to show that use of help options leads to improved listening comprehension ability.

Captions and Subtitles

- Use materials with captions to reinforce and confirm understanding of an aural text: for example, with a repeat listen. Captions can draw student attention to the difference between what they hear and the written form of the same message. This helps them direct attention to gaps in understanding during repeat listens.
- Captions can also help learners develop word segmentation skills and gain insight into their comprehension errors.
- Captions can become a crutch, allowing learners to resort to reading skills rather than develop appropriate listening strategies.

Podcasts

- Preparation or selection of appropriate materials needs careful attention, but distribution and access is easy for use at times convenient for learners and, thereby, extends listening practice beyond classroom time.
- Podcasts can be a useful teaching tool for metacognitive knowledge about L2 academic listening and note-taking skills.

Oral Computer-Mediated Communication

- Interactive listening practice can be expanded and reinforced similar to face-to-face listening contexts.

Developing Metacognitive Knowledge about L2 Listening in Multimedia Environments

We will conclude by returning to the scenario described at the beginning of this chapter to emphasize how textual support help options might be used profitably for listening development. By waiting until the third listen to consult a written portion of the text, Ms Nguyen is encouraging learners to first approach the text using their metacognitive knowledge about L2 listening as they would be obligated to do in real-life listening contexts. By encouraging learners to use the context to predict what they will hear, to monitor their comprehension, and to problem-solve along the way, she encourages them to activate and develop cognitive processes associated with real-life listening. Only after listening to the text twice, and attempting to comprehend the difficult parts by using all personal and contextual/visual resources available, do the learners consult select segments of the transcript track. At this point, learners listen to each segment as often as necessary in order to make the necessary sound–symbol connections that will enable them to hear and understand these words in the final uninterrupted listen to the text. This is how learners can learn how to listen and ultimately problem-solve by consulting the written text to resolve any remaining important points of difficulty. As they do this, learners continue to develop their word segmentation skills.

Use of any extraordinary support (i.e., help options) that would interfere with learners using only the cues that are available to them in real-life listening needs to be deferred if classroom practice, or practice in independent learning environments, is going to help learners develop their ability to listen efficiently and effectively. Such supports include: periodic comprehension checks to verify and correct comprehension along the way; captions or subtitles during initial listening efforts; written or pictorial annotations that require listeners to process extra information; and non-supporting visuals that detract from efficient processing of the audio. While these tools appear to have beneficial effects for vocabulary learning and increased sensitivity to sound–symbol relationships in the target language, they are not helpful for teaching learners to develop listening skills in contexts where these supports are not available. For purposes of listening practice, these help options should be consulted only when learners have exhausted all the cues that would be at their disposal, as if they were in a real-life listening context. Furthermore, based on the findings of research to date, learners may need to be taught meta-technical skills in order to make good choices and effectively use the various technological tools available to them in multimedia learning environments.

Summary

This chapter has explored the potential of technology for the teaching of L2 listening in multimedia environments by examining the most recent research evidence and weighing the results. We have examined literature on the use of technological tools such as video, textual supports such as transcripts and captions, and other options to help listeners mediate their comprehension efforts. The research evidence, up to now, is mixed and it appears that learners need to be taught some meta-technical skills if they are to benefit maximally from the technological tools available to support their listening development in multimedia environments. Based on the research evidence, we have provided some considerations for learning and teaching. Finally, we have considered the potential of this technology to prepare learners for real-life listening.

Discussion Questions and Tasks

1. A common teaching technique with video is to first have learners view the video without audio and then, in subsequent listens, listen with both video and audio. What would be the justification for such an approach to listening instruction? Based on what you know about listening comprehension, is this theoretically justifiable? Why?

2. This activity has three parts:

   (a) Choose a videotext and listen to it first with audio only and then listen/view with both audio and video. What enhanced or interfered with comprehension during the first listen? What strategies did you use? What strategies did you use for the second listen?

   (b) Choose a different video and, this time, listen/view this first time using both audio and video, followed by a second listen to the audio only. Note the strategies you used for each listen.

   (c) Discuss differences in facility of comprehension between the two approaches. Discuss any differences in strategy use prompted by the order of presentation.

3. If using captions for listening support, which would be most effective: captions in L1 or captions in L2? Justify your answer by referring to your knowledge about cognitive processing in L2 listening and the attentional constraints of working memory.

4. Compare the process approach used by Ms Nguyen in the opening scenario, referring to Table 6.1 on p. 110. Explain how this activity guides learners through the process of listening by (1) indicating where the stages delineated in Table 6.1 occur, and (2) how the different metacognitive processes at each stage are developed. Develop a worksheet that might accompany such an activity.

5. Danan (2004) concludes her review by confirming the use of subtitles and captions for improving listening "as long as viewers learn to take advantage of relevant strategies" (p. 76). What might be the relevant strategies (which Danan fails to provide)?

Suggestions for Further Reading

Hegelheimer, V., & Tower, D. (2004). Using CALL in the classroom: Analyzing student interactions in an authentic classroom. *System, 32*, 185–205.
A good study representative of research in this field, comparing use of help options with course performance. This study provides data on an application in actual use.

Hubbard, P. (Ed.). (2007). Technology and listening comprehension. *Language Learning & Technology, 11*, 1–117. Retrieved from http://llt.msu.edu/vol11num1/default.html

This special issue of *Language Learning & Technology* is dedicated to research on listening comprehension and technology. Of particular interest are three commentaries on the reported research and the possibilities of emerging technologies for teaching and researching listening.

Vanderplank, R. (2010). Déjà vu? A decade of research on language laboratories, television and video in language learning. *Language Teaching, 43*, 1–37.

An excellent, critical, and comprehensive review of the research literature (1999–2009) related to different technologies for use in language learning and teaching.

Winke, P., Gass, S., & Sydorenko, T. (2010). The effects of captioning videos used for foreign language listening activities. *Language Learning & Technology, 14*, 65–86.

A good study, with a large sample of participants, on the use of captions with a number of target languages. It includes both a quantitative and a qualitative component.

Chapter 12

Assessing Listening for Learning

Scenario

Today, Mme Boutin is doing a listening activity with her low-intermediate French class. After she provides the learners with a context for the oral text they will listen to (a radio talk show host calls a listener to inform her that she has won a contest), they complete the first part of a checklist of strategies on preparing for a listening task, in their notebooks. They read through this list of mental steps and prepare accordingly before listening to the text. After listening to the text twice, they complete the second part of the checklist, which systematically verifies the mental steps they carried out while listening. Mme Boutin then verifies comprehension of the text. The class discusses the strategies that helped them resolve some comprehension challenges and others that they did not resolve. Finally, Mme Boutin asks her learners to complete the third section of the checklist on goals for the next listening task: that is, they state what they will do next time based on what they have learned today.

Later this month, at the end of the unit, Mme Boutin will ask the learners in her class to complete a self-assessment checklist in their portfolios. This checklist summarizes the six listening objectives for the course in terms of what they can do, such as "I can catch the main point in short, clear simple messages and announcements." In the column after each objective, learners indicate whether they (1) can do this; (2) can do this with help; or (3) need more time and practice to attain this course objective. Mme Boutin's learners complete this checklist periodically and adjust their self-assessments, as necessary, to monitor their mastery of the listening objectives of the course.

At the end of the semester, and periodically throughout the course, Mme Boutin assesses listening skills in a more formal way through unit tests and the final exam. A mark is given for purposes of interim assessment, leading to a final mark for the course. Learners are asked to demonstrate a level of comprehension on the types of oral texts that meet the established listening objectives of the course. At the end of their high school studies, Mme Boutin's learners have the option of taking an international standardized examination. If they are successful, they receive a certificate attesting to their level of language competence, including listening comprehension.

Pre-reading Reflection

1. To what degree does the scenario reflect your experience in assessment of L2 listening skills? What is similar? What is different?
2. What is the teacher assessing today? What is the purpose of this assessment?
3. What is the purpose of the portfolio checklist? Why might this be useful?
4. What is the purpose of the unit tests and final exam?
5. What is the purpose of certification of language competence? Why might this be important to Mme Boutin's learners?
6. At each level of assessment, who is the audience for the outcome? Who will use the scores?

Introduction

In this book we argue for a comprehensive metacognitive approach to L2 listening instruction and present a wide range of tasks to guide language learners in listening development, in and out of the classroom. The end goal of a metacognitive approach is not only skill development: it is equally the development of learners who understand the challenges of L2 listening, think about their learning, know their own strengths and weaknesses as L2 listeners, can self-direct, and can manage their progress in listening. In other words, the goal is self-regulated learners who are aware of their own learning processes, the demands of their learning tasks, key listening skills, and a range of strategies that they apply and adapt to meet the needs of specific contexts. Progress toward this goal or achievement in L2 listening needs to be assessed periodically, regardless of what approach is used in teaching.

Assessment is an important part of learning and teaching. The goal of classroom assessment is, first of all, to provide learners, teachers, and parents with feedback on learner progress in listening development. A second goal, for more formal contexts, is to assign a mark or a level to learner listening performance for purposes of awarding credits, placement, or promotion. Finally, on a larger scale, assessment provides program administrators and school jurisdictions with information on the success of listening instruction in their language programs.

Comprehension, the product of listening, can be assessed by a variety of informal and formal methods. These methods range from learner-based measures such as self-assessment to more formal measures such as course-based examinations or standardized tests. Teachers assess learner progress in listening comprehension as it occurs during class time and, at the same time, through systematic assessment of the products of learning over the duration of a course. On the basis of these products (e.g., performance on a listening task) teachers can draw inferences about learner listening ability. Whatever form it takes, assessment ultimately involves a judgment of learner mastery of content and skills in relation to targeted course objectives or an established benchmark.

The word *assessment* comes from the Latin *assidere,* meaning *to sit beside.* This notion evokes the image of learner and teacher working together to improve learning and teaching. This perspective places an equally important emphasis on the process of listening as on the product. Involving learners in assessment has similar benefits to their active involvement in the learning process. Learners become aware of cognitive processes and develop metacognitive awareness of listening to help them better regulate their comprehension processes. Involving learners in assessment helps them reflect on their learning, set goals, monitor progress, and regularly evaluate their goals. This approach to teaching and assessment is key to successful learning; it leads to greater learner investment and motivation and, ultimately, autonomous language learners.

This chapter discusses L2 listening assessment within the framework of metacognition. We will examine the differences between two approaches to assessment, formative and summative, and show the importance of formative assessment for the development of self-regulated language learners. However, learners will periodically take some form of summative assessment to determine their level of listening development for purposes of promotion or certification. We will examine some examples of both formative and summative assessment, and then discuss some issues related to each approach in light of five important criteria for considering the use of an assessment tool: (1) validity; (2) reliability; (3) authenticity; (4) washback; and (5) practicality.

Approaches to Assessment: Formative and Summative

Formative assessment describes ongoing assessment and observation in the classroom. It is used by teachers to improve instructional methods and by learners to monitor their progress through the teaching and learning process. On the other hand, summative assessment is a judgment of learner listening ability after an instructional phase is complete, or a global judgment by an educational jurisdiction on the effectiveness of an instructional program. The purposes of these two broad approaches to assessment are fundamentally different, as can be seen in Table 12.1. These differences have important implications for the role of the learner/listener in the assessment process.

Formative assessment focuses on the process of learning. It seeks to enhance learning by providing learners with feedback on their progress in meeting targeted learning outcomes. It notes strengths and weaknesses, offers suggestions for improvement, and helps learners acquire the strategies that will lead to greater success. The results of formative assessment feed back into the classroom and are used by both teachers and learners for purposes of remediation. Teachers can adapt their teaching accordingly and learners can determine how to better focus their learning efforts. As such, formative evaluation is interested in learning processes, how learners can improve, and how they can acquire the strategies that will lead to greater success. This makes formative assessment continuous, with learners playing an integral role in the process. Formative assessment is often carried out through more informal methods, such as

Table 12.1 Differences Between Formative and Summative Assessment

	Formative Assessment	Summative Assessment
What?	• All objectives of the unit, a few at a time • Learning processes	• Selected course/program objectives, representative of the level assessed
Why?	• Provide feedback to student and teacher on progress in learning • Determine need for and/or type of remediation required	• Determine level for placement purposes • Course pass/failure • Certification
When?	• Continuous, as part of regular learning activities	• Periodic, at end of a course or program
How?	• Observation • Checklists • Portfolios	• Standardized tests • Achievement/Placement/Proficiency tests
By whom?	• Teacher • Student • Peer	• Teacher • Institution • Educational jurisdiction (school board, government)
Decision to make?	• Adjust teaching procedures • Adapt learning activities • Provide individual remediation on strategies and/or targeted skill(s)	• Award credits (promotion) • Certification • Program evaluation

self-assessment or peer assessment and teacher observation or checklists. It is never global, focusing instead on a limited number of specific course objectives at a time. Formative assessment is more often associated with anecdotal comments than a mark.

Summative assessment, on the other hand, focuses more on the product of learning. It measures mastery of course content against unit objectives at the completion of a course unit or ranks performance at the end of a period of instruction. The only involvement learners have in summative evaluation is taking the test. The result, however, is used to make decisions about their future, such as promotion to a higher level or issuing a certificate attesting to their level of language/listening proficiency. To that end, summative assessment is product-oriented and periodic. Results can also be used by the educational jurisdiction (school board or state) to assess how well a particular skill is taught (e.g., listening) and take action to improve the program, as required.

Summative assessment is done by means of achievement tests to measure learning of specific material, proficiency tests to measure an overall ability in a skill, or high-stakes standardized tests to measure L2 competence for purposes of university studies in the target language. Summative assessment is much broader in scope than formative assessment in that performance can be referenced against defined levels of a scale of language proficiency such as the CEFR (Common European Framework of Reference for Languages) or against the performance of a group on standardized tests, such as TOEFL.

Having clarified the main differences between formative and summative assessment, we will now examine some examples of each approach more closely.

Formative Assessment of L2 Listening

Several types of formative assessment instruments can be used to monitor development of listening skills and provide feedback to learners and teachers. These include learner checklists, questionnaires, listening diaries, teacher checklists, interviews, and, finally, portfolios. Although interim, summative-type assessments such as quizzes and unit tests can also provide valuable formative feedback, they will be discussed later under summative assessment instruments. Given the close link between listening practice that focuses heavily on process and formative assessment, some of the modes of assessment discussed in this chapter were already presented and illustrated in earlier chapters. In these cases, only cursory reference will be made here.

Learner Checklists

Learner checklists (see Figure 12.1) consist of a series of statements that identify certain behaviors or steps in the process of listening. These ele-

Before Listening	D1*	D2	D3	D4	D5
I understand what I have to do after listening and I have asked the teacher for clarifications as required.					
I have thought about the vocabulary of the topic of the text.					
I have thought about my knowledge about the topic of the text.					
I have made my predictions about what I think I might hear.					
I have prepared myself to pay attention and to concentrate on what I will hear.					
I have read the questions I need to answer, or any other material the teacher has given me.					
I have encouraged myself.					
After Listening					
I concentrated on the listening task.					
I tried to verify my predictions.					
I revised my predictions as required.					
I paid attention to key words that were stressed.					
I used my knowledge of the topic to help me guess the words I did not understand.					

*D = Date

TO IMPROVE MY LISTENING, THE NEXT TIME I WILL:

D1:

D2:

D3:

D4:

D5:

Figure 12.1. Checklist to Guide Listening Performance

ments are important in planning for listening, monitoring, and problem-solving during listening, and evaluating after listening. Checklists can help learners focus their attention while listening and self-assess their application of important strategies before and after a listening task. Learners read through a list of behaviors in the first section of the checklist after prediction and other pre-listening activities but before listening to the text itself. After listening, learners complete the second section, which helps them reflect on what they did as they were listening and what they found easy or difficult. When all the steps of the teaching activity have been completed, the learners may be asked to complete a third section of the checklist where they briefly state what they will do differently on the next listening task, based on their performance and reflection on the process.

On checklists, the response is either yes or no; learners tick the box after the statement. Checklists can be cumulative; one sheet may have different columns, identified by date, for each classroom listening activity. Cumulative checklists can be useful to learners and teachers for monitoring listening development over time. There may also be an area on a checklist for feedback from the teacher, either on what the learner has done and/or what the teacher has observed. Examples of helpful observations teachers can make on completed checklists include assessments of whether learners are responding honestly and realistically, based on teacher observation of overall classroom indicators, and suggestions for focused strategies for future listening efforts.

Checklists are particularly helpful for beginner-level listeners and less verbal learners who are more reluctant to participate in process-based class discussions about listening strategies. Completed checklists can be filed in the listening section of the learner portfolio (see later). Other checklist instruments, similar in focus but at a more advanced level, were presented earlier.

Questionnaires

Questionnaires that focus on important processes in listening can be used by learners for purposes of self-assessment, and by teachers for diagnostic purposes to determine direction for remediation. An instrument such as the MALQ taps learner awareness of important processes and strategies for L2 listening. The advantage of questionnaires is that they are easy to administer and can be administered periodically. Since they often use a rating scale (the MALQ uses a scale of 1 for strongly disagree to 6 for strongly agree), questionnaires facilitate comparison. They can be repeated at the end of a course or a unit to ascertain progress in the awareness of listening processes. Completed, dated questionnaires can be filed in the portfolio to track progress over time. Teachers can use completed questionnaires, such as the MALQ, to determine specific areas that are not as well developed: for example, how knowledge about texts is used in planning for listening, or the degree to which a learner evaluates listening strategy use.

Listening Diaries

Listening diaries or journals offer listeners an opportunity to express thoughts, feelings, and reactions to particular listening activities and listening efforts in general. The focus can be on listening initiatives outside of class, as well as activities in class. Entries can be wide-ranging, from progress toward goals or affective responses to risks taken. The format can be completely open; it is often useful, however, for teachers to provide some structure or prompts on what or when to write. Although diaries are intended for learner self-reflection, their potential for formative assessment is enhanced when teachers periodically respond to entries. Some specific observations teachers can make in response to diary entries include the following:

- Makes thorough preparations.
- Listening outside class shows evidence of effort.
- Spends time and effort analyzing listening problems.
- Reflects on performance in a listening event.
- Gives responses that show careful thought about the listening process and good comprehension of the listening input.
- Consciously plans for and uses listening strategies.
- Has developed a clear self-concept as an L2 listener.

By engaging in dialogue with learners, teachers can provide more personalized help to struggling listeners and also learn more about progress in listening by the class as a whole.

Teacher Checklists

Since listening is a covert process, observation is generally of limited value for assessing listening processes in one-way listening events. However, observation of interviews, or other interactive situations, can provide some insights into listener behavior in interactive listening. Behaviors that can be observed include use of clarification strategies, uptaking or back-channelling cues, along with speaking objectives for a given unit. Figure 12.2 presents a generic checklist in which teachers can insert the particular behaviors they would like to observe, related to the objectives of the unit under study. Other columns can be used for speaking objectives, since assessment of listening is not isolated in this context. Given that learners alternate in the roles of speaker and listener, assessment is usually done for two learners at one time.

Objectives: Legend Y=yes N=no ~=with help	Can understand instructions	Can follow directions	Asks for clarification when necessary	Etc.						
Student:										
Student:										
Student:										

Figure 12.2. Teacher Observation Checklist for Interactive Listening/Speaking

Interviews

One-on-one interviews regarding progress in listening offer in-depth, personalized insights into listener thought processes. We will discuss two types: think-alouds and stimulated recall.

Think-aloud is a procedure that attempts to tap thought processes during the act of listening (see the example in Chapter 3). It is based on the assumption that listeners are able to report what they are processing in working memory at that time. When the recording is stopped at predetermined intervals, learners are encouraged to "think aloud" after minimal prompts by the teacher. Think-aloud data can be useful to shed light on where and how listeners experience difficulties, as well as the strategies they do or do not use.

Stimulated recall is a version of the individual interview; teacher and learner together focus on information about listening already provided by the learner in another format, such as MALQ responses or a video of the learner interacting with another speaker. In order to gain greater insight into listening processes, the teacher asks the learner to comment, with the MALQ for example, on a low response to a specific item, a particular response pattern, or a significant change in questionnaire responses over time (pre-, mid-, and post-semester). A teacher–learner exchange on MALQ, presented in Figure 12.3, provides insight into change in learner response over time: that is, how reflection on what to do differently led the learner to focus harder.

Portfolios

Portfolios can be tools for learning, reflection, and goal-setting. Learners collect samples of many of the formative measurement tools described

Teacher: With regard to [MALQ] item 14 "After listening, I think back to how I listened, and about what I might do differently next time," you disagreed at first, then you slightly disagreed, now you strongly agree. Is that correct?

Student: I think, um, I think that's how I was making like, a mistake before: this is like, I would listen, but I wouldn't really decide: "O.K., next time . . .," I don't know, I think I didn't pay as much attention before as I do now before, but now, it's like: "O.K., next time, I have to figure this out," like more, like focus more that way, and maybe that will help me understand more . . .

Figure 12.3. Example of a Stimulated Recall Exchange

Source: Vandergrift, unpublished data

earlier, as well as some summative assessments, in a portfolio. Portfolios demonstrate learner efforts, progress, and achievements in learning (Genesee & Upshur, 1996), usually for all language skills.

Portfolios that just collect sample materials over time are not formative assessment tools in themselves. However, portfolios can incorporate a reflective component on past and future learning that makes them powerful formative assessment tools. An example of such a portfolio is the European Language Portfolio (ELP; Council of Europe, 2000). This tool, individualized and validated by country, contains three elements: (1) a language passport summarizing language experiences and qualifications; (2) a language biography designed to guide learners to plan, reflect on their learning, and assess progress toward their goals; and (3) a dossier containing a selection of work that best represents the learner's proficiency in the target language(s). The ELP has two principal functions. As a pedagogical tool, it fosters the development of learner autonomy. As a reporting tool, it documents the learner's various language learning experiences in a comprehensive manner, inside and outside the formal education system.

The ELP is referenced against the Common European Framework of Languages (CEFR) (Council of Europe, 2001), a common basis for defining language proficiency among the member countries of the Council of Europe. The CEFR defines levels of language proficiency along three broad levels of language performance on a continuum from no ability to near mastery: Basic (A), Independent (B), and Proficient (C). These broad bands are broken down into six global levels of performance against which to measure progress in language learning: A1, A2, B1, B2, C1, and C2. Use of this classification scheme is gaining international currency as a common standard.

The listening descriptors in Figure 12.4, from the CEFR self-assessment grid, include descriptors along the six global levels of language proficiency (Council of Europe, 2001, pp. 26–27). This grid forms the basis

Level	Descriptor
C2	Has no difficulty in understanding any kind of spoken language, whether live or broadcast, delivered at fast native speed. Can understand enough to follow extended speech on abstract and complex topics beyond his/her own field, though he/she may need to confirm occasional details, especially if the accent is unfamiliar.
C1	Can recognize a wide range of idiomatic expressions and colloquialisms, appreciating register shifts. Can follow extended speech even when it is not clearly structured and when relationships are only implied and not signaled explicitly. Can understand standard spoken language, live or broadcast, on both familiar and unfamiliar topics normally encountered in personal, social, academic, or vocational life. Only extreme background noise, inadequate discourse structure, and/or idiomatic usage influences the ability to understand.
B2	Can understand the main ideas of propositionally and linguistically complex speech on both concrete and abstract topics delivered in a standard dialect, including technical discussions in his/her field of specialization. Can follow extended speech and complex lines of argument provided the topic is reasonably familiar, and the direction of the talk is signposted by explicit markers.
B1	Can understand straightforward factual information about common everyday or job-related topics, identifying both general messages and specific details, provided speech is clearly articulated in a generally familiar accent. Can understand the main points of clear standard speech on familiar matters regularly encountered in work, school, leisure etc., including short narratives. Can understand enough to be able to meet needs of a concrete type provided speech is clearly and slowly articulated.
A2	Can understand phrases and expressions related to areas of most immediate priority (e.g., very basic personal and family information, shopping, local geography, employment) provided speech is clearly and slowly articulated.
A1	Can follow speech that is very slow and carefully articulated, with long pauses for him/her to assimilate meaning.

Figure 12.4. CEFR Level Descriptors for Overall Listening Comprehension

Source: COE, 2001, p. 66

for self-assessment in Part 1 (Passport) and Part 2 (Biography) of the ELP where learners identify current level of competence, set goals, monitor progress, and assess learning outcomes. The descriptors in Figure 12.5 depict what an L2 listener should be able to do at each of the six levels of interactive listening in the target language.

Part 2 (Biography) of the ELP is particularly suited to formative assessment. In the Biography section the descriptors for a level are broken down into smaller units for listeners to set goals and monitor progress within a given level. Figure 12.6 displays the finer grained, individualized descriptors for the B1 level in the Swiss ELP for young people and adults (Council of Europe, 2000; Lenz & Schneider, 2004). These descriptors become the goals against which learners track their progress periodically

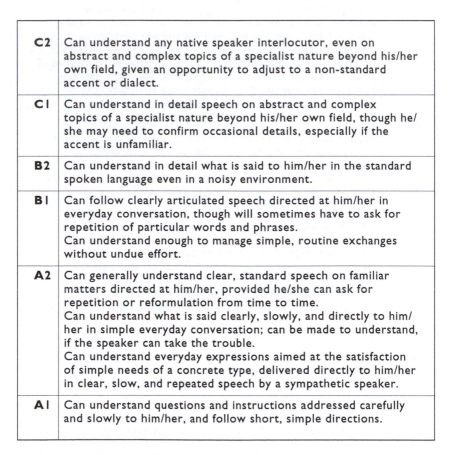

C2	Can understand any native speaker interlocutor, even on abstract and complex topics of a specialist nature beyond his/her own field, given an opportunity to adjust to a non-standard accent or dialect.
CI	Can understand in detail speech on abstract and complex topics of a specialist nature beyond his/her own field, though he/she may need to confirm occasional details, especially if the accent is unfamiliar.
B2	Can understand in detail what is said to him/her in the standard spoken language even in a noisy environment.
BI	Can follow clearly articulated speech directed at him/her in everyday conversation, though will sometimes have to ask for repetition of particular words and phrases. Can understand enough to manage simple, routine exchanges without undue effort.
A2	Can generally understand clear, standard speech on familiar matters directed at him/her, provided he/she can ask for repetition or reformulation from time to time. Can understand what is said clearly, slowly, and directly to him/her in simple everyday conversation; can be made to understand, if the speaker can take the trouble. Can understand everyday expressions aimed at the satisfaction of simple needs of a concrete type, delivered directly to him/her in clear, slow, and repeated speech by a sympathetic speaker.
AI	Can understand questions and instructions addressed carefully and slowly to him/her, and follow short, simple directions.

Figure 12.5. CEFR Level Descriptors for Understanding a Native Speaker Interlocutor

Source: COE, 2001, p. 75

Overall Descriptor for B1 Listening: Can understand straightforward factual information about common everyday or job-related topics, identifying both general messages and specific details, provided speech is clearly articulated in a generally familiar accent. Can understand the main points of clear standard speech on familiar matters regularly encountered in work, school, leisure etc., including short narratives. Can understand enough to be able to meet needs of a concrete type, provided speech is clearly and slowly articulated.	I can do	I can do with help of teacher or peer	My objective
Detailed Descriptors:			
I can follow clearly articulated speech directed at me in everyday conversation, though I sometimes have to ask for repetition of particular words and phrases.			
I can generally follow the main points of extended discussion around me, provided speech is clearly articulated in standard dialect.			
I can listen to a short narrative and form hypotheses about what will happen next.			
I can understand the main points of radio news bulletins and simpler recorded material on topics of personal interest delivered relatively slowly and clearly.			
I can catch the main points in TV programs on familiar topics when the delivery is relatively slow and clear.			
I can understand simple technical information, such as operating instructions for everyday equipment.			
(Additional goals related to course or program objectives)			

Figure 12.6. Self-Assessment Checklist for Level B1 (CEFR)

Based on Lenz & Schneider, 2004

as they take courses at the B1 level. In the three columns to the right of each descriptor, learners indicate whether they can perform the described behavior (1) on their own; (2) with help from a teacher or peer; or (3) not yet. As learners update this checklist at important moments during a course, they will become aware of progress in mastering the listening behaviors described for the level.

This brief description of the ELP demonstrates how a portfolio can be more than just a collection of language samples and self-assessment records. It can also serve as a formative assessment tool for setting goals, tracking progress, and evaluating learning against a well-defined benchmark such as the CEFR.

Self-report tools, essential for learning, need to be complemented by assessments that certify a learner's level of listening and language competence. This is done periodically (e.g., at the end of high school or university studies) through summative assessments such as a standardized examination referenced to the CEFR, or another well-established and internationally recognized benchmark such as the IELTS (International English Language Testing System). The ensuing certificate(s), filed in Part 3 (Dossier) and used to update Part 1 (Passport) of the ELP, can also be presented as an official record of language proficiency for purposes of work and future study in the target language.

Dynamic Listening Assessment

Dynamic assessment views learning and assessment as inextricably linked, so that there is no distinction between them. It is grounded in socio-cultural theory (Vygotsky, 1986). In this paradigm, learning becomes internalized and accessible for use later as the result of mediation with a teacher or another proficient target language speaker. Dynamic listening follows a pattern similar to an intensive interview process. After an initial attempt to complete a listening task, the learner works with the mediator, listening frequently to the oral text with mediation offered as problems arise. Mediation involves leading questions, hints, and prompts as learners work through their understanding of a text. The mediator may also provide linguistic and cultural explanations, as required and illustrated in Figure 12.7 (Ableeva, 2008). In this process, learning and assessment are intertwined and cannot be separated.

Given its one-on-one nature, dynamic assessment is able to give individualized instruction to listeners who may be in the same class but experience different types of comprehension problems. A recent study by Ableeva (2010) compared the results of a traditional listening test with dynamic listening assessment of intermediate-level learners of French. It demonstrated how mediation illuminated sources of poor performance on the traditional test and allowed for appropriate instruction, targeted to address identified problems.

Formative Assessment Tools: Summary

All of the formative assessment tools described earlier are useful for assessing the listening process, tracking progress, and promoting reflection on the development of metacognitive awareness about L2 listening. This does not mean, however, that formative assessment does not address

---

Student: . . . qu'est-ce que c'est belge? (what does it mean "belge"?)

Mediator: Belge? Belgian . . . donc, Léon de Bruxelles . . . Bruxelles c'est la capitale de la Belgique? Belgique (Belgian . . . so, Léon de Bruxelles . . . Brussels is the capital of Belgium)

Student: Ah, ok.

Mediator: et c'est un restaurant . . . quel restaurant? français? canadien? (and it's a restaurant . . . what kind of restaurant? French? Canadian?)

Student: Belgian.

Mediator: Oui, belge . . . ok . . . la Belgique c'est un pays . . . Belgium . . . en français on dit la Belgique et l'adjectif c'est belge, par exemple, un restaurant belge . . . (yes, Belgian . . . ok . . . la Belgique it's a country . . . Belgium . . . in French they say "la Belgique" and the adjective is belge, for example, a Belgian restaurant . . .)

Figure 12.7. Example of a Dynamic Assessment Exchange

Source: Ableeva, 2008, p. 74

the product of listening. Formative assessment tools are designed for use with assessment tasks that focus on comprehension. Verification of comprehension may be accompanied by a process-based class discussion about difficulties encountered and how these difficulties were or were not resolved. The verification exercise may be one found in the course teaching materials or in the pedagogical sequence. It may even involve a mark, as in a quiz.

The important thing, however, is that process-based assessment is interwoven with product-based assessment so that both learners and teachers become aware of what learners can do, related to the listening objectives of a particular unit, and what may need further development. Whether a mark is attached to the assessment or not, the goal is to provide feedback, in order to modify teaching and learning activities for the next lesson or assessment task.

Summative Assessment of L2 Listening

This section will briefly discuss some types of summative assessment tools familiar to most learners and teachers: quizzes, achievement tests, proficiency tests, and large-scale standardized tests.

Quizzes

Quizzes can serve both summative and formative roles in language assessment. They are usually based on a limited number of current unit or course objectives. L2 listening quizzes can be a variation of the listening practice regularly done in class. For example, a comprehension exercise (or quiz) and the resulting mark (e.g., 8/10) can be formative by providing feedback on progress in listening to certain types of texts and understanding vocabulary related to the current theme, as well as summative by providing a mark for purposes of unit assessment.

Achievement Tests

At the end of a course unit, learners often write a teacher-developed achievement test to assess what they know with regard to the objectives of that particular unit. In a four skills course, such a test will usually include a section where learners listen to one or more texts and complete a comprehension task, such as answering multiple-choice and/or open-ended questions, transferring information to a table, choosing a picture, ordering a set of pictures, etc. These tasks are likely similar to earlier quizzes. The resulting mark will contribute to a summative course assessment, for purposes of credit and promotion within the educational system and beyond. These tests can also be formative in nature, depending on when they occur in the timeline of a course.

Proficiency Tests

Listening proficiency tests are designed to assess global listening competence. They may be "in-house" measurement instruments developed and validated for a particular university or school jurisdiction, or they may be large-scale standardized tests. They are always summative since the goal is to provide information to the teacher, institution or school jurisdiction with regard to admission, placement, or certification. They can be used to place learners at an appropriate course level or in a particular type of language course, such as a course on listening development.

Proficiency tests are not tied to a particular course or curriculum. They may be referenced against a particular language framework such as the CEFR or the IELTS. They allow for the possibility of differential competence in the target language: for example, referenced against the CEFR, learner performance may result in placement at B2 for listening but only at A2 for writing.

Large-Scale Standardized Tests

At certain points in their educational trajectory, learners may take a large-scale standardized test to certify their proficiency level for purposes of placement, job qualifications, or study in the target language. Large-scale tests such as TOEFL or IELTS are usually required for admission to university by non-native applicants. These tests are often standardized so that results can be interpreted on a common scale. In contrast to achievement tests, standardized tests are administered and scored under a consistent set of procedures. Uniform conditions of administration are necessary to make it possible to compare results across individuals or schools. Although standardized tests might be helpful to decision makers, they are not necessarily helpful for the learners involved (Shohamy, 2001). The results of these types of tests often become the basis for important decisions about a learner's future, such as program placement, promotion, university acceptance, or graduation. When test results have serious consequences for a test taker's future, the requirements for evidence of test validity and reliability (see later) become correspondingly higher.

Summative Assessment Tools: Summary

The goal of summative assessment tools is to provide information to various stakeholder recipients (learner, parent, teacher, educational jurisdiction) on learner competence (e.g., L2 listening) at a certain point in time. There is generally no interest in assessing learning process: only the product of learner learning is of interest. The judgment made, based on the learner's performance, will likely have important implications for his or her future.

Choosing Formative and Summative Assessment Tools for L2 Listening

In their discussion of principles of language assessment, Brown and Abeywickrama (2010) ask some fundamental questions about the quality of an assessment tool and identify five "cardinal" criteria:

1. Validity: to what degree does it accurately measure what you want to measure?
2. Reliability: to what degree is it dependable?
3. Authenticity: to what degree is it representative of real-life language use?
4. Washback: to what degree does it provide useful feedback for the learner and influence the teaching process?

5. Practicality: to what degree is it amenable for classroom use, given administrative constraints?

The final section of this chapter will discuss each one of these criteria, how formative and summative assessment tools measure up against them, and issues for teachers to consider in choosing a mix of formative and summative assessment tools to fit their particular situations. Table 12.2 summarizes these issues.

Validity

Validity refers to the extent to which a test assesses what it proposes to assess. A test of L2 listening should measure comprehension ability only. It should not, for example, be a test of hearing, prior knowledge about a topic, other variables such as spelling in dictation, or reading long multiple-choice questions. The aspects of validity most important for the assessment of L2 listening comprehension are construct validity, content validity, and predictive validity.

Construct validity refers to clarity and specification of the essential theory on which the measurement instrument is based. It requires defining what needs to be assessed and then creating tasks to elicit the targeted knowledge and skills through appropriate texts and response items. Generally, the purpose of the assessment tool and the context of language use will guide construct definition (Buck, 2001). However, when it comes to general proficiency tests and overall classroom listening development, the construct for L2 comprehension cannot be as clearly defined. In this case, Buck proposes a default listening construct that assesses:

> the ability to (1) process extended samples of realistic spoken language, automatically and in real time; (2) understand the linguistic information that is unequivocally included in the text; and, (3) make whatever inferences are unambiguously implicated by the content of the passage. (2001, p. 114)

This construct represents the core of listening ability and is sufficiently flexible to fit most contexts and allow listeners to demonstrate their comprehension ability.

In related research, Wagner (2002) examined the construct validity of a video-based test. Using existing taxonomies of listening skills, he hypothesized that top-down and bottom-up factors would define the construct. Instead, the two factors that emerged were the ability to process (1) explicitly stated information, and (2) implicitly stated information. This outcome provides empirical support for the default construct proposed by Buck—in particular, the second and third components of that construct.

Table 12.2. Issues in Formative and Summative Assessment in Light of the Five Criteria for Assessment

Principle	Formative Assessment	Summative Assessment
Validity	• assessment tasks match learning tasks easily because assessment is integrated into learning process • assess specific learning objectives • assess both process and product • assess all learning objectives throughout the process of instruction	• must ensure that assessment tasks match learning tasks, particularly for proficiency and standardized tests • assess global or long-term objectives • assess only product • careful sampling required to assess a representative number of objectives and contexts
Reliability	• comprehension can only be inferred, often by means of reading or writing • self- and peer-assessment vary widely; hard to control variables • use multi-method assessment to compensate for variability	• comprehension can only be inferred, often by means of reading or writing • one-time assessments are problematic as fair assessment of skill levels. • the more serious the consequences of the test, the greater the need to ensure high reliability
Authenticity	• use of real-life language and tasks increases authenticity • focus on specific outcomes assesses skill in one context at a time	• use of real-life language and tasks increases authenticity • focus on broader range of tasks and contexts requires frequent shifts in context by listener
Washback	• high because close link between assessment and learning tasks provides regular, useful feedback for learner and teacher • immediate feedback allows student to adjust strategy use and improve learning	• high if assessment tasks match learning tasks but low if not congruent, which may affect learner attitudes to teaching tasks • usually no feedback to the student other than a mark
Practicality	• frequency requires planning course time well • high time requirements in teacher marking/review	• occasional; limited impact on teaching time • initial preparation of a test to ensure validity and reliability is a challenge • purchase of reliable standardized or commercial tests reduces preparation time

Content validity refers to the degree to which an assessment tool samples the listening knowledge and skills that teachers wish to measure. An assessment tool should measure the particular listening skills being learned in order to determine if the listener can successfully perform these skills. For example, a test for academic listening must, perforce, assess different skills than a test for everyday functional listening (e.g., shopping, answering the telephone). Content validity requires that what is assessed reflects the learning objectives and the listening tasks included in a teaching unit or a course.

Content validity is closely related to face validity, which is the subjective judgment by learners of the degree to which a test reflects what it is purported to assess. In short, if it is supposed to measure listening skills, does it look like it measures listening skills? For example, dictation, a widely used integrative test for listening, would not have a great deal of face validity as a summative assessment for learners who spent a semester listening to real-life oral texts. If a test does not appear to assess what learners have learned, they may perceive the test as unfair and this may affect their performance. A quick way to check for face validity is to ask a colleague to glance over a test or instrument and describe what it is measuring.

Predictive validity is the degree to which an instrument is able to accurately predict real-life listening performance. For example, if the goal of listening instruction is functional language use outside the classroom, the predictive validity of the instrument will be the degree to which the score accurately predicts the listener's ability to understand information in realistic spoken texts and make the necessary inferences implied in that information (based on Buck's default construct). With reference to the B1 level listening criterion and spoken interaction criterion of the Common European Framework of Reference for Languages (Council of Europe, 2001, p. 26), for example, the assessment instruments would assess the listener's ability to:

- understand the main points of clear standard speech on familiar matters regularly encountered in work, school, leisure, including short narratives; and
- clearly follow articulated speech directed at him/her in everyday conversation, though will sometimes have to ask for repetition of particular words and phrases.

In sum, all facets of validity are closely related, with construct validity as the overarching concept. In fact, validity is increasingly viewed as a unitary concept. In addition to what the test measures, validity has been broadened to include the inferences that are made from test scores and how these scores are used (Bachman, 1990; Messick, 1989). Assessment instruments that meet the closely related criteria of construct, content, and predictive validity will measure in a credible way what has been learned, based on listening objectives for the course, which, in turn, are referenced against a particular curriculum or an overarching language framework such as the CEFR or the IELTS. The evaluation of learner comprehension ability will demonstrate real-life listening behavior as closely as possible.

Validity in Formative and Summative Assessments

Validity in the assessment of authentic listening comprehension is best accomplished through tasks that evaluate the development of real-life listening skills. As noted earlier, listening practice is best conducted through authentic language tasks that are appropriate to the age, language level, and life experience of the learners. Given the important link between learning and assessment, it would be most appropriate to assess learner progress in listening through similar tasks. Buck (1997) argues that authentic language tasks should (1) use texts in natural, spoken language that are as realistic as possible; (2) replicate tasks that listeners are likely to encounter in real-life contexts; and (3) reflect the purpose for listening to the text: that is, require listeners to understand the information the text was created to communicate. Some examples, in addition to those presented in Chapter 9, include: listening to a restaurant advertisement for the telephone number in order to make a reservation; answering the telephone and writing down the essential information so that the intended recipient can call back; listening to a short video and taking notes in order to retell the story to a friend; or, listening to an interview or debate on a controversial topic in order to write a report for a newsletter.

Assessment tasks that parallel learning tasks also hold a high degree of face validity for learners. Learners find this kind of authentic assessment more motivating because they sense that what they are learning is related to their needs and can be used in real-life situations. Although the purposeful listening associated with real-life texts is both authentic and motivating, the reality of much of everyday listening is that we listen without any immediate need and retain the information for potential use in the future (Buck, 2001). This reality legitimates much of classroom listening practice and assessment where listeners seek to understand the main ideas and supporting details of a range of authentic, real-life oral texts.

To meet the criterion of validity, formative assessment instruments should target the specific objectives under instruction and teachers should initiate any necessary remedial instruction as soon as possible. The close relationship between teaching and formative assessment makes it easier to ensure validity. Examples of specific objectives include comprehension of unit vocabulary, specific types of questions in an interview, verifying information in a specific kind of text, or recognizing a structure being learned in the unit. Focusing on specific objectives at different points within a teaching unit informs both learners and teachers on progress made toward these objectives. It ensures an interim, formative assessment of all unit objectives and helps the teacher make decisions about which objectives need further instruction and assessment. Validity is further enhanced when the formative assessment instruments also monitor the process dimension of listening through monitoring and evaluation of strategies used, particularly by learners who are experiencing difficulty.

Summative assessment tools, on the other hand, are more global in nature. If they are achievement tests, they will assess progress in attaining the broader objectives of a course. If they are proficiency tests or standardized tests, they are usually not tied to a particular program and will not assess objectives and learning tasks of a specific program. Their validity lies in the degree to which the content and tasks in the test match the broad, global descriptions of listening ability.

Summative assessment tools cannot assess everything. Within the domain of general listening ability, they must carefully sample a limited but representative number of language tasks and contexts in order to meet validity standards. Finally, since most summative assessment tools are not interested in monitoring listening development, they would be less valid for courses where explicit development of metacognition is part of the learning objectives.

Reliability

Reliability is concerned with the degree to which one can rely on an assessment instrument to provide consistent and dependable results. In other words, a reliable instrument will provide similar results with a similar population under similar conditions. Reliability is always important, but it becomes particularly critical for high-stakes tests where the results may have significant impact on a learner's future. The goal of reliability is to have all learners demonstrate their true level of comprehension ability. Brown and Abeywickrama (2010) note that learners, teachers, instrument administration, and the instrument itself are all factors that contribute to the reliability of assessment.

Learner-related factors, such as fatigue, illness, or stress, are particularly pertinent in the assessment of listening. As noted earlier, anxiety plays a significant role in listening performance due to the ephemeral nature of the acoustic signal. This dimension of reliability can be enhanced by frequent listening practice with similar texts in regular classroom learning, without the threat of assessment. Some techniques to help learners reduce anxiety were presented in earlier chapters.

Teacher-related factors include potential bias in scoring, since reliable correction requires consistent judgment on the part of the marker. This becomes particularly pertinent for assessment methods and test items that are open-ended and subject to interpretation. The more high-stakes the test, the more important it is to have at least two scorers and to conduct periodic inter-rater reliability checks in order to ensure that scoring by all raters is consistent. An example is the scoring of free written recall protocols where learners write as much information as possible about what they understood, after listening to a passage.

Administration-related factors refer to the contextual factors that can affect test outcomes. These are particularly important for the assessment of listening, given that reliable results depend on the ability of all learners to hear the acoustic signal in the same way. In order to ensure this, there must be no distracting noises (e.g., ventilation, traffic outside) so that learners in all areas of the room can hear and see (in the case of video) equally well. In the case of multiple administrations of the same assessment, it is crucial that all groups hear the aural material in the same way and at the same time of the day, in addition to the factors already mentioned. In cases of live presentation (not recorded), it is important to respect similar pauses, repetitions, and listening conditions for all groups.

Test-related factors refer to the capacity of the assessment items to correctly measure comprehension of what the learners hear. Ambiguous items, for example, reduce the reliability of the testing instrument. This is also true of items that require learners to draw on information outside of a text or items that have more than one possible answer.

Reliability in Formative and Summative Assessment

Ensuring reliability is a challenge for formative assessment since much of it is based on learner self-assessment or peer assessment, which can vary greatly within and between learners. The implicit nature of listening requires learners to reflect on a range of unobservable knowledge and skills. A single instrument or the performance of a single task is not enough to provide learners with an accurate picture of their strengths and weaknesses. Using diverse instruments and tasks in formative assessment can help to increase effectiveness and reliability.

The practice of formative assessment is an emerging field. Over time, evidence-based research will find consensus on more reliable key indicators of progress in learning the process of listening. Research already shows that time spent on formative assessment can have positive impacts on the listening outcomes on more summative measures (Ross, 2005).

Multi-method assessment increases reliability in both formative and summative assessment. Frequent, systematic assessment through a variety of instruments by learner and teacher can provide a more reliable picture of learner listening ability. For example, reliability is enhanced when data from a learner questionnaire such as the MALQ is triangulated with some quiz results and listening diary entries to capture both the strengths and weaknesses of a learner with regard to L2 listening. The importance of multi-method assessment was underlined in a qualitative classroom study by Rea-Dickens and Gardner (2000) who found that critical decisions about learner advancement were often made based on inadequate observation data. This is particularly important when assessing listening comprehension on the basis of classroom observation: it is not always clear how much a learner understands unless the teacher verifies comprehension regularly and uses various types of formative assessment.

This is equally true for summative evaluation. Often important decisions about a learner's future are made based on the results of a one-time assessment that may not be a reliable representation of listening ability because of extenuating circumstances at the time of the test.

A major challenge for reliable assessment of listening is the elusive nature of the acoustic signal. Listening processes are difficult to measure in one definitive test, because they are not directly observable and they cannot be verified empirically. By their very nature, cognitive processes in listening interact in complex ways with different types of knowledge, changing as the process evolves, unlike writing or speaking. The product of listening is not directly observable either. Ultimately comprehension can only be inferred on the basis of task performance for both formative and summative assessment. The reliability of inferences may increase or decrease, depending on how we ask learners to demonstrate comprehension. As a general rule, the more serious the consequences of the assessment result, the greater the need to ensure a high level of reliability of the assessment instrument.

Since actual comprehension is not observable, it has to be demonstrated in some other way, without introducing reading or writing as confounding variables.[1] In this sense, reliability also intersects with validity. Pure listening comprehension is most appropriately measured through aural prompts and non-verbal verification options such as selecting from a choice of pictures or objects, sequencing pictures or other graphics, drawing a picture, tracing on a map, or performing a physical response. On the other hand, using aural prompts to assess listening comprehension raises other issues: memory becomes an intervening variable, since learner ability to demonstrate comprehension may depend on how much information they can hold in memory. Jotting down notes can compensate for memory constraints and enhance face validity of the test. Carrell, Dunkel, and Mollaun (2004) concluded that note-taking during a computer-based

---

1 In the case of interactive listening, it is possible to observe use of reception strategies such as clarification requests and appropriate back-channelling cues used to advance the conversation.

listening test may help L2 listeners, depending on the length of the lecture, the topic, and listener proficiency.

Authenticity

Authenticity in assessment refers to the degree to which real-life language use is reflected in the texts and tasks assessed. Listening passages that have the characteristics of unplanned speech are closer to the oral language used in everyday speech. The more an assessment uses dense, cognitively demanding texts intended for reading, the less it will reflect the principle of authenticity for listening. As noted in Chapter 8, listening texts containing unplanned speech share a number of characteristics, such as redundancies, false starts, and pauses that make them more "listenable" and easier to comprehend. Authenticity can also be enhanced through the choice of tasks used to assess comprehension. Tasks that require listeners to transfer comprehended information are more authentic in that they reflect real-life purposes for listening. An example is filling in a calendar, based on listening to a conversation between two friends about what they need to accomplish.

Authenticity in Formative and Summative Assessment

Authenticity in formative assessment is likely to be high because the instrument focuses on a limited number of learning objectives and texts closely related to the context and theme of the unit. If the learning objectives for the unit focus on authentic real-life listening skills, the assessment will then meet this criterion as well. Since formative assessment is focused on one theme, all listening tasks will be related to a similar context. On the other hand, authenticity in summative assessment can be a greater challenge because most tests will require learners to listen to texts representing a range of contexts. Such tests require listeners to constantly shift contexts, which does not reflect real-life listening and can affect learner performance.

Authenticity in summative evaluations can be increased or decreased by factors such as the speaker's accent and dialect. These factors can introduce a bias against listeners who may be less familiar with the accent used in the assessment tool (Major et al., 2002, 2005). This is less of a difficulty with formative assessment because familiarization with particular accents is often one of the specific objectives of a unit and the assessment will be designed to measure that objective.

Washback

The impact of assessment on classroom teaching is referred to as washback. The impact of washback often affects the curriculum, teacher, and learner actions and attitudes, resulting in behaviors that they would not do if it were not for the test (Alderson & Wall, 1993). The more a test reflects classroom learning activities (i.e., real-life listening tasks), the more beneficial the washback effects and the potential for the test to shape learner attitudes toward the value of these listening tasks. The inverse is also true: for example, if the final examination in a course uses a dictation or a listening cloze activity to test listening comprehension, the washback effects will be negative. If this is the case, learners may not consider authentic listening practice useful and teachers may choose not to develop real-life listening skills in class.

Washback also includes the potential of assessment tools to provide feedback to guide future learning efforts. Since immediate feedback to learners is an essential part of formative assessment, washback is inherent in formative assessment tools. If this feedback is to be beneficial to learners, however, it must go beyond mere judgment of whether the targeted objectives have been mastered or not. The diagnostic dimension of formative assessment should provide learners with precise feedback on strengths and weaknesses. This can be feedback on process (specific listening strategies and skills), or product (language-related issues such as vocabulary). Appropriate feedback can increase learner ownership of their progress to becoming successful L2 listeners.

Washback in Formative and Summative Assessment

The positive washback effects of formative assessment can foster learner motivation for learning. Becoming more aware of listening processes and understanding appropriate strategy use alters learner attributions and builds learner self-efficacy for listening tasks and expectations for success. Learners can attribute their difficulty to ineffective strategy use rather than inherent inabilities, if their efforts are not successful. As learners attribute success to use of effective strategies, knowledge about how to listen will be strengthened, facilitating the likelihood of strategy transfer (Chamot et al., 1999). This is consistent with the views of Deci and Ryan (1985) who contend that a learner's sense of self-determination and intrinsic motivation is enhanced when teachers support learner autonomy and provide informative feedback.

The built-in washback element of formative assessment can also reduce anxiety because assessment is a regular part of the learning process. Both washback and face validity are enhanced when assessment and learning are interwoven in formative assessment.

On the other hand, washback in summative assessment requires specific attention by the teacher. It is rarely part of a summative approach to assessment. An extreme example is a mark without any explanation. Teachers can provide feedback on summative assessments, such as achievement tests, through more detailed notes of explanation for the results on particular items or scheduling face-to-face meetings to discuss the meaning of the results of a particular summative assessment.

Practicality

Practicality refers to the feasibility of using a particular assessment instrument in the context of a particular classroom and course of instruction. Time is likely the most important factor. In addition, administration-related factors, such as availability of equipment and time, affect the results of testing and need to be taken into consideration by the teacher in the choice or design of assessment instruments.

Practicality in Formative and Summative Assessment

Assessment of listening presents more complex practical challenges than assessment of reading or writing, by comparison. A significant practical factor in formative assessment is the amount of time required for administration of the tools and feedback to the learners. Formative assessment is labor-intensive and, in order to be useful, it needs to be systematic.

Practical factors in summative evaluation are different. The time needed to adequately and fairly sample language from the desired range of listening contexts and create appropriate response formats within a particular instrument may be a challenge. Use of commercial tests may reduce preparation time, but choice of tests for a particular class and context can also be a challenge. Administration factors need to be considered when summative tests are given in larger groups, for example, or in circumstances different from the usual class, such as standardized tests.

Formative and Summative Assessment: Other Considerations

Both formative and summative assessments have their place in learning and teaching L2 listening. Determining the appropriate mix and choice of particular instruments will depend on the circumstances of a particular class and teacher.

Some of the factors involved in listening assessment have received attention in research, providing guidance for teachers to make strategic choices for assessment of listening in their courses. Response format has a significant effect on listening test performance in both formative and summative assessment. Cheng (2004) determined that learners completing multiple-choice cloze items outperformed learners who completed traditional multiple-choice items who, in turn, outperformed learners who completed open-ended questions.

The placement of the comprehension question in relationship to the text, if both are presented orally, also has consequences. If the question comes after the text, listeners are more likely to respond incorrectly than if the question is given before the text (Tsui & Fullilove, 1998). Three different formats for multiple-choice questions were investigated by Yanagawa and Green (2008). Listeners who previewed only the question stems and listeners who previewed both the question stems and the answer options performed at similar levels. However, listeners who previewed only the answer options obtained significantly lower results.

In general, more reliance on formative assessment will enhance metacognitive awareness of listening processes. However, it is legitimate to ask whether the time and energy given to the reflection, goal-setting, and feedback involved in formative assessment will actually lead to improved learning outcomes. An important study by Ross (2005) demonstrated that formative assessment methods can have a positive impact on L2 listening success. Differences in TOEFL listening and reading sub-scores for a large cohort of Japanese learners of English were tracked, over a period of eight years, for any evidence of change in test performance as a result of a shift in classroom assessment from product-oriented, summative procedures to more process-oriented, formative approaches. The rationale for introducing a formative approach was predicated on the idea that self-assessment and peer assessment would increase learner investment and motivation. The formative assessment measures were primarily a combination of self-assessment and peer-assessment as part of the grading criteria for the listening courses.

Three analyses of achievement and proficiency growth pointed to gains in listening for the formative assessment cohort, but not in reading. To explain these results, Ross (2005) speculates that shifting the locus of control to learners through more "process-oriented portfolios, self-assessment, peer-assessment, group projects and cooperative learning tasks" (p. 337) may lead to increased learner engagement. The design of the study was not experimental, and thus does not permit strong causal inference. However, the overall picture suggests that formative approaches enhance motivation, and so indirectly influence achievement (Ross, personal communication, September 9, 2010).

Summary

Assessment is an important part of learning for the learner. It can also help teachers and school authorities review and improve programs of instruction. Key to these results is seeing assessment as a learning activity.

For listening, this chapter has emphasized the value of formative assessment as a learning tool. In addition to monitoring progress, formative assessment enhances metacognitive knowledge about listening, which is an essential component to becoming a successful L2 listener.

A mix of formative and summative assessment is desirable and can be effective. Regular formative assessments, reinforced by occasional summative assessments on a broader level and at strategic points in the learning cycle, can provide feedback on progress made and confirmation of achievement in proficiency. This will result in increased motivation to continue the complex task of listening development. Formative assessment can be perceived by teachers as a burden; however, when it becomes part of learning, it is woven into regular classroom learning activities.

Whether formative or summative, assessment tools need to be evaluated against the criteria of validity, reliability, authenticity, washback, and practicality. An assessment strategy for a particular course will take all these factors into consideration, along with the particular circumstances of the learners and program. Careful implementation of an effective assessment strategy will contribute to the goal of helping learners learn to listen through an emphasis on both the process and product of listening.

Discussion Questions and Tasks

1. "All tests are assessments but not all assessments are tests" (Brown & Abeywickrama, 2010, p. 123). What does this statement mean to you? Discuss its relevance for the assessment of L2 listening.

2. Given what you now know about listening processes, can you explain the results of the research studies dealing with multiple-choice test formats (pp. 265–66)?

   (a) Cheng (2004)
   (b) Yanagawa and Green (2008)
   (c) Tsui & Fullilove (1998)

3. Examine a listening test for the types of listening passages, tasks, and response formats used. Evaluate the test from the perspective of the five criteria discussed in this chapter.

4. Examine the listening activities in a textbook and accompanying learner exercise book. Are there any formative assessment activities included? What does the teacher's guide include with regard to strategy development and formative assessment?

5. How can one combine assessment of both product and process in one formative assessment instrument? Take a listening activity from the textbook you examined and create a formative assessment instrument that allows for assessment of both process and product.

Suggestions for Further Reading

Brown, H. D., & Abeywickrama, P. (2010). Beyond tests: Alternatives in assessment. In H. Douglas Brown (Ed.), *Language assessment: Principles and classroom practices* (2nd ed.) (pp. 122–155). Whiteplains, NY: Pearson Longman.
A chapter on alternatives in assessment that presents and discusses the pros and cons of a number of options to the traditional test.

Buck, G. (2001). *Assessing listening.* Cambridge, UK: Cambridge University Press.
Chapter 3: Approaches to assessing listening (pp. 61–94)
An introduction to three approaches to assessing listening (discrete-point, integrative, and communicative), the main ideas associated with each approach, as well as examples for each.
Chapter 5: Creating tasks (pp. 116–153)
A good discussion of how to develop listening tasks in the light of the construct of listening adopted, including the following: (1) task characteristics; (2) interaction between task and test-taker; (3) use of comprehension questions; and (4) evaluating and modifying listening tasks.
Chapter 6: Providing suitable texts (pp. 154–193)
An overview of many practical issues related to providing test takers with suitable samples of spoken language, how to select or create the texts and how to present them to the test taker.

Ross, S. J. (2005). The impact of assessment method on foreign language proficiency growth. *Applied Linguistics, 26,* 317–342.
This empirical study examines the effects of formative assessment on the listening and reading performance of a large cohort of learners on a high-stakes summative assessment. Although somewhat technical, it provides evidence for the positive impact of formative assessment on growth in listening.

Thompson, I. (1995). Assessment of second/foreign language listening comprehension. In D. Mendelsohn, & J. Rubin (Eds.), *A guide for the teaching of second language listening* (pp. 31–58). San Diego, CA: Dominie Press.
A good, readable overview of many of the issues related to valid and reliable assessment of listening comprehension.

Epilogue: Synthesis of Issues Related to Teaching and Learning Listening

In the Prologue we introduced a number of common perceptions about teaching and learning second language (L2) listening. We asked you to reflect on how much you agreed or disagreed with these statements, and to keep them in mind as you read through the book.

Now that you have finished reading the book, have your beliefs changed? How have the research findings confirmed or changed your understanding of L2 listening? Has the approach to listening instruction and development discussed and exemplified in this book changed or added to your own thinking about listening comprehension and methods of teaching and learning L2 listening?

We will close the book with a brief overview of the issues in the Prologue. Our discussion will be based on the research and the principles for teaching and learning L2 listening presented throughout this book.

1. Compared to the other language skills, listening is a passive activity

On the surface, listening may appear to be a relatively passive skill. After all, there is nothing that can be observed. Listening processes are very difficult to access, because of their covert nature. However, listeners are engaged in a number of cognitive processes as they construct meaning. They perceive sounds, segment words, accumulate these into meaningful units, register stress and intonation, and retain all of these. They also interpret all the detailed inputs within the immediate and larger context of the utterance. Managing all of these processes in real time, given the constraints of working memory, is an enormous feat. In fact, prolonged listening under less than ideal circumstances can quickly lead to physical and mental exhaustion.

Listening is hard work and, contrary to popular opinion, listeners are very active as they seek to understand a message. This is particularly true for L2 listeners whose knowledge of the target language is incomplete and who often must compensate for gaps in understanding. Continuing to direct attention to the text or interlocutor and maintaining concentration add to the cognitive demands of the task.

L2 listeners may develop a passive approach to listening in the target language because they do not feel in control: they feel they are at the mercy of the sound stream or the speaker. It is important for learners to realize that they can be proactive in their approach to a listening text. When they attempt to anticipate what they will hear, based on their accumulated linguistic, prior, and metacognitive knowledge, listeners can better regulate their comprehension. If they anticipate correctly, what they understand will reinforce their predictions. If they are wrong, they can problem-solve to discover the reason for the difference. Either way, the likelihood of understanding and remembering can exceed what they would have understood when they did nothing to manage their listening. This is why planning, predicting, monitoring, problem-solving, and evaluation are such powerful listening and learning tools.

2. The important thing in teaching instruction is that students get the right answer

An accurate understanding of the desired information is an important goal for L2 listening instruction. Typically, the main goal of communicative listening activities is successful comprehension. However, with a focus on the product of listening, every activity becomes a test of learner listening ability, rather than a means for understanding the social and cognitive nature of developing and using these listening skills. Although a focus on the product of listening allows teachers to verify comprehension, the answer (correct or incorrect) neither helps learners gain insight into the comprehension process nor helps them learn how to listen better. Furthermore, an exclusive interest in the right answer often creates a high level of anxiety, which has negative impacts on the efficiency of working memory.

Learners need opportunities to learn the process of listening, just as they are taught the process of writing, for example. They need to acquire the metacognitive skills involved in successful comprehension so that they can better regulate these processes and become more successful listeners. Teacher guidance and scaffolded listening practice are valuable for demystifying the processes involved in successful listening and help make explicit to novice listeners the implicit processes of skilled listeners.

By integrating metacognitive activities with everyday listening activities, teachers can help learners become aware of the various processes that are involved in L2 listening. In turn, learners can apply this knowledge to their listening development beyond the classroom to explore their own self-concept as listeners, use appropriate strategies, or identify factors that influence their own performance in different listening tasks.

3. Learner anxiety is a major obstacle in L2 listening

Learner factors that contribute to high anxiety are perceptions that listening is the most difficult skill and largely beyond their control. Classroom factors that contribute to anxiety are the focus on product and the association of listening with evaluation of comprehension. In combination, these factors can lead to low confidence levels, a limited sense of self-efficacy, and a feeling by learners that they are incapable of improving their listening abilities. This affects progress in learning.

The way we teach listening can contribute to or reduce anxiety. When the focus is the product of listening, listening activities often become a test of listening ability; learners are expected to reveal how much they have understood or, more often, what they have not understood, leading to anxiety about listening. On the other hand, teaching approaches that focus on the process of listening can facilitate the acquisition of L2 listening skills and gradually help learners take control of their own listening development, which can reduce anxiety. Practice without the threat of direct teacher evaluation allows learners to use working memory to full capacity and understand more, which in turn increases learner self-confidence in their ability to listen with success.

Pre-listening activities can also help alleviate anxiety by better preparing learners for what they will hear. Building schematic knowledge helps learners anticipate content and the potential occurrence of certain words. Discussion helps them recognize words they already know in print but not yet in spoken form. These elements of pre-listening activities can facilitate word recognition and lexical segmentation.

It is useful for learners to identify which situations create anxiety. With this knowledge, they can use appropriate strategies to deal with listening situations that they find problematic. It will also help them recognize that the whole process of learning to listen need not cause anxiety, even if some moments are stressful. Although high levels of anxiety can be debilitating, a certain level of anxiety can give learners the "edge" to concentrate harder and be more successful.

4. Listening means understanding words, so teachers just need to help learners understand all the words in the sound stream

Research on the role of vocabulary in listening success demonstrates that it is a very significant factor; recent studies demonstrate that up to 50 percent of success in listening ability could be explained by vocabulary knowledge. This reality points to the importance of instruction in both lexical knowledge and word recognition skills for the L2 listener.

Pre-listening discussion can help learners recognize words they know in print but cannot easily identify in connected speech. Learners are often unable to make the sound–script connection because they are not able to segment the sounds of the word from surrounding words or, in some cases, they do not recognize the word because of their own inaccurate or different pronunciation of it.

Time spent on post-listening perception activities can increase learner knowledge of sounds and phonological rules for recognizing words. Repeated exposure to unfamiliar sounds and knowing how some sounds change in connected speech will help beginning- and intermediate-level learners develop more reliable word segmentation skills. At post-listening stage, learners no longer feel the pressure that often occurs during real-time listening; they can now pay attention to isolated features of speech and build up their metacognitive knowledge of authentic speech. During these activities, learners often realize that the words they could not recognize are actually words they know.

Research also indicates that some L2 listeners are able to successfully compensate for a weaker linguistic base. This suggests that these learners are very strategic in their approach to the listening task. Teaching learners to compensate for gaps in understanding by inferencing on the basis of what is known demonstrates what is characteristic of successful learners. A metacognitively orientated pedagogical sequence and other metacognitive activities can help learners to skillfully orchestrate metacognitive processes and achieve comprehension, in spite of gaps in understanding.

5. Teaching listening through video is better than audio alone

The visual component offered by videotext elicits a positive affective response to learning; but the measurable impact of adding a visual component for listening comprehension is less certain. Attention to the listening task, the visual, and the audio may be too demanding or distracting. The reality is that the visual content in many videotexts often does not closely match the audio. When the two are not congruent, listeners become distracted and can no longer concentrate adequately on the audio, frustrating the comprehension process. Therefore, a key consideration in choosing videotext for listening instruction is ensuring a close match between the content of the images and the audio input, especially for learners at lower levels of language proficiency. When the visual supports the audio, comprehension is greatly facilitated for beginner-level listeners. Listeners at higher proficiency levels are more capable of dealing with a mismatch between audio and video, particularly if the topic is well known to them.

Most of the studies investigating the use of videotext have been carried out in the context of assessment. Given the stress of assessment, the potential for distraction, and the need to move eye contact between the monitor and the test materials, great care is needed in choosing to include a visual component with test material. When opting for videotext as testing prompts, assessors need to ask if the material chosen will assess the ability to understand the target language or the ability to interpret the accompanying visual without a need to attend to the linguistic input.

When teachers choose to make extensive use of videotext, instruction in media literacy may be required. Understanding the nature of different types of visuals and texts (e.g., the difference between news clips, interviews, comedy, and stories), as well as strategies for mediating both video and audio for comprehension purposes, are important for effective use of visuals to enhance listening comprehension.

6. Learners who have good listening ability in their first language will also become good L2 listeners

L2 learners already possess an acquired listening competence in their first language (L1).

The degree to which L1 listening ability might contribute to L2 listening ability has only recently been examined. Results suggest that L1 listening ability is, indeed, one of many factors that contribute to success in L2 listening. The close links between literacy in L1 and L2 have also been observed in a number of studies related to L2 reading and L2 writing. The relationship is particularly strong between languages that have a similar typology and use the same alphabet.

Research suggests that skilled L2 listeners are able to transfer their L1 listening skills to listening in another language. The good news for less skilled L2 listeners, however, is that they can benefit from metacognitive instruction for L2 listening that raises their awareness about the listening process and teaches effective strategies for managing comprehension and overall listening development. Recent research has demonstrated that this kind of instruction can lead to improved listening ability.

Determining the potential contribution of L1 listening to L2 listening ability is important because, in our assessment of L2 listening ability, we may inadvertently be assessing L1 listening ability.

7. Interactive listening, in conversation with another speaker, is more difficult than one-way listening (i.e., radio and television)

Some features of interactive listening can in fact make it easier. First of all, listeners can clarify meaning or ask their interlocutor to slow down or repeat what was said. The opportunity to seek clarification makes inter-active listening less demanding. Second, listeners in interactive situations often have some kind of shared experience or communicative goal, such as common life experiences or an interview, to facilitate interpretation. In each of these situations, the context provides a backdrop against which (1) to predict content, and (2) to monitor interpretation as the interaction unfolds.

Some interactive listening events can be equally or more demanding than one-way listening. When listeners are expected to reply, for exam-ple, they must prepare and formulate an appropriate response as they process the speech of their interlocutor. This adds significantly to the cognitive load, because they must attend to the speaker's message, clarify understanding when comprehension is uncertain, and begin to formulate a response. Listeners must allocate their limited attentional resources to both comprehension and production in swift succession.

The social and affective demands of some interactive listening tasks may also be very high. How listeners deal with a comprehension problem in interactive situations depends on factors such as willingness to take risks, fear of losing face, assertiveness, and motivation. The degree to which these variables influence the interaction will depend on the relationship between the interlocutors. Status relationships can affect comprehension and the freedom to negotiate meaning. Finally, the face-to-face nature of interactive listening also requires attention to non-verbal signals, body language, and culturally bound cues, which can add to or change the literal meaning of an utterance.

8. When teachers provide learners with the context for a listening activity, they give away too much information

Listening is a process of matching new input with what one already knows about a topic. In many real-life situations we already have a context for understanding what we hear. In others, such as turning on the radio, we approach listening "cold" and it takes us a short time to "tune in" to the topic, which then provides us with a conceptual framework to inter-pret what we hear. In the classroom, when teachers provide learners with the context before beginning a listening activity, they are only providing information usually available to listeners in real-life listening situations.

Providing learners with contextual information for L2 listening helps them activate various knowledge sources to interpret what they hear. Learners use information about the topic to activate their store of prior knowledge and predict what they might hear. Similarly, they use infor-mation about text type to activate their textual/discourse knowledge and predict the possible types of speech they might hear and how the input might be organized. Then, guided by their metacognitive knowledge, learners use this information to activate potential scenarios and related vocabulary, make logical predictions, and activate appropriate strategies to compensate for any inadequate linguistic knowledge. This information can also be used to monitor their unfolding interpretation as they listen as well as evaluate their understanding after listening.

Contextual information can be provided through discussion, reading, or visuals. Helping learners "tune into" the listening input immediately reduces the cognitive burden of listening significantly and also helps to reduce anxiety about listening.

9. Letting students listen on their own, according to their interests, is the best way to develop listening skills

Listening outside the language classroom is useful for learners; if the learning is left to chance, however, it may not occur. On the other hand, preparing students in class with the metacognitive tools for listening outside class, along with task-based practice, increases the potential for learning from those experiences. Preparation gives learners the confidence to move beyond easily comprehensible listening texts to select input that is slightly more challenging, which stimulates greater learning.

Activities that bridge from the classroom to real-life listening experiences can engage learners in situations with a high level of communicative authenticity and develop their metacognitive knowledge about the features of a range of listening texts. If learners become familiar with the structure of different types of texts, they can anticipate the overall structure of the discourse and apply relevant comprehension skills and strategies to achieve better understanding. When teachers introduce different genres and plan tasks that sensitize learners to the types of communication associated with each genre, learners develop metacognitive knowledge about texts that can be used to enhance comprehension.

Listening projects that are part of classroom instruction can also help students further develop their own listening skills. Those who do not have a habit of practicing beyond the classroom may begin to do so. For learners who are already trying to improve their listening proficiency on their own, the skills and thinking processes they develop through classroom instruction will help them become more effective in their out-of-class listening efforts. Since listening projects give learners the opportunity to report back what they do when they listen on their own, they will also benefit from teacher and peer discussion about their listening experiences. This creates a cycle of learning that provides crucial continuity between formal and informal ways of learning to listen.

10. Captions and subtitles are useful tools for learning to listen

The use of L2 captions and subtitles (here after captions) can lead to better word identification and, ultimately, vocabulary learning. Captions can play a role in the development of L2 skills by reinforcing and confirming understanding of a listening text, and directing listener attention to gaps in understanding during repeat listens. Consulting captions to note differences between what they hear and the written form of the message can help listeners improve word segmentation skills and give them greater insight into their comprehension errors.

With regard to comprehension of content, however, it is not clear whether comprehension with captions is a result of listening or reading. Captions can become a crutch if learners resort to reading rather than developing appropriate listening strategies. In order to overcome this limitation, captions should only be consulted after learners have attempted to understand the text as a whole, using the prediction, inferencing, monitoring, and other strategies they would use in real-life listening contexts. This is equally true for the use of text transcripts.

Written support is usually not available in authentic, real-time listening; therefore learners need to learn to rely only on the acoustic signal and relevant contextual factors, along with metacognitive knowledge, to construct the meaning of what they hear. More research needs to verify the potential of captions to improve comprehension through comparison with a comprehension measure where listeners can only refer to cues available in real-life listening contexts.

Appendix A
Strategies for L2 Listening Comprehension With Examples From Learners

1. Planning: Developing awareness of what needs to be done to accomplish a listening task, developing an appropriate action plan and/or appropriate contingency plans to overcome difficulties that may interfere with successful completion of a task.

Advance organization:
Clarifying the objectives of an anticipated listening task and/or proposing strategies for handling it.

- *I read over what we have to do.*
- *I try to think of questions the teacher is going to ask.*
- *I have two months to prepare for my listening paper.*

Self-management:
Understanding the conditions that help one successfully accomplish listening tasks, and arranging for the presence of those conditions.

- *I try to get in the frame of mind to understand French.*
- *I put everything aside and concentrate on what she is saying.*
- *I need to be more focused.*

2. Focusing attention: Avoiding distractions and heeding the auditory input in different ways, or keeping to a plan for listening development.

Directed attention:
Attending **in general** to the listening task and ignoring distraction; maintaining attention while listening.

- *I listen really hard.*
- *I pick out the words that are familiar so that . . .*
- *I tried to concentrate on carrying out my plan.*

Selective attention:
Attending to **specific aspects** of language input or

- *I listen for the key words.*
- *I pay special attention to adjectives.*

situational details that assist in understanding and/or task completion.	• *Because I hear "also," then I concentrate on the words after "also."*

3. Monitoring: Checking, verifying, or correcting one's comprehension or performance in the course of a task.

Comprehension monitoring: Checking, verifying, or correcting understanding at the local level.	• *There's one word I didn't hear. Er . . . the something is . . . er . . . protects eyes, some other I can't remember.* • *But actually I know this meaning, but it does not make sense to me in this sentence.*
Double-check monitoring: Checking, verifying, or correcting understanding across the task during the second time through the oral text.	• *If I could listen the next sentences, the following sentence, then maybe I can have the correct choice.* • *Sunny in the morning, that's not making sense . . . (earlier) it sounded like a cold front, something doesn't make sense to me anymore.*

4. Evaluation: Checking the outcomes of listening comprehension or a listening plan against an internal or an external measure of completeness, reasonableness, and accuracy.

Performance evaluation: Judging one's overall execution of the task.	• *How close was I? (at end of a think-aloud report)* • *I was saying to myself, mm . . . did I guess right? How can eyebrow protect the ultra-violet light to our eyes . . . I think what I know influence my understanding and comprehension.*
Strategy evaluation: Judging one's strategy use.	• *I don't concentrate too much to the point of translation of individual words because then you just have a whole lot of words and not how they're strung together into some kind of meaning.*
Problem identification: Identifying what needs resolution or what part of	• *Okay, I'm wrong, so I need to be more attentive and see what's going on . . .*

the task still needs to be completed.

- *So I need to think about what I missed, um, how I can, hear it, and kind of keep trying again.*
- *I just memorise the word in my mind, how the word is pronounced, and when the teacher says it again, or in some other time, I will sometimes, I will ask the teacher.*

Substitution:
Selecting alternative approaches, revised plans, or different words or phrases to accomplish a listening task.

- *That way of listening didn't help me. I'm now watching many video recordings instead.*
- *I should stop translating so much ... maybe guess more.*
- *Sometimes in Chinese I need to repeat the sentence in my, in my thinking, but in English, I have no time, so I have to think about a picture.*

5. Inferencing: Using information within the text or conversational context to guess the meanings of unfamiliar language items associated with a listening task, to predict content and outcomes, or to fill in missing information.

Linguistic inferencing:
Using known words in an utterance to guess the meaning of unknown words.

- *I use other words in the sentence.*
- *I try to think of it (the word) in context and guess.*
- *(Heard "adiposity") Is it means, again means the store, it gives out energy? ... Deposit. I thought of ... it's a word used in banking ... I think there is some relationship, I guess.*
- *I use the sound of words to relate to other words I know.*

Voice and paralinguistic inferencing:
Using tone of voice and/or paralinguistics to guess the meaning of unknown words in an utterance.

- *I listen to the way the words are said.*
- *I guess, using tone of voice as a clue.*

Kinesic inferencing:
Using facial expressions,

- *I try to read her body language.*

body language, and hand movements to guess the meaning of unknown words used by a speaker.

- *I read her face.*
- *I use the teacher's hand gestures.*

Extralinguistic inferencing:
Using background sounds and relationships between speakers in an oral text, material in the response sheet, or concrete situational referents to guess the meaning of unknown words.

- *I guess on the basis of the kind of information the question asks for.*
- *I comprehend what the teacher chooses to write on the board to clarify what she is saying.*

Between parts inferencing:
Using information from different parts of the text to guess at meaning.

- *Because in the beginning she said "race," so maybe it was a horse race . . .*
- *You pick out things you do know and in the whole situation piece it together so that you know what it does mean.*

6. Elaboration: Using prior knowledge from outside the text or conversational context and relating it to knowledge gained from the text or conversation in order to embellish one's interpretation of the text.

Personal elaboration:
Referring to prior experience personally.

- *I think there is some big picnic or a family gathering, sounds like fun, I don't know . . .*
- *You know . . . maybe they missed, because that happens to me lots just miss accidentally and then you call up and say, "Well, what happened?"*

World elaboration:
Using knowledge gained from experience in the world.

- *When I heard the first sentence talk about the animal, I looked for the information in my memory about this. So with this information I listened.*
- *I guessed that it might be the beach. Because I know that it is a problem with the beaches there's too much ultra-violet light.*

Academic elaboration:
Using knowledge gained in academic situations.

- *[I know that] from doing telephone conversations in class.*

- *I relate the word to a topic we've studied.*
- *I try to think of all my background in French.*

Questioning elaboration:
Using a combination of questions and world knowledge to brainstorm logical possibilities.

- *Something about 61, restaurant, 61. Maybe it's the address.*
- *Um, he said he started, probably fixing up his apartment, something about his apartment. Probably just moved in, um, because they're fixing it up.*

Creative elaboration:
Making up a story line, or introducing new possibilities into an event.

- *Sounded like introducing something, like it says here is something but I can't figure out what it is, it could be like . . . one of the athletes, like introducing some person or something.*
- *I guess there is a trip to the Carnival in Quebec so maybe it is like something for them to enter a date, to write, or draw . . .*

Visual elaboration:
Using mental or actual pictures or visuals to represent information.

- *I make pictures in my mind for words I know, then I fill in the picture that's missing in the sequence of pictures in my mind.*
- *I have known something about camel, so you talk about hump, just like a picture showing before me, I can see two humps . . .*

7. Prediction: Anticipating the contents and the message of what one is going to hear.

Global prediction:
Anticipating the gist or the general contents in a text.

- *I can understand this sentence because I have known something about camel . . . if you don't say anything more I will still know what you're going to say . . .*

Local prediction:
Anticipating details for specific parts of a text.

- *Because in the first sentence it says the hump . . . maybe the next sentence is on what the use of the hump, what's the*

importance to the camel, so it also
helps me to understand.

8. Contextualization: Placing what is heard in a specific context in order to prepare for listening or assist comprehension.

Linguistic contextualization:

Relating a word or a phrase heard to an environment where the word has appeared before.

- *I don't know the word's exact meaning, but I remember the word is on the road—"hump"*
- *Theoretically? Is it related to theory?*
- *(Heard "insulates") I think of grammar. I think it's a verb, "insurates" . . . to protect. Insure, does it mean to protect?*

Schematic contextualization:

Relating a clue to some factual information in long-term memory.

- *And the last sentence, "It can store food" and that's something at the back of the camel, so I can relate to former sentence and the meaning, even though the word and the whole sentence I didn't know.*

9. Reorganizing: Transferring what one has processed into forms that help understanding, storage, and retrieval.

Summarization:

Making a mental or written summary of language and information presented in a listening task.

- *I remember the key points and run them through my head, "What happened here and what happened here?" and get everything organized in order to answer the questions.*

Repetition:

Repeating a chunk of language (a word or phrase) in the course of performing a listening task.

- *I sound out the words.*
- *I say the word to myself.*

Grouping:

Recalling information based on grouping according to common attributes.

- *I try to relate the words that sound the same.*
- *I break up words for parts I might recognize.*

Note taking:

Writing down key words

- *I write down the word.*

and concepts in abbreviated
verbal, graphic, or
numerical form to assist
performance of a listening
task.

- *When I write it down, it comes to my mind what it means.*

10. Using linguistic and learning resources: Relying on one's knowledge of the first language or additional languages to make sense of what is heard, or consulting learning resources after listening.

Translation:
Rendering ideas from one
language to L1 in a
relatively verbatim manner.

- *I . . . this word came to my brain, that is "shou duan, fang fa, shou duan." It's mechanism. The way . . . the strategy.*
- *I'll say what she says in my head, but in English.*
- *A little voice inside me is translating.*

Transfer:
Using knowledge of one
language (e.g., cognates) to
facilitate listening in
another.

- *I try to relate the words to English.*
- *I use my knowledge of other languages: English to understand German and Portuguese (primarily sound) to understand French.*

Deduction/induction:
Consciously applying
learned or self-developed
rules to understand the
target language.

- *I use knowledge of the kinds of words such as parts of speech.*
- *I think it is an adverb or a verb . . . I think this word was not very important.*

Resourcing:
Using available reference
sources of information
about the target language,
including dictionaries,
textbooks, and prior work.

- *I think usually I just listen on, and I remember that word, and I'll go consult the dictionary later, but I will not stop at this point.*

11. Cooperation: Working with others to get help on improving comprehension, language use, and learning.

Seeking clarification:
Asking for explanation,
verification, rephrasing, or
examples about the
language and/or task.

- *I'll ask the teacher.*
- *I'll ask for a repeat.*
- *I heard "designed by a committee." What's the meaning of "designed by a committee"?*

> • *I didn't know what the nurse said, then I asked, I asked someone beside me translate it to me.*

Joint task construction:
Working together with someone other than an interlocutor to solve a problem, pool information, or check a learning task.

> • *I like doing listening lessons with Mary. We talk a lot and help each other understand the difficult parts.*
> • *I learnt from the other students how to improve my listening.*

12. Managing emotions: Keeping track of one's feelings and not allowing negative ones to influence attitudes and behaviors.

Lowering anxiety:
Reducing anxiety through the use of mental techniques that make one feel more competent to perform a listening task.

> • *I think of something funny to calm myself down.*
> • *This time, the strategy that I induct is to be relaxed ... don't be nervous ... just continue.*

Self-encouragement:
Providing personal motivation through positive self-talk and/or arranging rewards for oneself during a listening activity or upon its completion.

> • *I try to get what I can.*
> • *O.K ... my hunch was right.*
> • *I tell myself that everyone else is probably having some kind of problem as well.*

Taking emotional temperature:
Becoming aware of, and getting in touch with, one's emotions while listening, in order to avert negative ones and make the most of positive ones.

> • *Okay I'm getting mad 'cause I don't understand.*
> • *In my listening practice, I keep myself relaxed and calm.*
> • *I was very anxious because I had to speak on the phone in English ... I wrote down some words first.*

Based on Goh (2002b), O'Malley & Chamot (1990), Oxford (1990), Vandergrift (1997)

Appendix B

Metacognitive Awareness of Listening Questionnaire (MALQ)

The MALQ is a 21-item questionnaire with five distinct factors significantly related to L2 listening comprehension success: Problem-Solving, Planning and Evaluation, Mental Translation, Person Knowledge, and Directed Attention. The MALQ can be used in different L2 instructional settings to raise student awareness of the process of listening, to positively influence students' approach to listening tasks, and to increase self-regulated use of comprehension strategies.

The instrument on the following page can be reproduced for self-assessment, research, or diagnostic purposes. Please contact the authors for information on scoring the questionnaire and interpreting results.

Larry Vandergrift: lvdgrift@uottawa.ca
Christine Goh: christine.goh@nie.edu.sg

Metacognitive Awareness of Listening Questionnaire (MALQ)

The statements on the following page describe some strategies for listening comprehension and how you feel about listening in the language you are learning. Do you agree with them? This is not a test, so there are no "right" or "wrong" answers. By responding to these statements, you can help yourself and your teacher understand your progress in learning to listen. Please indicate your opinion after each statement. Circle the number which best shows your level of agreement with the statement.

	Strongly disagree	Disagree	Slightly disagree	Partly agree	Agree	Strongly agree
I like learning another language	1	2	3	4	5	6

1. Before I start to listen, I have a plan in my head for how I am going to listen.	1	2	3	4	5	6
2. I focus harder on the text when I have trouble understanding.	1	2	3	4	5	6
3. I find that listening is more difficult than reading, speaking, or writing in English.	1	2	3	4	5	6
4. I translate in my head as I listen.	1	2	3	4	5	6
5. I use the words I understand to guess the meaning of the words I don't understand.	1	2	3	4	5	6
6. When my mind wanders, I recover my concentration right away.	1	2	3	4	5	6
7. As I listen, I compare what I understand with what I know about the topic.	1	2	3	4	5	6
8. I feel that listening comprehension in English is a challenge for me.	1	2	3	4	5	6
9. I use my experience and knowledge to help me understand.	1	2	3	4	5	6
10. Before listening, I think of similar texts that I may have listened to.	1	2	3	4	5	6
11. I translate key words as I listen.	1	2	3	4	5	6
12. I try to get back on track when I lose concentration.	1	2	3	4	5	6
13. As I listen, I quickly adjust my interpretation if I realize that it is not correct.	1	2	3	4	5	6
14. After listening, I think back to how I listened, and about what I might do differently next time.	1	2	3	4	5	6
15. I don't feel nervous when I listen to English.	1	2	3	4	5	6
16. When I have difficulty understanding what I hear, I give up and stop listening.	1	2	3	4	5	6
17. I use the general idea of the text to help me guess the meaning of the words that I don't understand.	1	2	3	4	5	6
18. I translate word by word, as I listen.	1	2	3	4	5	6
19. When I guess the meaning of a word, I think back to everything else that I have heard, to see if my guess makes sense.	1	2	3	4	5	6
20. As I listen, I periodically ask myself if I am satisfied with my level of comprehension.	1	2	3	4	5	6
21. I have a goal in mind as I listen.	1	2	3	4	5	6

Appendix C

Online Resources for Listening Practice

BBC: Learning English
http://www.bbc.co.uk/worldservice/learningenglish/multimedia/

British Council: Learn English
http://www.britishcouncil.org/learnenglish-central-skills-listening.htm

CBC: ESL: Learning English with the CBC
http://www.cbc.ca/ottawa/esl/lessons.html

CNN
CNN News channel site, with video clips and links plus daily quiz
http://www.cnn.com

English as a Second Language (ESL) Podcasts
http://a4esl.org/podcasts/

EnglishEnglish.com
http://englishenglish.com/listening_skills.htm

English Language Listening Lab Online (ELLLO)
http://www.elllo.org

English Listening Lounge (ELL)
http://englishlistening.com

English Online France
Resources for students and teachers of English as a foreign language
http://eolf.univ-fcomte.fr/

ESL: Listening
http://iteslj.org/links/ESL/Listening/

ESL Monkeys
English as second language online resources
http://www.eslmonkeys.com

Focus English
Everyday English in conversation
http://focusenglish.com/dialogues/conversation.html

Graded English language dictations free online
http://dictationsonline.com/

Hollywood.com
Hollywood trailers, synopses, film interviews
http://www.hollywood.com

Internet Movie Database
www.imdb.com

L2 Listening Site
Rodrigo Bedoya's webpage for metacognitive instruction and listening
(contains original worksheets by the author)
http://sites.google.com/site/l2listeningsite/

Lauri's ESL Website listening activities
http://fog.ccsf.cc.ca.us/~lfried/activity/listening.html

LEO Network
Learning English online network
http://learnenglish.de

Many Things
Audio for ESL/EFL—Jokes in English (MP3 files)
http://www.manythings.org/listen/

Oscar
The Academy Awards: official site of the Oscars
http://www.oscar.com

Randall's ESL Cyber Listening Lab
http://www.Esl-lab.com

Spotlight
http://www.spotlightradio.net/listen/

Storyline Online
http://storylineonline.net/

Takako's Great Adventure
http://international.ouc.bc.ca/takako/

Using English for Academic Purposes (UEfAP)
http://www.uefap.com/links/linkfram.htm

VOA Learning English
http://www1.voanews.com/learningenglish/home/

References

Ableeva, R. (2008). The effects of dynamic assessment on L2 listening comprehension. In J. P. Lantolf & M. E. Poehner (Eds.), *Sociocultural theory and the teaching of second languages* (pp. 57–86). London: Equinox.

Ableeva, R. (2010). Dynamic assessment of listening comprehension in second language learning. (Unpublished doctoral dissertation). Pennsylvania State University, University Park, PA. Retrieved from http://etda.libraries.psu.edu/theses/approved/WorldWideFiles/ETD5520/Ableeva_PS_Thesis_FINAL.pdf

Afflerbach, P., Pearson, P. D., & Paris, S. G. (2008). Clarifying differences between reading skills and reading strategies. *The Reading Teacher, 61,* 364–373.

Alderson, J. C., & Wall, D. (1993). Does washback exist? *Applied Linguistics, 14,* 115–129.

Alexander, P. A. (2008). Why this and why now? Introduction to the special issue on metacognition, self-regulation, and self-regulated learning. *Educational Psychology Review, 20,* 369–372.

Al-jasser, F. (2008). The effect of teaching English phonotactics on the lexical segmentation of English as a foreign language. *System, 36,* 94–106.

Altenberg, E. P. (2005). The perception of word boundaries in a second language. *Second Language Research, 21,* 325–358.

Anderson, A., & Lynch, T. (1988). *Listening.* Oxford: Oxford University Press.

Anderson, J. R. (1995). *Cognitive psychology and its implications* (4th ed.). New York: Freeman.

Arnold, J. (2000). Seeing through listening comprehension exam anxiety. *TESOL Quarterly, 34,* 777–786.

Atkinson, D. (2002). Toward a sociocognitive approach to second language acquisition. *The Modern Language Journal, 86,* 525–545.

Bachman, L. F. (1990). *Fundamental considerations in language testing.* Oxford: Oxford University Press.

Bacon, S. M. (1992). The relationship between gender, comprehension, processing strategies, and cognitive and affective response in foreign language listening. *The Modern Language Journal, 76,* 160–178.

Baddeley, A. D. (2000). The episodic buffer: A new component of working memory? *Trends in Cognitive Sciences, 4,* 417–423.

Baddeley, A. (2003). Working memory and language: An overview. *Journal of Communication Disorders, 36,* 189–208.

Baker, L. (2002). Metacognition in comprehension instruction. In C. Block &

M. Pressley (Eds.), *Comprehension instruction: Research-based best practices* (pp. 77–95). New York: Guilford Press.

Bandura, A. (1993). Perceived self-efficacy in cognitive development and functioning. *Educational Psychologist, 28*, 117–148.

Bernhardt, E. B., & Kamil, M. L. (1995). Interpreting relationships between L1 and L2 reading: Consolidating the linguistic threshold and the linguistic interdependence hypotheses. *Applied Linguistics, 16*, 16–34.

Biggs, J. (1999). *Teaching for quality learning at university.* Buckingham, UK: Society for Research into Higher Education.

Bird, S. A., & Williams, J. N. (2002). The effect of bimodal input on implicit and explicit memory: An investigation into the benefits of within-language subtitling. *Applied Psycholinguistics, 23*, 509–533.

Blau, E. K. (1990). The effect of syntax, speed, and pauses on listening comprehension. TESOL Quarterly, *24*, 746–753.

Block, C., & Pressley, M. (Eds.). (2002). *Comprehension instruction: Research-based best practices.* New York: Guilford Press.

Bonk, W. (2000). Second language lexical knowledge and listening comprehension. *International Journal of Listening, 14*, 14–31.

Borkowski, J. G. (1996). Metacognition: Theory or chapter heading? *Learning and Individual Differences, 8*, 391–402.

Brett, P. (1997). A comparative study of the effects of the use of multimedia on listening comprehension. *System, 25*, 39–53.

Brown, G. (1987). Twenty-five years of teaching listening comprehension. *English Teaching Forum, 25*, 11–15.

Brown, G. (1990). *Listening to spoken English.* Harlow: Longman.

Brown, G., & Yule, G. (1983). *Discourse analysis.* Cambridge: Cambridge University Press.

Brown, H. D., & Abeywickrama, P. (2010). Beyond tests: Alternatives in assessment. In H. Douglas Brown (Ed.), *Language assessment: Principles and classroom practices* (2nd ed.) (pp. 122–155). Whiteplains, NY: Pearson Longman.

Bruer, J. T. (1998). Education. In W. Brechtel & G. Graham (Eds.), *A companion to cognitive science* (pp. 681–690). Massachusetts: Blackwell Publishers Ltd.

Buck, G. (1995). How to become a good listening teacher. In D. Mendelsohn & J. Rubin (Eds.), *A guide for the teaching of second language listening* (pp. 113–128). San Diego, CA: Dominie Press.

Buck, G. (1997). The testing of listening in a second language. In C. Clapham & D. Corson (Eds.), *Encyclopedia of language and education, Vol. 7: Language testing and assessment* (pp. 65–74). Netherlands: Kluwer Academic Publishers.

Buck, G. (2001). *Assessing listening.* Cambridge, UK: Cambridge University Press.

Burns, A., Joyce, H., & Gollin, S. (1996). *I see what you mean: Using spoken discourse in the classroom.* Sydney: National Centre for English Language Teaching and Research.

Call, M. E. (1985). Auditory short-term memory, listening comprehension, and the input hypothesis. *TESOL Quarterly, 19*, 765–781.

Carrell, P., Dunkel, P., & Mollaun, P. (2004). The effects of note taking, lecture length, and topic on a computer-based test of EFL listening comprehension. *Applied Language Learning, 14,* 83–105.

Carter, R., & McCarthy, M. (1997). *Exploring spoken English.* Cambridge: Cambridge University Press.

Chamot, A.U. (1995). Learning strategies and listening comprehension. In D. Mendelsohn & J. Rubin (Eds.), *A guide for the teaching of second language listening* (pp. 13–30). San Diego, CA: Dominie Press.

Chamot, A.U., Barnhardt, S., El-Dinary, P.B., & Robbins, J. (1999). *The learning strategies handbook.* White Plains, NY: Longman.

Chang, A. C.-S. (2009). Gains to L2 listeners from reading while listening vs. listening only in comprehending short stories. *System, 37,* 555–760.

Chang, A. C.-S., & Read, J. (2006). The effects of listening support on the listening performance of EFL learners. *TESOL Quarterly, 40,* 375–397.

Cheng, H. (2004). A comparison of multiple-choice and open-ended response formats for the assessment of listening proficiency in English. *Foreign Language Annals, 37,* 544–555.

Chiang, J., & Dunkel, P. (1992). The effect of speech modification, prior knowledge and listening proficiency on EFL lecture learning. *TESOL Quarterly, 26,* 345–374.

Chung, J. M. (2002). The effects of using two advance organizers with video texts for the teaching of listening in English. *Foreign Language Annals, 35,* 231–241.

Cohen, A. D. (1998). *Strategies in learning and using a second language.* New York: Addison-Wesley Longman.

Cohen, A. D. (2007). Coming to terms with language learner strategies: Surveying the experts. In A. D. Cohen & E. Macaro (Eds.), *Language learner strategies: 30 years of research and practice* (pp. 29–45). Oxford: Oxford University Press.

Cohen, A. D., & Macaro, E. (2007). *Language learner strategies: 30 years of research and practice.* Oxford, UK: Oxford University Press.

Coniam, D. (2001). The use of audio or video comprehension as an assessment instrument in the certification of English language teachers: A case study. *System, 29,* 1–14.

Conrad, L. (1985). Semantic versus syntactic cues in listening comprehension. *Studies in Second Language Acquisition, 7,* 59–69.

Cook, M., & Liddicoat, A. J. (2002). The development of comprehension in interlanguage pragmatics: The case of request strategies in English. *Australian Review of Applied Linguistics, 25,* 19–39.

Council of Europe (2000). *The common European portfolio.* Retrieved from http://www.coe.int /T/DG4 /Portfolio /?L=E&M=/main_pages/ introduction. html

Council of Europe (2001). *A common European framework of reference for languages: Learning, teaching, assessment.* Cambridge: Cambridge University Press.

Cross, J. D. (2009a). Diagnosing the process, text and intrusion problems responsible for L2 listeners' decoding errors. *Asian EFL Journal, 11,* 31–53.

Cross, J. D. (2009b). Effects of listening strategy instruction on news videotext comprehension. *Language Teaching Research, 13,* 151–176.

Cross, J. (2010). Raising L2 listeners' metacognitive awareness: A socio-cultural theory perspective. *Language Awareness, 19*(4), 281–297.

Cubillos, J. H., Chieffo, L., & Fan, C. (2008). The impact of short-term study abroad programs on L2 listening comprehension skills. *Foreign Language Annals, 41,* 157–185.

Cutler, A. (2001). Listening to a second language through the ears of a first. *Interpreting, 5,* 1–23.

Cutler, A., & Carter, D.M. (1987). The predominance of strong initial syllables in the English vocabulary. *Computer Speech & Language, 2,* 133–142.

Danan, M. (2004). Captioning and subtitling: Undervalued language learning strategies. *Meta, 49,* 67–77.

Davis, M. H., & Johnsrude, I. S. (2007). Hearing speech sounds: Top-down influences on the interface between audition and speech perception. *Hearing Research, 229,* 132–147.

Davis, P., & Rinvolucri, M. (1988). *Dictation: New methods, new possibilities.* Cambridge: Cambridge University Press.

De Bot, K. (1992). A bilingual production model: Levelt's speaking model adapted. *Applied Linguistics, 13,* 1–24.

Deci, E., & Ryan, R. (1985). *Intrinsic motivation and self-determination in human behavior.* New York: Plenum.

Deci, E. L., & Ryan, R. M. (1995). Human autonomy: The basis for true self-esteem. In M. H. Kernis (Ed.), *Efficacy, agency, and self-esteem* (pp. 31–48). New York: Plenum.

Dinsmore, D. L., Alexander, P. A., & Loughlin, S. M. (2008). Focusing the conceptual lens on metacognition, self-regulation, and self-regulated learning. *Educational Psychology Review, 20,* 391–409.

Dipper, L., Black, M., & Bryan, K. L. (2005). Thinking for speaking and thinking for listening: The interaction of thought and language in typical and non-fluent comprehension and production. *Language and Cognitive Processes, 20,* 417–441.

Dörnyei, Z. (2005). *The psychology of the language learner: Individual differences in second language acquisition.* Mahwah, NJ: Erlbaum.

Dörnyei, Z., & Kormos, J. (1998). Problem-solving mechanisms in L2 communication: A psycholinguistic perspective. *Studies in Second Language Acquisition, 20,* 349–385.

Dudley-Evans, A. (1994). Genre analysis: An approach for text analysis for ESP. In M. Coulthard (Ed.), *Advances in Written Text Analysis* (pp. 219–228). London: Routledge.

Dunkel, P. (1986). Developing listening fluency in L2: Theoretical principles and pedagogical considerations. *The Modern Language Journal, 70,* 99–106.

Eckerth, J. (2009). Negotiated interaction in the L2 classroom. *Language Teaching, 42,* 109–130.

Eilam, B., & Aharon, I. (2003). Students' planning in the process of self-regulated learning. *Contemporary Educational Psychology, 28,* 304–334.

Elkhafaifi, H. (2005). Listening comprehension and anxiety in the Arabic language classroom. *The Modern Language Journal, 89,* 206–220.

Eysenck, M. W. (1993). *Principles of cognitive psychology.* New York, NY: Erlbaum.

Farrell, T. C., & Mallard, C. (2006). The use of reception strategies by learners of French as a foreign language. *The Modern Language Journal, 90*, 338–352.

Field, J. (1998). Skills and strategies: Towards a new methodology for listening. *ELT Journal, 52*, 110–118.

Field, J. (2001). Finding one's way in the fog: Listening strategies and second-language learners. *Modern English Teacher, 9*, 29–34.

Field, J. (2003). Promoting perception: Lexical segmentation in second language listening. *ELT Journal, 57*, 325–334.

Field, J. (2007). Looking outwards, not inwards. *ELT Journal, 61*, 3–38.

Field, J. (2008a). *Listening in the language classroom*. Cambridge: Cambridge University Press.

Field, J. (2008b). Bricks or mortar: Which parts of the input does a second language listener rely on? *TESOL Quarterly, 42*, 411–432.

Firth, A., & Wagner, J. (1997). On discourse, communication, and (some) fundamental concepts in SLA research. *The Modern Language Journal, 81*, 285–300.

Firth, A., & Wagner, J. (2007). Second/foreign language learning as a social accomplishment: Elaborations on a reconceptualized SLA. *Modern Language Journal, 91*, 800–819.

Flavell, J. H. (1976). Metacognitive aspects of problem solving. In L. B. Resnick (Ed.), *The nature of intelligence* (pp. 231–235). Hillsdale, NJ: Erlbaum.

Flavell, J. H. (1979). Metacognition and cognitive monitoring: A new area of cognitive-developmental inquiry. *American Psychologist, 34*, 906–911.

Flowerdew, J., & Miller, L. (1992). Student perceptions, problems and strategies in L2 lectures. *RELC Journal, 23*, 60–80.

Flowerdew, J., & Miller, L. (1996). Lecturer perceptions, problems and strategies in second language lectures. *RELC Journal, 27*, 23–46.

Flowerdew, J., & Miller, L. (2005). *Second language listening: Theory and practice*. New York: Cambridge University Press.

Flowerdew, J., Miller, L., & Li, D. (2000). Chinese lecturers' perceptions, problems and strategies in lecturing in English to Chinese-speaking students. *RELC Journal, 31*, 116–138.

Foster, P. (1998). A classroom perspective on the negotiation of meaning. *Applied Linguistics, 19*, 1–23.

Foster, P., & Ohta, A. (2005). Negotiation for meaning and peer assistance in second language classrooms. *Applied Linguistics, 26*, 402–430.

French, L. (2003). Phonological working memory and L2 acquisition: A developmental study of Quebec francophone children learning English. (Unpublished doctoral dissertation). Université Laval, Canada.

Garcia, P. (2004). Pragmatic comprehension of high and low level language learners. *TESL-EJ, 8*. Retrieved from http://tesl-ej.org/ej30/a1.html

Gardner, R.C., & MacIntyre, P. D. (1992). A student's contribution to second language acquisition. Part 1: Cognitive variables. *Language Teaching, 25*, 211–220.

Genesee, F., & Upshur, J. A. (1996). *Classroom-based evaluation in second language education*. New York: Cambridge University Press.

Ginther, A. (2002). Context and content visuals and performance on listening comprehension stimuli. *Language Testing, 19*, 133–167.

Goh, C. (1997). Metacognitive awareness and second language listeners. *ELT Journal, 51*(4), 361–369.

Goh, C. (1998). How learners with different listening abilities use comprehension strategies and tactics. *Language Teaching Research, 2*, 124–147.

Goh, C. (1999). What learners know about the factors that influence their listening comprehension. *Hong Kong Journal of Applied Linguistics, 4*, 17–42.

Goh, C. (2000). A cognitive perspective on language learners' listening comprehension problems. *System, 28*, 55–75.

Goh, C. (2002a). *Teaching listening in the language classroom*. Singapore: SEAMEO Regional Language Centre.

Goh, C. (2002b) Exploring listening comprehension tactics and their interaction patterns. *System, 30*, 185–206.

Goh, C. C. M. (2002c). Learners' self-reports on comprehension and learning strategies for listening. *Asian Journal of English Language Teaching, 12*, 46–68.

Goh, C. (2008). Metacognitive instruction for second language listening development: Theory, practice and research implications. *RELC Journal, 39*(2), 188–213.

Goh, C. (2010). Listening as process: Learning activities for self-appraisal and self-regulation. In N. Harwood (Ed.), *Materials in ELT: Theory and practice* (pp. 179–206). Cambridge: Cambridge University Press.

Goh, C., & Taib, Y. (2006). Metacognitive instruction in listening for young learners. *ELT Journal, 60*, 222–232.

Grabe, W. (2009). *Reading in a second language: Moving from theory to practice*. Cambridge: Cambridge University Press.

Graham, S. (2003). Learner strategies and advanced level listening comprehension. *Language Learning Journal, 28*, 64–69.

Graham, S. (2006). Listening comprehension: The learners' perspective. *System, 34*, 165–182.

Graham, S., & Macaro, E. (2008). Strategy instruction in listening for lower-intermediate learners of French. *Language Learning, 58*, 747–783.

Graham, S. J., Santos, D., & Vanderplank, R. (2010). Strategy clusters and sources of knowledge in French L2 listening comprehension. *Innovation in Language Learning and Teaching, 4*, 1–20.

Grgurović, M., & Hegelheimer, V. (2007). Help options and multimedia listening: Students' use of subtitles and the transcript. *Language Learning & Technology, 11*, 45–66.

Griffiths, R (1990). Facilitating listening comprehension through rate-control. *RELC Journal, 21*, 55–65.

Griffiths, R. (1991). Speech rate and listening comprehension further evidence of the relationship. *TESOL Quarterly, 25*, 230–235.

Gruba, P. (2004). Understanding digitized second language videotext. *Computer Assisted Language Learning, 17*, 51–82.

Gruba, P. (2007). *Decoding visual elements in digitized foreign newscasts*. Retrieved from http://www.ascilite.org.au/conferences/singapore07/procs/gruba.pdf

Gu, Y., Hu, G., & Zhang, L. J. (2009). Listening strategies of Singaporean primary pupils. In R. Silver, C. C. M. Goh, & L. Alsagoff (Eds.), *Language learning in new English contexts* (pp. 55–74). London: Continuum International Publishing.

Guichon, N., & McLornan, S. (2008). The effects of multimodality on L2 learners: Implications for CALL resource design. *System, 36*, 85–93.

Gullberg, M., & McCafferty, S. G. (2008). Introduction to gesture and SLA: An integrated approach. *Studies in Second Language Acquisition, 30*, 133–146.

Hacker, D. J., Dunlosky, J., & Graesser, A C. (Eds.). (2009). *Handbook of metacognition in education.* Mahwah, NJ: Erlbaum/Taylor & Francis.

Hagoort, P., & Levelt, W. J. M. (2009). The speaking brain. *Science, 326*, 372–373.

Halliday, M. A. K. (1985). *Spoken and written language.* Oxford: Oxford University Press.

Hancock, D. (2004). Cooperative learning and peer orientation effects on motivation and achievement. *The Journal of Educational Research, 97*, 159–166.

Harley, B. (2000). Listening strategies in ESL: Do age and L1 make a difference? *TESOL Quarterly, 34*, 769–776.

Harley, B., & Hart, D. (2002). Age, aptitude and second language learning on a bilingual exchange. In P. Robinson (Ed.), *Individual differences and instructed language learning* (pp. 301–330). Amsterdam: Benjamins.

Harris, T. (2003). Listening with your eyes: The importance of speech-related gestures in the language classroom. *Foreign Language Annals, 36*, 180–187.

Hegelheimer, V., & Tower, D. (2004). Using CALL in the classroom: Analyzing student interactions in an authentic classroom. *System, 32*, 185–205.

Hernández, S. S. (2004). The effects of video and captioned text and the influence of verbal and spatial abilities on second language listening comprehension in a multimedia learning environment. (Unpublished doctoral dissertation). New York University, New York.

Horwitz, E. (1986). Preliminary evidence for the reliability and validity of a foreign language anxiety scale. *TESOL Quarterly, 20*, 559–564.

Horwitz, E. (2010). Foreign and second language anxiety. *Language Teaching, 43*, 154–167.

Horwitz, E. K., & Young, D. (1991) *Language anxiety: From theory and research to classroom implications.* Englewood Cliffs, NJ: Prentice Hall.

Horwitz, E. K., Tallon, M., & Luo, H. (2009). Foreign language anxiety. In J. C. Cassady (Ed.), *Anxiety in schools: The causes, consequences, and solutions for academic anxieties* (pp. 96–118). New York: Peter Lang.

Howatt, A.P.R. (1984). *A history of English language teaching.* Oxford: Oxford University Press.

Hoven, D. (1999). A model for listening and viewing comprehension in multimedia environments. *Language Learning & Technology, 3*, 88–103.

Hubbard, P. (Ed.), (2007). Technology and listening comprehension. *Language Learning & Technology, 11*, 1–117. Retrieved from http://llt.msu.edu/vol11num1/default.html

Hulstijn, J. H. (2001). Intentional and incidental second language vocabulary learning: A reappraisal of elaboration, rehearsal and automaticity. In P. Robinson (Ed.), *Cognition and second language instruction* (pp. 258–286). Cambridge: Cambridge University Press.

Hulstijn, J. H. (2003). Connectionist models of language processing and the training of listening skills with the aid of multimedia software. *Computer Assisted Language Learning, 16*, 413–425.

Hulstijn, J. H. (2011). Explanations of associations between L1 and L2 literacy skills. In M. S. Schmid & W. Lowie (Eds.), *Modeling bilingualism: From structure to chaos* (pp. 85–111). Amsterdam: Benjamins.

Imhof, M., & Janusik, L. (2006). Development and validation of the Imhof-Janusik listening concepts inventory to measure listening conceptualization differences between cultures. *Journal of International Communication Research, 35*, 79–98.

Ito, K., & Strange, W. (2009). Perception of allophonic cues to English word boundaries by Japanese second language learners of English. *Journal of the Acoustical Society of America, 125*, 2348–2360.

Jensen, E. D., & Vinther, T. (2003). Exact repetition as input enhancement in second language acquisition. *Language Learning, 53*, 373–428.

Johnson, K. (1996). *Language teaching and skill learning*. London: Blackwell.

Johnson, K., & Morrow, K. (Eds.). (1981). *Communication in the classroom*. Harlow: Longman.

Jones, L. (2004). Testing L2 vocabulary recognition and recall using pictorial and written test items. *Language Learning & Technology, 8*, 122–143.

Jones, L. (2006). Listening comprehension in multimedia environments. In L. Ducate & N. Arnold (Eds.), *Calling on CALL: From theory and research to new directions in foreign language teaching* (pp. 99–125). San Marcos, TX: CALICO.

Jones, L., & Plass, J. (2002). Supporting listening comprehension and vocabulary acquisition in French with multimedia annotations. *The Modern Language Journal, 86*, 546–561.

Jung, E. H. (2003). The role of discourse signaling cues in second language listening comprehension. *The Modern Language Journal, 87*, 562–577.

Kellerman, S. (1992). "I see what you mean": The role of kinesic behaviour in listening and implications for foreign and second language learning. *Applied Linguistics, 13*, 239–258.

Kemp, J. (2010). The listening log: Motivating autonomous learning. *ELT Journal, 64*(4), 385–395.

Kintsch, W. (1998). *Comprehension: A paradigm for cognition*. New York: Cambridge University Press.

Kluwe, R. H. (1982). Cognitive knowledge and executive control: Metacognition. In D. R. Griffin (Ed.), *Animal mind—human mind* (pp. 201–224). Berlin: Springer-Verlag.

Krashen, S. (1985). *The input hypothesis: Issues and implication*. Harlow and New York: Longman.

Krashen, S. (1996). The case for Narrow Listening. *System, 24*, 97–100.

Lantolf, J. P. (2000). *Sociocultural theory and second language learning*. Oxford University Press.

Lantolf, J. P., & Thorne, S. L. (2006). *Sociocultural theory and the genesis of second language development*. Oxford: Oxford University Press.

Larsen-Freeman, D. (1986). *Techniques and principles in language teaching*. New York: Oxford University Press.

Lee, B., & Cai, W. (2010). The effects of language proficiency on unfamiliar word processing in listening comprehension. *Hong Kong Journal of Applied Linguistics, 12*, 61–82.

Lee, J., & Schallert, D. L. (1997). The relative contribution of L2 language proficiency and L1 reading ability to L2 reading performance: A test of the threshold hypothesis in an EFL context. *TESOL Quarterly, 31*, 713–739.

Lenz, P., & Schneider, G. (2004). A bank of descriptors for self-assessment in European language portfolios. Strasbourg: Council of Europe.

Levelt, W. J. M. (1989). *Speaking: From intention to articulation.* Cambridge, MA: The MIT Press.

Levelt, W. J. M. (1993). Language use in normal speakers and its disorders. In G. Blanken, J. Dittmann, H. Grimm, J. C. Marshall & C.-W. Wallesch (Eds.), *Linguistic disorders and pathologies* (pp. 1–15). Berlin: De Gruyter.

Levelt, W. (1995). The ability to speak: From intentions to spoken words. *European Review, 3*, 13–23.

Lightbown, P. M., & Spada, N. (2006). *How languages are learned* (3rd ed.). Oxford: Oxford University Press.

Liu, X. L. (2005). Teaching academic listening. In P. F. Kwah & M. Vallance (Eds.), *Teaching ESL to Chinese learners* (pp. 70–79). Singapore: Pearson Longman.

Liu, X. L., & Goh, C. (2006). Improving second language listening: Awareness and involvement. In T. S. C. Farrell (Ed.), *Language teacher research in Asia* (pp. 91–106). Alexandria, VA: TESOL.

Long, D. R. (1990). What you don't know can't help you. *Studies in Second Language Acquisition, 12*, 65–80.

Lund, R. J. (1991). A comparison of second language listening and reading comprehension. *The Modern Language Journal, 75*, 196–204.

Lynch, T. (1995). The development of interactive listening strategies in second language academic settings. In D. J. Mendelsohn & J. Rubin (Eds.), *A guide for the teaching of second language listening* (pp. 166–185). San Diego, CA: Dominie Press.

Macaro, E., Graham, S., & Vanderplank, R. (2007). A review of listening strategies: Focus on sources of knowledge and on success. In E. Macaro & A. Cohen (Eds.), *Language learner strategies: 30 years of research and practice* (pp. 165–185). Oxford: Oxford University Press.

Macaro, E., Vanderplank, R., & Graham, S. (2005). *A systematic review of the role of prior knowledge in unidirectional listening comprehension.* London: EPPI-Centre, Social Science Research Unit, Institute of Education, University of London.

MacIntyre, P. (2002). Motivation, anxiety and emotion in second language acquisition. In P. Robinson (Ed.), *Individual differences and instructed language learning* (pp. 45–68). Amsterdam: Benjamins.

Major, R., Fitzmaurice, S. F., Bunta, F., & Balasubramanian, C. (2002). The effects of non-native accents on listening comprehension: Implications for ESL assessment. *TESOL Quarterly, 36*, 173–190.

Major, R. C., Fitzmaurice, S. F., Bunta, F., & Balasubramanian, C. (2005). Testing the effects of regional, ethnic and international dialects of English on listening comprehension. *Language Learning, 55*, 37–69.

Mareschal, C. (2007). Student perceptions of a self-regulatory approach to second language listening comprehension development. (Unpublished doctoral dissertation). University of Ottawa, Canada.

Markham, P., & Peter, P. (2003). The influence of English language and Spanish language captions on foreign language listening/reading comprehension. *Journal of Educational Technology Systems, 31*, 331–341.

Markham, P., Peter, L., & McCarthy, T. (2001). The effects of native language vs. target language captions on foreign language students' DVD video comprehension. *Foreign Language Annals, 34*, 439–445.

Marslen-Wilson, W. D., & Tyler, L. K. T. (1980). The temporal structure of spoken language understanding. *Cognition, 8*, 1–71.

Mayer, R. E. (2001). *Multimedia learning*. Cambridge: Cambridge University Press.

Mayer, R. E. (2002). Cognitive theory and the design of multimedia instruction: An example of the two-way street between cognition and instruction. *New Directions for Teaching and Learning, 89*, 55–71.

McCarthy, M., & Carter, R. (1995). Spoken grammar: What is it and how can we teach it? *ELT Journal, 49*, 207–218.

McMinn, S. W. J. (2010). Podcasting possibilities: Increasing time and motivation in the language learning classroom. Retrieved from http://www.eifel.org/publications/proceedings/ilf08/contributions/improving-quality-of-learning-with-technologies/McMinn.pdf

Mecartty, F. (2000). Lexical and grammatical knowledge in reading and listening comprehension by foreign language learners of Spanish. *Applied Language Learning, 11*, 323–348.

Mendelsohn, D. (1994). *Learning to listen*. San Diego, CA: Dominie Press.

Mendelsohn, D. (1998). Teaching listening. *Annual Review of Applied Linguistics, 18*, 81–101.

Messick, S. (1989). Validity. In R. Linn (Ed.), *Educational measurement* (3rd ed.) (pp. 13–103). Washington, DC: American Council on Education/Macmillan.

Miller, L. (2009). Engineering lectures in a second language: What factors facilitate students' listening comprehension? *Asian EFL Journal, 11*, 8–30.

Mills, N., Herron, C., & Cole, S. (2004). Teacher-assisted versus individual viewing of foreign language video: Relation to comprehension, self-efficacy, and engagement. *CALICO Journal, 21*, 291–316.

Mills, N., Pajares, C., & Herron, C. (2006). A re-evaluation of the role of anxiety: Self-efficacy, anxiety and their relation to reading and listening proficiency. *Foreign Language Annals, 39*, 276–295.

Morley, J. (1999). Current perspectives on improving aural comprehension. *ESL Magazine, 2*(1), 16–19.

Morley, J. (2001). Aural comprehension instruction: Principles and practices. In M. Celce-Murcia (Ed.), *Teaching English as a Second or Foreign Language* (3rd ed.) (pp. 81–106). Boston, MA: Heinle & Heinle.

Moyer, A (2006). Language contact and confidence in second language listening comprehension: A pilot study of advanced listeners of German. *Foreign Language Annals, 39*, 255–275.

Munby, J. (1978). *Communicative syllabus design*. Cambridge: Cambridge University Press.

Nathan, P. (2008). Cooperative learning and metacognitive awareness in second language listening comprehension. (Unpublished Master's thesis). National Institute of Education, Nanyang Technological University, Singapore.

Nelson, T. O. (1996). Consciousness and metacognition. *American Psychologist, 51*, 102–16.

Nisbet, J., & Shucksmith, J. (1986). *Learning strategies*. London: Routledge and Kegan Paul.

Noels, K.A., Pelletier, L., Clément, R., & Vallerand, R. (2000). Why are you learning a second language? Motivational orientations and self-determination theory. *Language Learning, 50*, 57–85.

O'Bryan, A., & Hegelheimer, V. (2007). Integrating CALL into the classroom: The role of podcasting in an ESL listening strategies course. *ReCALL, 19*, 162–180.

Ockey, G. J. (2007). Construct implications of including still image or video in computer-based listening tests. *Journal of Pragmatics, 38*, 1928–1942.

Oller, J. W. (1979). *Language tests at school*. Harlow: Longman.

O'Malley J.M., & Chamot, A.U. (1990). *Learning strategies in second language acquisition*. Cambridge: Cambridge University Press.

O'Malley, J. M., Chamot, A. U., & Küpper, L. (1989). Listening comprehension strategies in second language acquisition. *Applied Linguistics, 10*, 418–437.

Oxford, R. (1990). *Language learning strategies: What every teacher should know*. New York: Newbury House.

Paivio, A. (1986). *Mental representation: A dual-coding approach*. New York: Oxford University Press.

Paris, G., & Winograd, P. (1990). How metacognition can promote academic learning and instruction. In B. F. Jones & L. Idol (Eds.), *Dimensions of thinking and cognitive instruction* (pp. 15–51). Hillsdale, NJ: Lawrence Erlbaum.

Perkins, D. (1995). *Outsmarting IQ: The emerging science of learnable intelligence*. New York: The Free Press.

Pica, T. (1994). Research on negotiation: What does it reveal about second-language learning conditions, processes, and outcomes? *Language Learning, 44*, 493–527.

Pintrich, P. R. (2000). The role of goal orientation in self-regulated learning. In M. Boekaerts, P.R. Pintrich, & M. Zeidner (Eds.), *Handbook of self-regulation* (pp. 451–502). San Diego, CA: Academic Press.

Pressley, M. (2002). Metacognition and self-regulated comprehension. In A. Farstrup & S. Samuels (Eds.), *What research has to say about reading instruction* (pp. 291–309). Newark, DE: International Reading Association.

Pujolà, J.-T. (2002). CALLing for help: Researching language learning strategies using help facilities in a web-based multimedia program. *ReCALL, 14*, 235–262.

Rader, K. E. (1991). *The effects of three different levels of word rate on the listening comprehension of third-quarter university Spanish learners*. (University Microfilms No 91–05, 192). Columbus, OH: Ohio State University.

Rea-Dickens, P., & Gardner, S. (2000). Snares and silver bullets: Disentangling the construct of formative assessment. *Language Testing, 17*, 215–243.

Renandya, W. A., & Farrell, T. S. C. (2011). "Teacher the tape is too fast!" Extensive listening in ELT. *ELT Journal, 65*, 53–59.

Richards, J. (1983). Listening comprehension: Approach, design and procedure. *TESOL Quarterly, 16*, 153–168.

Richards, J. C. (2005). Second thoughts on teaching listening. *RELC Journal, 36*(1), 85–92.

Rixon, S. (1981). The design of materials to foster particular listening strategies. *ELT Document Special, 121*, 68–106.

Robin, R. (2007). Learner-based listening and technological authenticity. *Language Learning & Technology, 11*, 109–115.

Robinson, P. (2002). *Individual differences and instructed language learning.* Amsterdam: John Benjamins.

Rogers, C. V., & Medley, F. W. (1988). Language with a purpose: Using authentic materials in the foreign language classroom. *Foreign Language Annals, 21*, 467–478.

Rose, K. R., & Kasper, G. (Eds.). (2001). *Pragmatics in language teaching.* Cambridge: Cambridge University Press.

Ross, S. J. (2005). The impact of assessment method on foreign language proficiency growth. *Applied Linguistics, 26*, 317–342.

Rost, M. (1990). *Listening in language learning.* Harlow: Longman.

Rost, M. (2005). L2 Listening. In E. Hinkel (Ed.), *Handbook of research in second language teaching and learning* (pp. 503–527). Mahwah, NJ: Erlbaum.

Rost, M. (2007). "I'm only trying to help": A role for interventions in teaching listening. *Language Learning & Technology, 11*, 102–108.

Rost, M., & Ross, S. (1991). Learner use of strategies in interaction. Typology and teachability. *Language Learning, 41*, 235–273.

Roussel, S. (2008). Les stratégies d'autorégulation de l'écoute et leur influence sur la compréhension de l'orale chez des apprenants de l'allemand langue seconde. (Unpublished doctoral dissertation). Université de Toulouse 2, France.

Roussel, S., Rieussec, A., Nespoulous, J.-L., & Tricot, A. (2008). Des baladeurs MP3 en classe d'allemand: L'effet de l'autorégulation matérielle de l'écoute sur la compréhension auditive en langue seconde. ALSIC, 11. Retrieved from http://alsic.revues.org/index413.html

Rubin, J. (1975). What the good language learner can teach us. *TESOL Quarterly, 9*, 41–51.

Sakai, H. (2009). Effect of repetition of exposure and proficiency level in L2 listening tests. *TESOL Quarterly, 43*, 360–371.

Salaberry, M. R. (2001). The use of technology for second language learning and teaching: A retrospective. *The Modern Language Journal, 85*, 39–56.

Sanders, L. D., Neville, H. J., & Woldorff, M. G. (2002). Speech segmentation by native and non-native speakers: The use of lexical, syntactic, and stress-pattern cues. *Journal of Speech, Language and Hearing Research, 45*, 519–530.

Schoonen, R., Hulstijn, J., & Bossers, B. (1998). Metacognitive and language-specific knowledge in native and foreign language reading comprehension: An empirical study among Dutch students in Grades 6, 8 and 10. *Language Learning, 48*, 71–106.

Seo, K. (2002). The effect of visuals on listening comprehension: A study of Japanese learners' listening strategies. *International Journal of Listening, 15*, 57–81.

Sheerin, S. (1987). Listening comprehension: Teaching or testing? *ELT Journal, 4*, 126–131.

Shohamy, E. (2001). *The power of tests: A critical perspective on the uses of language tests.* Harlow: Pearson Education.

Shohamy, E., & Inbar, O. (1991). Construct validation of listening comprehension tests: The effect of text and question type. *Language Testing, 8,* 23–40.

Skehan, P. (1998). *A cognitive approach to language learning.* Oxford: Oxford University Press.

Skehan, P. (2003). Task-based instruction. *Language Teaching, 36,* 1–14.

Smidt, E., & Hegelheimer, V. (2004). Effects of online academic lectures on ESL listening comprehension, incidental vocabulary acquisition and strategy use. *Computer Assisted Language Learning, 17,* 517–556.

Staehr, L. S. (2009). Vocabulary knowledge and advanced listening comprehension in English as a foreign language. *Studies in Second Language Acquisition, 31,* 577–607.

Stern, H. H. (1975). What can we learn from the good language learner? *Canadian Modern Language Review, 31,* 304–318.

Stern, H. H. (1983). *Fundamental concepts of language teaching.* Oxford: Oxford University Press.

Sueyoshi, A., & Hardison, D. M. (2005). The role of gestures and facial cues in second-language listening comprehension. *Language Learning, 55,* 661–699.

Suvorov, R. (2009). Context visuals in L2 listening tests: The effects of photographs and video vs. audio-only format. In C. A. Chapelle, H. G. Jun & I. Katz (Eds.), *Developing and evaluating language learning materials* (pp. 53–68). Ames, IA: Iowa State University.

Taguchi, N. (2005). Comprehending implied meaning in English as a foreign language. *The Modern Language Journal, 89,* 543–562.

Taguchi, N. (2008). The role of learning environment in the development of pragmatic comprehension: A comparison of gains between EFL and ESL learners. *Studies in Second Language Acquisition, 30,* 423–452.

Thompson, I. (1995). Assessment of second/foreign language listening comprehension. In D. Mendelsohn & J. Rubin (Eds.), *A guide for the teaching of second language listening* (pp. 31–58). San Diego, CA: Dominie Press.

Tremblay, R. (1989). *Production orale non-interactive.* Montréal: Centre Éducatif et Culturel.

Tsui, A., & Fullilove, J. (1998). Bottom-up or top-down processing as a discriminator of L2 listening performance. *Applied Linguistics, 19,* 432–451.

Tyler, M. (2001). Resource consumption as a function of topic knowledge in nonnative and native comprehension. *Language Learning, 51,* 257–280.

Underwood, M. (1989). *Teaching listening.* Harlow: Longman.

Ur, P. (1984). *Teaching listening comprehension.* Cambridge: Cambridge University Press.

Vandergriff, I. (2006). Negotiating common ground in computer-mediated versus face-to-face discussions. *Language Learning & Technology, 10,* 110–138.

Vandergrift, L. (1997a). The strategies of second language (French) listeners: A descriptive study. *Foreign Language Annals, 30,* 387–409.

Vandergrift, L. (1997b). The Cinderella of communication strategies: Receptive strategies in interactive listening. *Modern Language Journal, 90,* 338–352.

Vandergrift, L. (1998). Successful and less successful listeners in French: What are the strategy differences? *The French Review, 71*(3), 370–394.

Vandergrift, L. (1999). Facilitating second language listening comprehension: Acquiring successful strategies. *ELT Journal, 53*, 168–176.

Vandergrift, L. (2002). It was nice to see that our predictions were right: Developing metacognition in L2 listening comprehension. *Canadian Modern Language Review, 58*, 556–575.

Vandergrift, L. (2003a). Orchestrating strategy use: Toward a model of the skilled second language listener. *Language Learning, 53*, 463–496.

Vandergrift, L. (2003b). From prediction through reflection: Guiding students through the process of L2 listening. *The Canadian Modern Language Review, 59*, 425–440.

Vandergrift, L. (2004). Learning to listen or listening to learn? *Annual Review of Applied Linguistics, 24*, 3–25.

Vandergrift, L. (2005). Relationships among motivation orientations, metacognitive awareness and proficiency in L2 listening. *Applied Linguistics, 26*, 70–89.

Vandergrift, L. (2006). Second language listening: Listening ability or language proficiency? *The Modern Language Journal, 90*, 6–18.

Vandergrift, L. (2007). Recent developments in second and foreign language listening comprehension research. *Language Teaching, 40*, 191–210.

Vandergrift, L. (2010). Researching listening in applied linguistics. In B. Paltridge & A. Phakiti (Eds.), *Companion to research methods in applied linguistics* (pp. 160–173). London: Continuum.

Vandergrift, L., & Bélanger, C. (1998). The National Core French Assessment Project: Design and field-test of formative evaluation instruments at the intermediate level. *Canadian Modern Language Review, 54*, 589–622.

Vandergrift, L., Goh, C., Mareschal, C., & Tafaghodtari, M. H. (2006). The Metacognitive Awareness Listening Questionnaire (MALQ): Development and validation. *Language Learning, 56*(3), 431–462.

Vandergrift, L., & Tafaghodtari, M. H. (2010). Teaching learners how to listen does make a difference: An empirical study. *Language Learning, 65*, 470–497.

Vandergrift, L., Weinberg, A., & Knoerr, H. (2010, June). Developing metacogitive awareness for L2 academic listening. Paper presented at the annual meeting of Canadian Association of Applied Linguistics, Montreal.

Vanderplank, R. (2010). Déjà vu? A decade of research on language laboratories, television and video in language learning. *Language Teaching, 43*, 1–37.

Veenman, M., Van Hout-Wolters, B., & Afflerbach, P. (2006). Metacognition and learning: Conceptual and methodological considerations. *Metacognition and Learning, 1*, 3–14.

Verdugo, D., & Belmonte, I. A. (2007). Using digital stories to improve listening comprehension with Spanish young learners of English. *Language Learning & Technology, 11*, 87–101.

Victori, M., & Lockhart, W. (1995). Enhancing metacognition in self-directed language learning. *System, 23*, 223–234.

Vogely, A. (1999). Addressing listening comprehension anxiety. In D. J. Young (Ed.), *Affect in foreign language and second language learning: A practical guide to creating a low-anxiety classroom atmosphere* (pp. 106–123). New York: McGraw-Hill.

Vygotsky, L. (1986). *Thought and language*. Cambridge, MA: The MIT Press.

Wagner, E. (2002). Video listening tests: A pilot study. *Working Papers in TESOL & Applied Linguistics, 2.*

Wagner, E. (2007). Are they watching? Test-taker viewing behaviour during an L2 video listening test. *Language Learning & Technology, 11,* 67–86.

Wagner, E. (2008). Video listening tests: What are they measuring? *Language Assessment Quarterly, 5,* 218–243.

Wagner, E. (2010). Test-takers' interaction with an L2 video listening test. *System, 38,* 280–291.

Wang, M. C., Haertel, G., & Walberg, H. J. (1990). What influences learning? A content analysis of review literature. *Journal of Educational Research, 84,* 30–43.

Weber, A., & Cutler, A. (2006). First-language phonotactics in second-language listening. *Journal of the Acoustical Society of America, 119,* 597–607.

Wenden, A. (1987). Metacognition: An expanded view of the cognitive abilities of L2 learners. *Language Learning, 37,* 573–594.

Wenden, A. (1991). *Learner strategies for learner autonomy.* Harlow: Prentice Hall.

Wenden, A. (1998). Metacognitive knowledge and language learning. *Applied Linguistics, 19,* 515–537.

Wenden, A. (2001). Metacognitive knowledge in SLA: The neglected variable. In M. P. Breen (Ed.), *Learner contributions to language learning: New directions in research* (pp. 44–64). Harlow: Pearson Education.

Wenden, A. (2002). Learner development in language learning. *Applied Linguistics, 23,* 32–55.

Wenden, A., & Rubin, J. (Eds.) (1987). *Learner strategies in language learning.* Harlow: Prentice-Hall.

White, G. (1998). *Listening.* Oxford: Oxford University Press.

White, G. (2006). Teaching listening: Time for a change in methodology. In E. Usó-Juan & A. Martínez-Flor (Eds.), *Current trends in the development and teaching of the four language skills* (pp. 111–135). Berlin: Mouton de Gruyter.

Wilberschied, L., & Berman, P. M. (2004). Effect of using photos from authentic video as advance organizers on listening comprehension in an FLES Chinese class. *Foreign Language Annals, 37,* 534–543.

Willis, J. (1996). *A framework for task-based learning.* Harlow: Longman.

Willis, J. (2005). Introduction: Aims and explorations into tasks and task-based teaching. In C. Edwards & J. Willis (Eds.), *Teachers exploring tasks in English language teaching* (pp. 1–12). Basingstoke: Palgrave Macmillan.

Wilson, M. (2003). Discovery listening—improving perceptual processing. *ELT Journal, 57,* 335–343.

Winke, P., Gass, S., & Sydorenko, T. (2010). The effects of captioning videos used for foreign language listening activities. *Language Learning & Technology, 14,* 65–86.

Wolff, D. (1989). Identification of text-type as a strategic device in L2 comprehension. In H. W. Dechert & M. Raupach (Eds.) *Interlingual processes* (pp. 137–150). Tubingen: Gunter Nann.

Yanagawa, K., & Green, A. (2008). To show or not to show: The effects of item stems and answer options on performance on a multiple-choice listening comprehension test. *System, 36,* 107–122.

Yanguas, I. (2010). Oral computer-mediated interaction between L2 learners: It's about time! *Language Learning & Technology, 14*, 72–93.

Young, L. (1994). University lectures—macro-structure and micro-features. In J. Flowerdew (Ed.), *Academic listening: Research perspectives* (pp. 159–176). New York: Cambridge University Press.

Young, M. Y. C. (1997). A serial ordering of listening comprehension strategies used by advanced ESL learners in Hong Kong. *Asian Journal of English Language Teaching, 7*, 35–53.

Zeidner, M., Boekaerts, M., & Pintrich, P. (2000). Self-regulation: Directions and challenges for future research. In M. Boekaerts, P. Pintrich, & M. Zeidner (Eds.), *Handbook of self-regulation* (pp. 749–768). New York: Academic Press.

Zeng, Y. (2007). Metacognitive instruction in listening: A study of Chinese non-English major undergraduates. (Unpublished Master's thesis). National Instituteof Education, Nanyang Technological University, Singapore.

Zhang, D., & Goh, C. (2006). Strategy knowledge and perceived strategy use: Singaporean students' awareness of listening and speaking strategies. *Language Awareness, 15*, 199–219.

Zhao, Y. (1997). The effects of listeners' control of speech rateon second language comprehension. *Applied Linguistics, 18*, 49–68.

Zimmerman, B. J., & Schunk, D. H. (2001). *Self-regulated learning and academic achievement*. Mahwah, NJ: Erlbaum.

Index

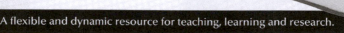